SATIRE
AND THE
TRANSFORMATION
OF GENRE

SATIRE

AND THE
TRANSFORMATION
OF GENRE

LEON GUILHAMET

UNIVERSITY OF PENNSYLVANIA PRESS
PHILADELPHIA · 1987

Library of Congress Cataloging-in-Publication Data

Guilhamet, Leon.
Satire and the transformation of genre.

Bibliography: p.
Includes index.
1. Satire, English—History and criticism.
2. Literary form.   3. Dryden, John, 1631–1700—
Criticism and interpretation.   4. Pope, Alexander.
1688–1744—Criticism and interpretation.
5. Swift, Jonathan, 1667–1745—Criticism and
interpretation.   6. English literature—18th
century—History and criticism.   I. Title.
PR931.G85   1987   827'.009   86-30715
ISBN 0-8122-8053-9 (alk. paper)

Designed by Adrianne Onderdonk Dudden

*To W. Jackson Bate, and in memory of
Francis Fergusson and Mark Van Doren*

CONTENTS

PREFACE

Despite advances in our knowledge of satiric literature over the last thirty years or so, the status of satire as a genre remains cloudy at best. The primary purpose of this book is to address the question of that status by suggesting several ways in which we can approach satire as a genre while avoiding conventional and superficial distinctions between prose and verse satire.

One of the weaknesses in genre study since Aristotle's *Poetics* has been a penchant to view themes and characters as generic traits. In the study of satire, this approach is reflected in Alvin Kernan's influential "disorderly and crowded" scene of satire and the more mechanical but pragmatic observations that women and politics are preferred satiric topics. Of course, as tradition exerts its influence, some themes are favored over others. It is a mistake, though, I believe, to define any genre by strictly thematic issues.

At the same time that we limit our concern for theme, we may need to broaden our sense of structure. Certain structures, such as the symposium and the familiar letter, for example, lay thematic obligations on their authors that can be ignored only at great peril. But both of these, in all their variations, are generic structures in their own right. A certain thematic freight is transported by every formal structure, and since external formal structures are regularly borrowed by satire, some themes associated with those forms may find their way into satire as well. It is our critical obligation to distinguish between themes formally transported and those which are inessential and variable. Indeed, I would go even further to argue that much of what is perceived as theme in satire is really a residue of form.

Perhaps the major argument of this study is that satire is known essentially by its form. If this contention has any merit at all, satire emerges with much more coherent generic possibilities than theorists have been willing to grant. As a corollary to this proposition, albeit one which I cannot even begin to explore here, there is the probability that the other genres can be better approached from a broader formal viewpoint. Since the generic qualities of satire have been so widely ignored and underestimated, however, to do them justice here will require a focused and sustained effort. Because a keen sense of other generic norms is essential to an understanding of how satire works, in the end it is not possible to deal with satire or any other genre apart from the larger generic system.

I have grounded my generic approach to satire in mimetic theory, partly because I believe it is the best theory of art Europe has ever had, despite wide variance in opinion as to what is represented, and also because all the satirists considered here, to the extent that they were concerned about theory at all, accepted some version of mimetic theory. Recent adaptations of mimesis to modern hermeneutics by Barbara Herrnstein Smith and Joel Weinsheimer have underscored the utility of mimetic concepts in thoroughly modern contexts. My own mimetic view, though not so broadly applicable as Weinsheimer's, for example, is nonetheless applied flexibly enough to require a few preliminary words of explanation.

Aristotle, of course, calls tragedy the imitation of an action (praxis); the neoclassicists stressed the imitation of nature, by which they usually, but not exclusively, meant human nature. Many brilliant interpretations of Aristotle's meaning, such as those by Erich Auerbach, Francis Fergusson, and the Chicago Critics, have enriched us in our own century, and I am greatly indebted to them. My own theory of imitation arose from the need to explain the complexities that I was seeing in satire. To comprehend what was happening, it was necessary to expand my sense of what mimesis was, to include aspects of parody and the eighteenth-century formal imitation. If nature can be imitated, why should rhetorical or belletristic structures be arbitrarily omitted from nature? This is especially true of the neoclassical conception of nature, which included human nature in a prominent place. If literary art is the finest expression of the human verbal capacity, why should it not be deemed a proper object of other mimetic art? It seems to me that it was and is, and that the concept of the literary imitation is an attempt to recognize this fact. One of the achievements of the eighteenth century was the stretching of the concept of mimesis to include all manner of creation. In the process, practitioners of mimesis and theorists of the concept altered it completely. And by making it more capacious and flexible, they opened the way for what came to be known as nonmimetic theories.

Throughout this book I regard imaginative or creative literature as mimetic. This category includes all the major literary genres, including satire. History, oratory, scientific writing, and like forms I regard as natural discourse, which purportedly deals directly with a real world I believe to exist. The poet, dramatist, or satirist, on the other hand, creates fictions that deal less directly, but sometimes more pointedly, with that same real world. Poetry, drama, and satire are all mimetic because of their essential fictional status. Of course, I should make clear that nonmimetic works often make substantial use of fictional techniques. Determining whether a work is history or a novel may not be an easy task for this reason and for the additional one that mimetic works may contain substantial nonmimetic materials. The essential job of classification belongs to the genre critic.

The problem with critical approaches that do not recognize some separation between mimetic and nonmimetic structures is that the crucial distinction between the real world and that of the imagination may be lost. That much Romantic theory leads to solipsism illustrates the perils of expressiveness. One of the reasons that the work of the satirists provides such pungent commentary on the real world is that it relies on the mimetic-nonmimetic distinction for its aesthetic success. Whether or not an imaginative view of experience is "truer to life" is not the point. The important thing to notice is that the two verbal structures are distinct from one another, despite their apparent similarities. They possess, in some respects, a different order of being. One exists within an aesthetic range determined by its genre and fictional pattern. The other is a direct verbal means of solving problems or addressing situations in the real world. It exists as a form of pragmatic action. On the other hand, mimetic art, as Plato recognized, is a step further removed from reality than is nonmimetic creation. Nevertheless, its power is not diminished on that account. Indeed, fiction, which mimesis implies, can enlist the power of myth and tradition, which natural discourse cannot command on its own.

Since I cite a substantial number of literary works in the course of this study, I have included dates in parentheses for nearly all of them where they are mentioned for the first time. Most of the dates designate the first edition, but I have silently substituted the date of composition when it is known and when it places the work more precisely. This is done entirely as a courtesy to my readers; I have no intention of providing a handy compendium or the suggestion of one.

Anyone who writes a scholarly book incurs more obligations than he can properly discharge in a preface. Still, some of my more obvious debts can at least be mentioned. Vincent Carretta, Paul J. Korshin, Charles T. Mark, and Betty W. Rizzo read the manuscript at various points in its later stages and offered substantial and helpful suggestions. An important impetus at a critical time was a National Endowment for the Humanities seminar in satire at Brown University, which I was privileged to attend during the summer of 1980. Edward A. Bloom, who directed that seminar, was kind enough to read and comment on some preliminary versions of parts of this book. An early draft of my introduction was read at Nassau Community College in 1981 and a portion of my reading of *The Rape of the Lock* was presented at the annual meeting of the American Society for Eighteenth-Century Studies in 1983. The libraries of Brown University, City College, Hunter College, Rutgers University, and Yale Univesity, and the New York Public Library proved substantial resources. I am grateful for whatever assistance and encouragement I had from persons and institutions.

1

INTRODUCTION

How to tell a satire remains a problem despite some very good work on the subject over the last thirty years. Definitions, thematic analyses, studies of formal verse and Menippean satire, historical accounts, and studies which stress origins, pictorial and emblematic associations, political and historical explanations, and rhetorical techniques have enriched our understanding of satire. It is fair to say, too, that the status of satire has risen in the scholarly world and, perhaps, even with the public at large.[1] Yet excellent as this body of work is, serious students must reflect that several basic issues regarding satire remain unresolved. Although Alvin Kernan could write of an "accepted view of satire"[2] with some confidence in 1984, he seems to have been referring to the acceptance of satire as a major form rather than to widespread agreement about how it works and what exactly it is. The satisfaction that many seem to take in the condition of scholarship in this area may come from a consideration of how far we have come rather than of how far we have to go. What tranquillity there is in the field seems to me the result more of basic confusions than of universal accord.

The issue of the persona is one where the battle lines have been clearly drawn. Persona may seem a quaint and old-fashioned issue more than thirty years after Maynard Mack drew our attention to its importance in his classic study, "The Muse of Satire" (1951). With such influential commentators as John Traugott and the late Irvin Ehrenpreis denying the validity of the concept or fixing our attention elsewhere, persona remains an issue of the utmost importance for those concerned with the aesthetics of satire.[3]

The genre-mode distinction is, by all odds, in much worse shape. It is perhaps well and good when book-length studies appear in which satire's status as a genre is denied. Although an important aspect of the subject is ignored, such books can still tell us much about modal satire, rhetorical technique, and thematic continuities. But when a commentator, refusing to grapple with the issue, refers to satire without any distinction as to genre or mode, we may be permitted to demur. Works which are clearly concerned with modal questions are referred to, erroneously, as dealing with generic considerations. Form and theme are cheerfully confused. All this arises from the assumption on the part of many on the periphery of satire studies that satire is a known phenomenon, defined and circumscribed for all time.[4] There are still others, of a stronger intellectual cast, who, believing that the universe of words is a wondrous mystery, refuse to run the risk of formulating a distinction. Against all such evasions this book is written, but countering them is not its primary purpose. Above all, I intend to engage certain substantive issues with regard to satire which impinge upon its generic status. In short, I want to make a case for my conviction that to understand satire, it is necessary to know it as a genre.

This study, then, is actuated not only by the assumption that satire is a genre, but that its generic status can be defined and is worth knowing, or at least that its limits can be better understood. A certain amount of classification is unavoidable—a prospect that, within limits, need not be contemplated with regret. "Classifying," Claude Lévi-Strauss has written, "as opposed to not classifying, has a value of its own, whatever form the classification may take."[5] Lévi-Strauss is thinking of the primitive mind coming to terms with nature or the scientist attempting to surpass it, but the significance of his structuralist viewpoint for the study of literature is axiomatic. Whatever we may postulate as its source, I am persuaded with Northrop Frye that there is a universe of words in which the most significant constellations are great works of literature. The first stage in getting to know this universe is classification. For the primitive mind attempting to bring order out of chaos and Frye doing much the same thing in the universe of words, classification of some kind is the first step.

So it surely was as well when Francesco Sansovino, in his *Discorso in materia della satira* (1560), classified satire according to style (humble, low), subject matter (low, not high or magnificent), kinds of persons depicted (humble, e.g., servants, sinners), and the nature of imitation (direct, without adornment or artifice). Sansovino's approach, which Bernard Weinberg considers typical of Renaissance Italian commentaries on satire,[6] is by no means contemptible. Through its classifications within a hierarchy of genres, it tells us a good deal about what the Renaissance thought of satire. We may dismiss it or quarrel with it, but we cannot deny that Sansovino has taken us farther toward understanding satire than those who have never raised a question or ventured a distinction.

Genre, like language, is a system of signs; like language, it is incomplete in any single example of the kind or even in the works of any one practitioner. Like language, too, genre can be approached either synchronically or diachronically. The synchronic approach deals essentially with the timeless aspects of genre, those qualities that satires have in common rather than those that make them unique. In the case of satire these unifying qualities tend to be formal or structural rather than thematic, ethical, or psychological. Diachrony concerns the changes a genre undergoes as the product of historical relationships. Like language, genre is variable, not fixed.[7] But also, like language, genre does not respond in predictable ways to diachronic forces.

My approach will stress the synchronic for several reasons. First of all, I am interested in satire primarily as an art form. Satire, even more than other genres, draws much of its artistic power from its generic tradition. Far from providing us with a full understanding of the aesthetics of satire, modern criticism has left much to be done. Also, before we can properly evaluate diachronic influences, we must take the synchronic relationships of a work of art fully into account. But having said this, there is no way diachrony can be ignored, especially since I survey approximately two thousand years of satire. The impact of history, social and political, and of individual style will need to be dealt with even as I focus on generic matters. Important as genre is in satire, a single-minded concentration would tend to be reductive. In Part 2, I intend to present coherent interpretations of some major satires based on my observations regarding genre in this introduction and Part 1. Definitive sorting out of the timebound and the timeless will not always be possible.

Adding to the complexity of this undertaking, but simplifying it too, is the fact that I focus on one literary period, at least in Part 2. Extending from *Mac Flecknoe* (1682) and *Absalom and Achitophel* (1681) to *The New Dunciad* (1742) is the relatively short period when the finest satire ever composed in any language was published. Although the reasons for the preeminence of three major satirists—Dryden, Swift, and Pope—and their appearance over such a short span of time are a constant topic of speculation, it seems to me that the answers are more likely to be found in the satires themselves than in any special historical or social conditions. Again, this is not to deny the influence of social, economic, or political history on literature. Rather, it is simply a safer procedure to grasp the achievement represented by these satires with respect to structure and meaning than in terms of wholly external influences. As I have already observed, however, the synchronic-diachronic distinction can hardly be absolute. My preference for the synchronic should be understood primarily as a matter of emphasis.

What has been written on satire as genre has centered on one or the other of two accepted forms: formal verse satire and Menippean satire. The first of these has been rigorously defined as to its component parts. It is a verse dialogue between a satirist speaker and an *adversarius*. The rhetorical attack is more or less sharply focused on a single vice, and a single, related virtue is promoted somewhere in the course of the debate. With Lucilius as its designated inventor and Horace, Persius, and Juvenal as distinguished practitioners, formal verse satire enjoys unassailable stature among the kinds of satire.

The concept of formal verse satire seems to have emerged in English criticism with the preference for Juvenal over Horace among seventeenth-century satirists and critics. Although borrowing much from the *De Satyrica* (1605) of the French classicist Isaac Casaubon, Dryden's *Original and Progress of Satire* (1693) marks a turning point for English criticism. But Dryden's theory of satire, influential as it has undoubtedly been, may not be an accurate statement of generic realities.

After giving what he calls "the history of satire," Dryden turns finally to a definition of satire, which he takes from Heinsius, the celebrated Dutch scholar:

> Satire is a kind of poetry, without a series of action, invented for the purging of our minds; in which human vices, ignorance, and errors, and all things besides, which are produced from them in every man, are severely reprehended; partly dramatically, partly simply, and sometimes in both kinds of speaking; but for the most part figuratively, and occultly; consisting in a low familiar way, chiefly in a sharp and pungent manner of speech; but partly, also, in a facetious and civil way of jesting; by which either hatred or laughter, or indignation, is moved.[8]

Dryden dismisses Heinsius's definition as "obscure and perplexed," which it surely is in some respects. But much more to the point, he characterizes it as a description "accommodated to the Horatian way; and excluding the works of Juvenal and Persius, as foreign from that kind of poem."[9]

Dryden is generally correct that Heinsius's definition pertains more to Horace than to Juvenal and Persius, but he is wrong in excluding the latter two entirely. Dryden's purpose in dismissing Horace's mixed form and low diction is to make a case for what he calls "perfect satire," which lashes only one vice.[10] Although in *An Essay of Dramatic Poesy* (1668), Dryden mounted an interesting defense of the English use of underplots,[11] by 1679 he stated the belief that "the ancient method, as 'tis the easiest, is also the most natural and the best."[12] This preference for the single plot is consistent with his belief that action and plot are virtually synonymous terms.[13] If, as Aristotle contends, a single action is best, it follows that a single plot is also preferable.[14] This same kind of thinking may be adapted to satire without visible strain. Like Casaubon before him, Dryden identifies multiple arguments in Horace's satires. Therefore, he rejects Horace's approach in favor of the practice of a single argument exemplified in the satire of Persius, Juvenal, and their great French successor, Boileau.[15]

Dryden recognizes that because of the derivation of the word *satura*, which "signifies a dish plentifully stored with all variety of fruits and grains,"[16] it may prove irrelevant to object to a lack of unity in Horace's *sermones*. But, again, the method of Persius, that of Juvenal, "who calls his poems a *farrago*, which is a word of the same signification with *satura*,"[17] and finally the authority of Boileau carry the day. Dryden's impact on later satirists would suggest that a neoclassical concept of unity and method, amenable to a fairly rigid formulation of rules, was to dominate early eighteenth-century practice. Although much theory of satire follows Dryden in this regard, practice seems to deviate from theory in several respects.

The second universally recognized form of satire is nearly no form at all. Menippean satire, usually regarded as a mixture of prose and verse, is too vague a generic concept to offer us much guidance. Taking its name from a Greek Cynic philosopher, Menippus, who was reputed to have pioneered the form, it would seem to carry a substantial residue of philosophy along with it. Lucian's use of the character Menippus in so many of his satires suggests a strong Menippean influence. But Menippus's satires have not survived, and our knowledge of those by Varro, his Roman successor, permits only the merest speculation.[18]

But the distinction between verse satire and Menippean satire may be a false one if Heinsius's description of Horace has any authority. Horace's own account of Lucilius shows that satire in its early development did not have anything like the unified action demanded by Dryden. Whether a satire is in verse, prose, or a combination of the two seems relevant only with regard to the skills of the satirist, not in the development or even in the essential structure of satire. Horace may well have realized this when he denied that his satires were poems at all. A *satura* or *sermo* is what it is. To call it a poem or prose fiction is to misrepresent it or allude to its borrowing capacity. Clearly Horace thought of his satires as part of a genre. Indeed, Heinsius's definition seems to fit prose satire or a mixture of prose and verse as well as it does Horace's *sermones*. Also it is not irrelevant to Persius and Juvenal, although Casaubon, Boileau, and Dryden thought otherwise. But Dryden himself recognizes the insignificance of the distinction between prose and verse in satire when he cites Spenser's *Mother Hubberds Tale* and his own *Mac Flecknoe* and *Absalom and Achitophel* as English examples of the Varronian form, although none is mixed with prose.[19]

In addition to the perennial ratifiers of Menippean conventions, there is a small body of modern critical opinion that regards mixtures other than verse and prose as essential components of satire. In his *Problems of Dostoevsky's Poetics*, first published in Russia in 1929, Mikhail Bakhtin examines what he calls "menippea" (not necessarily satiric). In this genre he finds "a wide use of inserted genres: novellas, letters, oratorical speeches, symposia, and so on. . . ."[20] He recognizes many other patterns traceable to genre mixing, such as "the threshold dialogue" and "social utopia," which are genres in themselves. Limiting himself to medieval satire in general and John Skelton in particular, A. R. Heiserman discovers the employment of "various mixtures of literary conventions which sometimes . . . appear as elaborate fictions, and sometimes as more subtle 'supposicyons' of 'arte'."[21] He goes on to note that conventional objects "were attacked by conventional mixtures of conventions."[22] J. P. Sullivan's recognition of multiple genres in the Menippean form also provides a basis for the contention that the mixing of prose and verse is only one way of indicating the more essential use of multiple genres in a single satiric form.[23]

Genre mixing throughout literature is more widespread than has commonly been supposed. Some of the most illuminating work on the subject appeared in Rosalie Colie's brief posthumous book, *The Resources of Kind* (1973).[24] Both Ralph Cohen and Ralph W. Rader have made significant contributions to our awareness of the same phenomenon in eighteenth-century literature.[25] But whatever the importance of genre mixing among other forms, nowhere is it more functional than in satire. In fact, in a high proportion of satires, the mingling of different generic strategies provides a key to the structure and dynamics of the work of art.

Before examining the structure of satire, one must come to terms with satire as mode, or what is usually called the satiric. Since few commentators possess a very clear idea of the genre of satire, there is a tendency to ignore any distinction between genre and mode. Further, the comic and the satiric are virtually left undistinguished from one another. This leads to critics' mistaking comic works allied to the tradition of satire for generic satires. Indeed, almost any work containing some satire as mode has been considered a satire by one critic or another. Recent critical studies have treated such works as *Gargantua and Pantagruel* (1532 or 1533–52), *The Anatomy of Melancholy* (1621), *The Vicar of Wakefield* (1766), and *Tristram Shandy* (1759–67) as satires or dominantly satiric books.[26] A refutation of these claims would require full analyses of the works in question, but my following distinction between satiric mode and comic mode will provide a first step.[27]

Finally, there are works that possess the formal structure of satire, but do not contain modal satire and therefore cannot be called satires in any modern sense of that word. Among some of the most important of these are Boethius's *Consolation of Philosophy* (524 A.D.) and the earlier works, Aulus Gellius's *Noctes Atticae* (180 A.D.), Athenaeus's *Deipnosophists* (192 A.D.), Macrobius's *Saturnalia* (early fifth century?), and Martianus Capella's *Marriage of Philology and Mercury* (410–39 A.D.).

Aristotle defines the ridiculous as a mistake or deformity which does not cause pain or harm to others.[28] This is the essence of the comic. Plato in the *Philebus*, on the other hand, takes a moralist's view and defines the ridiculous as "a certain kind of badness."[29] Plato's bias applies more accurately to the satiric than to the comic. If comedy presents its ridiculous objects as things of no importance, the harmlessly ugly or base,[30] satire interprets the ridiculous as harmful or destructive, at least potentially. This harm may come to others or even to the object of satire himself. In comedy, on the other hand, we are shown a fool who is just part of the nature of things. But the object of satire is unnatural, perverse in some specific way. He has perverted his nature, knowingly or unconsciously, and, even where the satire is mild, he is implicated in some evil. The division between knaves and fools is relevant here, at least for a start, if we are to understand the distinction between the satiric and the comic. Comic butts are fools, satiric butts are knaves. Unfortunately, however, the distinction will not hold up indefinitely: satire, like comedy, identifies fools as well as knaves. The difference, however, is that satiric fools bring harm to themselves or, of greater importance, to others and perhaps to us, the audience or readers. The danger, however, is usually not immediate, and in reading satire of an earlier period, the modern reader must adjust the variables to allow for contemporary relevance. In eighteenth-century imitation of classical satire, the author showed his wit by making the adjustments for his audience. Such accommodation suggests that satire is more timebound than comedy. Part of the danger inherent in the satiric object stems from the threat of time. The comic fool, on the other hand, is timeless and harmless; this perception by the audience releases tension and leads to laughter. The satiric fool, however, raises tensions. Though we may laugh at first, our laughter presently yields to serious concern. We soon recognize, though sometimes not immediately, that we are not in the realm of the comic. Another mode entirely, which employs many of the same techniques as the comic, has us in its grip. But the vision is not a pleasant one. Satire has a palpable design upon us.

As Elder Olson has pointed out, the ridiculous is found in opposition to the good, on the one side, and the serious, on the other.[31] The comic functions chiefly in contrast to the serious; the satiric in opposition to the good. In other words, the comic shows us what we can regard as benign or of no concern at all, whereas satire points out what is in contrast to the good. Both make use of the ridiculous, but each mode bears a different relationship to it.

The basic difference between the satiric and the comic is that the satiric reinterprets the ridiculous in an ethical light. The satiric employs comic techniques of ridicule, but discovers harm and even evil in the ridiculous. The ridiculous that is proper to satire cannot be reconciled to the good at the conclusion of a comic plot. Rather the evil or perversity is isolated in expectation of some moral correction. The correction comes from the satire itself, as the evildoer is, to use a Renaissance phrase, "stripped and whipped." But neither tone nor technique is geared to effect a reconciliation. Most satire employs comic techniques of diminution or reductionism,[32] but in satire the ugly and deformed are also harmful. One paradox of satire is that it reveals its objects as both contemptible and terrifying.

In satire, the contemptible and the terrifying are often embodied in the unnatural. In the medieval animal fable and satire, *Speculum Stultorum* (twelfth century), Brunellus the ass, dissatisfied with his short tail, desires a longer one. This clearly unnatural passion receives explicit treatment as such. Of course, the ass fails to achieve the end he seeks, succeeding only in losing most of the tail he has. Juvenal presents the best classical example of a satirist who depicts unnatural acts in abundance, whether sexual, religious, or economic. The great English Augustans carry on this tradition with splendid intensity. Dryden's Achitophel, Zimri, and Corah, to name just a few, are all unnatural in different ways. But their animosity to their lawful lord, King David, unites them in one great perversion. Pope's Sporus, an amphibean of sexual perversity, is one of the most fiendishly brilliant portraits in all of satire. The worst indictment Swift can bring against European Yahoos in the fourth part of *Gulliver's Travels* (1726) is that they, unlike their more primitive brothers in Houyhnhnmland, are capable of unnatural vices. Since acts against nature seem to excite both contempt and horror at once, they become part of a successful strategy for satire.

At this point it may be objected that the harmful and unnatural can be found in literary works that are not satiric. Iago in *Othello* (1603–4) comes at once to mind, and other characters of a more heroic turn, such as Macbeth and Milton's Satan, promptly follow. But objects of the satiric and figures of evil in other genres, such as tragedy or epic, can be distinguished by the presence or absence of a comic dimension. Satiric objects are both ridiculous and terrifying. Iago, Macbeth, and Satan are never ridiculous, even when reductionist techniques are applied to them. It may be argued that the devils reduced to hissing serpents in book 10 of *Paradise Lost* (1674) are treated satirically. That, of course, is entirely possible, since the satiric can be found in any other genre, but no one would argue that the satiric is a dominant mode in any of these three works. Neither Iago, Macbeth, nor Satan is essentially ridiculous. Zimri, Sporus, and Mac Flecknoe are completely ridiculous, but they are also harmful and dangerous. Satire, thus, depends on the reader's ability to take a comic and serious view of an object at the same time. This is not as difficult as we might expect, however, because we combine contempt and terror in our reactions to behavior that we regard as unnatural or perverse.

Pope's portrait of Atticus in the *Epistle to Arbuthnot* (1734) may furnish us with examples of how a satiric profile can vary between comic and serious responses. Since Addison, successful in the arts, will brook no competition, Pope sees him in the unnatural posture of an Ottoman sultan who kills his own brothers to assure himself a peaceful reign:

> Shou'd such a man, too fond to rule alone,
> Bear, like the *Turk*, no brother near the throne. . . .
> (197–98)[33]

Atticus is represented as "scornful," "jealous," and possessed of "hate for Arts that caus'd himself to rise . . ." (199–200), all dangerous rather than merely ridiculous traits. But some comic qualities follow in a succession of contemptible deceits:

> Damn with faint praise, assent with civil leer,
> And without sneering, teach the rest to sneer;
> Willing to wound, and yet afraid to strike,
> Just hint a fault, and hesitate dislike;
> Alike reserv'd to blame, or to commend,
> A tim'rous foe, and a suspicious friend,
> Dreading ev'n fools. . . .
>
> (201–7)

Here timidity seems to rule Atticus; his behavior, from the "leer" to the dread of fools, is more comic than serious; and yet he is capable of wounding, even if he lacks the capacity to strike. The divided response to Atticus reflects the two essential tendencies of the satiric toward the comic and serious:

> Who but must laugh, if such a man there be?
> Who would not weep, if *Atticus* were he!
>
> (213–14)

The final weeping response in the passage proves that Atticus, with his genius and achievements, is far from lacking consequence. Even the starving Grub Street hacks of the *Dunciad,* who have elicited so much sympathy from those who seek to devalue Pope, are a potent threat because of their power to corrupt whatever they touch or utter, from word to literary work. Whatever we may think, Pope does not see them as harmless objects of ridicule. If he did, they would be mere comic figures. But they become perverse and unnatural when they bring their lack of talent to bear on literature. An insufficiency of talent, Pope understands, translates not into ineffectuality but rather into positive evil. Whether the thresher becomes a poet or the linen draper a prime minister, the act and result are equally perverse. What we in an egalitarian society value, Dryden, Swift, and Pope found utterly unnatural and represented as such. When the man suited for a less demanding and responsible profession becomes a poet, he exerts a power of evil beyond the fact of his poetic incompetence. If the majority of men could judge of merit there would be no danger. But in this fallen world, perversity wins its way by blandishments which have nothing to do with deserts. Superficialities of personality or affectations of learning obscure judgment until the worse is thought to be the better course. At this point, however, the satirist comes in; he tears off the mask of deceit and penetrates the veil of ignorance to reveal evil, like Duessa, in all its loathsome filthiness. Satire effects a transformation from the false, alluring shape to the real one.

Presented in a certain way, transformation is a source of the ridiculous. When human beings attempt a metastasis from what is natural to what is perverse and harmful, they become proper objects of ridicule. In his "Preface" to *Joseph Andrews* (1742), Henry Fielding maintains that affectation is the source of the ridiculous, and further subdivides his categories into vanity and hypocrisy. But Fielding never distinguishes between the ridiculous in comedy and in satire. Vanity may be thought of as primarily a comic vice, and hypocrisy, which is usually more serious, may be satiric. But such a distinction can only be tentative pending an analysis of the context in which a vice is viewed. In *Tom Jones* (1749), for example, characters such as Blifil, George Seagrim, Ensign Northerton, Lady Bellaston, and Lord Fellamar represent character types that receive severe treatment in the course of the novel. Despite their existence in the comic world of Fielding's fiction, an inclination to mete out harm, even though finally aborted or nullified, marks them as objects of satire.

But it is the metamorphosis into something harmful or perverse that is the focus of a good deal of satire. In his First Satire of the First Book, Horace meditates at length on the discontent men have with the place nature has assigned to them. Juvenal's Tenth Satire and Johnson's great imitation of it, *The Vanity of Human Wishes* (1749), ponder the disasters that follow our attempt to emerge from obscurity. In Samuel Butler's *Hudibras* (1662–80) religious reformation leads inexorably to transformation of the most grotesque kind. Tailors and tinkers metamorphose quixotically into knights of a dangerously enthusiastic breed. Passions for novelty, fashion, and other chimeras result in the deformation of character, form, and human nature itself.

Although modal satire, which can be found in virtually any genre, is a necessary condition for satire, it is not a sufficient one. The same is true for comic ridicule which should not be mistaken for modal satire or treated as a sufficient cause of formal satire. The essential integrants of generic satire are a combination of modal satire and variable rhetorical and generic structures which are borrowed and de-formed. The dynamic of satire transforms these components into a new generic identity.

David B. Morris has recently suggested that satire is a special kind of fiction which cannot be fully understood within the norms for other genres. Morris is certainly right in reminding us of "the distinctive, strange, and compelling language of satirical fictions."[34] Satire is, indeed, unique in many ways. Nevertheless, it is not so peculiar that we should consider placing it outside the class of mimetic works.

Since Aristotle, apparently in response to Plato's theory of art, argued that tragedy or poetry was not an action, but the imitation of an action, there has been a good deal of controversy over what poetry imitates. Barbara Herrnstein Smith has advanced a persuasive viewpoint which may prove helpful here. She has begun by distinguishing between natural and fictive discourse:

> By 'natural discourse,' I mean here all utterances—trivial or sublime, ill-wrought or eloquent, true or false, scientific or passionate—that can be taken as someone's saying something, somewhere, sometime: i.e., as the verbal acts of real persons on particular occasions in response to particular sets of circumstances. . . . that utterance—cannot recur, for it is historically unique.[35]

Fictive discourse, on the other hand, *represents* such natural utterances or verbal events. It is a linguistic structure, not a linguistic event. To quote Smith once again, fictive discourse "may be distinguished from other mimetic artforms . . ." and "from other verbal compositions. As a mimetic artform, what a poem distinctively and characteristically represents is not images, ideas, feelings, characters, scenes, or worlds, but *discourse*. Poetry does, like drama, represent actions and events, but exclusively verbal ones."[36] By poetry she means all verbal mimesis.

Unfortunately Smith does not deal directly with satire. Indeed, satire that has an immediate political or personal purpose might cause some difficulty to her theory. What distinguishes such satire from purely rhetorical, nonmimetic structures, such as a political broadside that has a practical function and no application beyond it?

The first step in identifying a work as a satire is to differentiate natural discourse and fictive discourse. If the rhetorical structure or logical sequence of a satiric speech or discourse is excessively disrupted by fictive techniques, it is likely to be a generic satire. Such techniques include irony, genre mixing, the use of a persona. An abundance of such strategies causes a malformation or deformation of the text. This leads to a generic transformation to satire. If, however, the fictive devices remain subordinate to the purpose of natural discourse, there is no deformation and, consequently, no generic change from rhetoric to fiction. The primary distinction between modal satire and generic satire is that in the former there is no generic transformation.

A key point in our understanding of satire is its role as a borrower of forms. These forms, as we shall see, may be mimetic or nonmimetic. Indeed, this appropriation of other forms is unique to satire and is one of its chief identifying characteristics.[37]

The extent of that borrowing is also an important consideration and provides us with a significant distinction between simple and complex satire. If a satire restricts its borrowing to rhetorical (nonmimetic) forms or makes use of only one literary (mimetic) structure, it is simple satire. The term "simple" refers merely to there being only one dynamic change or transformation. This corresponds roughly to what many Renaissance and eighteenth-century critics referred to as "unmixed" satire. What separates it from complex satire is this relatively simple structural dynamic and curtailed length. The simple satire also maintains a single basic rhetorical pattern, even when a mimetic structure is the host form.

The basic rhetorical patterns imitated by simple satire correspond roughly to the major categories of classical oratory: demonstrative (epideictic), deliberative (public), and judicial (forensic). These categories enable us to establish the same kind of formal unity for satire that rhetorical theory instituted for the oration, showing us that satires, like orations, can have fundamentally different actions and temporal schemes and yet remain part of a larger generic grouping. That satires fit as comfortably into these categories as they do underscores the close relationship between satire and rhetoric. In some respects all satires are imitations of rhetorical structures. They become satires by deforming the rhetorical structures with strategies calculated to disrupt the normal logic of the rhetorical text.

Even simple satire may be classified as primarily demonstrative, deliberative, or judicial, depending upon its rhetorical and satiric purpose. Even so, it may parody a literary form; and if it does so, it remains simple by not employing any additional generic structures. The parody of a belletristic form becomes satire by the introduction of elements which de-form the host structure while preserving an essentially rhetorical movement or action. The pattern of simple satire extends from one basic host form to formal satire. Once additional generic or rhetorical structures (if the host form is rhetorical) are introduced in the process of deformation, the resulting satire is complex.

Complex satire begins in the same way as simple satire, with a host structure—rhetorical, belletristic, or popular. Like simple satire, it de-forms the host structure by means of modal satire, comic ridicule, and ironic devices. The only difference is the much more elaborate use of additional genres and styles so that the form becomes preeminently mingled satire. As in all satire, the introduction of formations contradictory to the purposes of the host genre de-forms that structure and transforms it into satire. The dynamic of complex satire consists of more than one formal strategy working in relation with one another. Complex satire thus differs from the simple kind only in its much more ambitious use of competing formations and its tendency to become encyclopedic, if not in bulk, then at least in the range of its satiric applications.

Although the rhetorical pattern of its simple phase may be readily recognizable, a complex satire employs such a range of rhetorical and generic strategies that no one category can represent it satisfactorily. In a work such as A *Tale of a Tub* (1704), however, the imitated pattern of a deliberative discourse remains dominant. The wide variety of rhetorical and belletristic strategies employed disrupts the text in other ways than obscuring its basic structure.

The method of imitating another form in satire is parody. Parody of itself, though, does not constitute satire. A comic technique, parody is a primary reagent by which the transformation from borrowed or imitated form to the shape of satire is achieved. Other means associated with parody are an inconsistent or unreliable narrator or persona, illogical shifts in intention or design, introduction of a variety of literary or rhetorical structures, and extreme hyperbole. These characteristics tend to overlap and are commonly identified as belonging to parody.

A more specific technique of parody found in most of the satires discussed in Part 2 of this study is the mock-heroic. The mock-heroic is a comic form or, as mode, a kind of comic ridicule employed in simple and complex satires. As a form of parody, it is not essentially satiric, but is an important reagent for the deformation of epic in the transformation to satire. In complex generic satire, the mock-heroic regularly joins with modal satire and other strategies to transform the imitated structure.

The use of the mock-heroic suggests an important feature of complex satire, namely, its scope. Complex satire employs a wide variety of imitated

forms primarily because it undertakes to satirize something far more complicated and comprehensive than a single individual or limited group. Individual complex satires may seem to focus on persons, such as Shadwell and
Cibber, but they are usually far more ambitious than that. The complexity of
these satires is analogous to that of epic, and like epic, they paint on a broad
canvas. Like epic, too, they employ a wide variation in style well-suited
to present a full and complex view of society. Unlike epic, however, which
normally praises a nation or culture, these satires depict national or cultural
values as being in a state of crisis, if not total collapse.

A general statement about how the mingling of genres produces a satiric
effect may be in order before proceeding to a closer examination of individual
satires. Here again, comic theory can be of assistance. The reductionism
often identified with satire[38] is really a comic technique. Reductionism becomes satiric only when an opposing magnification of harm enters into the
satire. Thus the reduction in stature which the object of satire undergoes
serves not to render him harmless, as in comedy, but to magnify his evil. But
how is this deflation and concurrent amplification achieved?

D. H. Monro has provided some helpful commentary when he explains
the comic by "the linking of disparates, . . . the collision of different mental
spheres, . . . the obtrusion into one context of what belongs in another."[39]
For satirists throughout the first half of the eighteenth century at least, these
"different mental spheres" correspond to genres. In other words, each genre—
tragedy, comedy, pastoral, epic, georgic—has a certain texture, that is, images, style, diction, characters, associated with it. When we are sensitive to
generic subtleties, we immediately react when a shift in style, for example,
takes place within a context governed by another style. Rosalie Colie expressed the concept well when she identified the underlying literary theory of
the Renaissance in the following terms:

> namely, that a literary kind stands for a kind of subject, a kind of con-
> tent, literary and intellectual; and also that some references to a sub-
> ject or content may be taken as metaphors for a whole kind.[40]

No one ascribes greater importance to genre than E. D. Hirsch does when he
argues that "an interpreter's preliminary generic conception of a text is con-
stitutive of everything that he subsequently understands, and . . . this remains the case unless and until that generic conception is altered."[41]

Although attitudes toward genre were changing during the period in which they wrote, the major English satirists—Dryden, Swift, and Pope—possessed a full grasp of generic integrity more kindred with the earlier Renaissance than with later periods. This facility with generic norms gave them a particular advantage in the composition of satire.

The mixing of genres in satire, a phenomenon we shall encounter repeatedly in the course of this study, serves a purpose similar to that in comedy: the reduction or deflation of satiric objects and the magnification of their perversity and consequent harm. But in comedy only the first part of this process takes place. Satiric objects, like comic ones, are normally defined in terms of one generic pattern, and then are put in action in the context of another. This results in incongruity or what Monro calls "inappropriateness."[42] The ineffectuality of a character from one genre trying to act in the context of one to which he is totally foreign is a source of the ridiculous. When the inappropriateness becomes positively harmful, modal satire occurs.

The idea of satire, even simple satire, as primarily a mixed form, may convey a sense of formal confusion. Indeed Alvin Kernan, in what has become a classic perception, describes the satiric scene as essentially chaotic;

> Every author of satire is free to stress the elements of the scene which appear most important to him, but beneath the divergencies of the surface the satiric scene remains fundamentally the same picture of a dense and grotesque world of decaying matter moving without form in response only to physical forces and denying the humane ideal which once molded the crowd into a society and the collection of buildings into a city.[43]

However disordered the milieu under attack, it does not follow that the form of satire, despite its imitation of chaos, is similarly chaotic. Indeed, the generic fragments, while dissecting the modern world, find connections with the idealized traditions of antiquity. As mediator between the real and the ideal, satire sets its gaze squarely on the worst of what is real. Sometimes the utopian vision or panegyrical flight captures for a short while a side of paradise. But whether or not specifically utopian material is present, the use of conventional genres, or even scraps of those genres, implies the existence in the past of an order prior to the dislocation characteristic of the modern world. When we recognize that satire was a vision of chaos in the ancient world as well, the powers of renewal unique to that form seem invested with a special potency. One of satire's many paradoxes is that in apparently having no particular form, it transforms such miscellany into a generic structure. Indeed, that form emerges from the combustible dynamic of mixed literary styles. Further, the relationship of each satire to others in its tradition establishes a pattern or format which is unmistakable. No genre is more dependent on its tradition than is satire.

PART 1
THE SIMPLE
STRUCTURES OF
SATIRE

2
DEMONSTRATIVE SATIRE

At the close of his fine panegyrical poem, *Eleonora* (1692), Dryden reveals how satire may emerge from praise. In a long apostrophe to the lady's soul, he presents himself as a poet who

> dares to sing thy Praises, in a Clime
> Where Vice triumphs, and Vertue is a Crime:
> Where ev'n to draw the Picture of thy Mind,
> Is Satyr on the most of Humane Kind:
> Take it, while yet 'tis Praise; before my rage
> Unsafely just, break loose on this bad Age;
> So bad, that thou thy self had'st no defence,
> From Vice, but barely by departing hence.
> (363–70)[1]

Since the very act of extolling Eleonora's virtues implies a comparison of them with the defects of most other human beings, the poet must restrain himself from emulating Juvenal and breaking into a satiric vein: *Difficile est saturam non scribere*. The conceit is functional, since it provides an explanation for Eleonora's death, but, even more important, it points to an intimate connection between praise and satire. For Dryden, whenever he delivers himself of a panegyric—and he composed many a one—a satire is always implied in the praise. What Dryden was doubtless aware of when he wrote these lines is the structural similarity between panegyric and satire. Both fall under demonstrative oratory in classical rhetorical theory. As Aristotle has it, "cere-monial oratory of display either praises or censures somebody."[2] Further, Aris-totle goes on to identify each kind of rhetoric with a kind of time. The demonstrative or "ceremonial orator is . . . concerned with the present, since all men praise or blame in view of the state of things existing at the time, though they often find it useful also to recall the past and to make guesses at the future."[3]

The most impressive demonstrative or epideictic oratory that survives is in the form of state orations. Perhaps the most famous one of all is that deliv-ered by Pericles in the second book of Thucydides' *History of the Peloponnesian War* (fifth century B.C.). Panegyric is demonstrative oratory, usually in poeti-cal form. Satire, whether verse or prose, is the opposite of panegyric, con-demning rather than praising, although, as we shall see, satire often contains panegyrical passages. As we have seen in Dryden's *Eleonora*, panegyric can contain satiric passages and possess the potential to turn to satire. This rela-tionship between satire and panegyric often results in elaborate mixing of the two modes. When a panegyric is delivered, we are always aware that there may be an effect opposite to that intended. This is what Pericles seems to mean when in the exordium of his oration, he comments on the perils of praise:

> The favourable hearer, and he that knows what was done, will perhaps think what is spoken short of what he would have it, and what it was: and he that is ignorant, will find somewhat on the other side which he will think too much extolled; especially if he hear aught above the pitch of his own nature. For to hear another man praised finds pa-tience so long only, as each man shall think he could himself have done somewhat of that he hears. And if one exceed in their praises, the hearer presently through envy thinks it false.[4]

Although satire is at similar risk, it may prosper by envy. Yet if that satire is too brutal, the object of satire may receive sympathy, thus blunting its effect. Since the satirist is usually regarded as overly sensitive to human foibles, such sympathy may be generated even without undue brutality.

Though seemingly antithetical to one another, satire and panegyric are really close cousins. Whenever one is dominant, the other is implied. That is surely why no formal distinction is made between praise and blame in demon-strative rhetorical theory.

Despite the widespread acceptance of the views of Fred N. Robinson and

Robert C. Elliott that magic and curse are the roots from which later satire has sprung,[5] many theorists, because of their demands for fiction or irony in satire, have failed to treat curse and invective as satire. It is true that this kind of satire is something of an embarrassment to anyone dealing with the complexities of later masters, but the family resemblance cannot be denied. Further, once it is seen that satire in its primary forms is analogous to rhetorical form, much of the difficulty vanishes. Curse or invective, of course, does not conform to the pattern of demonstrative orations. But the denunciatory format is there, and, indeed, there is use of imagery and other rhetorical techniques. Let us consider two examples from Archilochus (seventh century B.C.).

After wishing his enemy shipwrecked, Archilochus imagines him carried off by waves and washed ashore, where

> Thracians with their shaggy hair . . . seize him all nude. Then will he feel a thousand different pangs eating the bread of slavery; his body stiff with cold and covered half with kelp left by the surf of the sea. There may he lie with chattering teeth, at his last gasp, flat on his face, like a dog, cast up by currents on the very farthest shore. . . . how I should love to see him, the man who wronged me, trampled our oath, who once was a friend.[6]

Even in its fragmentary form, we can see the essential demonstrative structure as Aristotle describes it. Archilochus, of course, does more than guess at the future; his curse has the force of incantation. But having vividly foreseen the future, the satirist recalls the past to reveal the reason for his animosity. It is the present condition of his enemy, however, which is the reason for the poem in the first place. The former friend has violated an oath and, until now, has gone unpunished. While attacking its object in his present state, the curse looks forward to his future punishment.

Another poem by Archilochus focuses on the present degraded state of Lycambes who, according to tradition, went back on his word to give Archilochus his daughter in marriage:

> What is this, old Lycambes, what is this you have done? What god has robbed you of your wits? You used to be a clever man, but now, look you are the butt of every joke in town. You have defiled the greatest bond of all, the fellowship of bread and salt.[7]

Here the action is more clearly in the present, although, again, a broken oath in the past is cited as the cause of present ills. Short, compact, even fragmentary, the Archilochan invective, except for its poetic form, is similar to demonstrative oratory.

Although early forms of satire, invective and curse, bear a striking resemblance to demonstrative rhetoric, even as satire became a mimetic art, it preserved its affinity for rhetorical form. This is true, I believe, because satire took a dual path in its development towards rhetorical form as well as towards mimesis. The persuasive quality of so much satire also kept it under the influence of rhetoric.

There is, of course, much disagreement about the early forms which served as a basis for satire's development. Many of the ones mentioned as satiric prototypes, however, are forms of philosophical debate, and, as such, are strongly rhetorical. Robert C. Elliott mentions the Cynic diatribe, the chria, the mime, Atellan farce, the beast fable, and the Theophrastan character.[8] Northrop Frye sees satire beginning "with the Greek *silloi* which were pro-scientific attacks on superstition."[9] Another possible source, specifically for formal verse satire, is the parabasis of Old Comedy. A clearly rhetorical form, the parabasis is marked off from the main dramatic action. Since its purpose is commentary and criticism, it is not an unworthy candidate for status as a precursor of more highly developed satiric forms.

What emerges from this potpourri of early forms is the attitude among scholars of satire that satiric form is a confused issue. The fact that all these forms did contribute to the development of satire and can be found as component parts of many later satires leads to a conclusion which needs to be stated clearly. The reason for the multitude of forms related to satire is twofold. First, satire is by its nature a borrower of forms. Second, these forms, like simple satire, are essentially rhetorical, a fact that accounts for a host of similarities between them.

Although I have identified oratorical form, especially the demonstrative or epideictic kind, with early satiric manifestations, they are not identical. Whether satire predated rhetoric, or rhetoric satire is much like the question of the chicken or the egg. But rhetoric in its simplest expressions would seem to presuppose the more complex forms of tragedy, epic, and satire. If that is so, it may be accurate to say that satire borrows a rhetorical form even as it may borrow a literary or belletristic form as it moves into the complex phase.

"The Satire on the Bards," traditionally ascribed to Taliesin (sixth century?) and contained in the medieval Welsh tale *Gwion Bach and Taliesin,* is a good example of early demonstrative satire. The poem consists of a series of charges against bards who misuse their talent. The poem concludes with the following stanza:

> I do not revile your minstrelsy,
> For God gave that to ward off evil blasphemy;
> But he who practices it in perfidy
> Reviles Jesus and his worship.[10]

Throughout, the poem maintains the present tense appropriate to demonstrative rhetoric and employs no overt techniques of irony or indirection. The invective becomes satire through mimetic art.

To conclude this discussion of demonstrative satire, I should like to examine a poem that, while essentially demonstrative, shows a substantial tendency toward incorporating other rhetorical forms. This poem is Cleveland's celebrated "The Rebel Scot" (1642–43).

Clearly in the manner of Juvenal, Cleveland's poem is modeled on the verse satires of Hall and Marston. The uncontrollable anger characteristic of this tradition and of Marston especially is evident:

> I am all on fire,
> Not all the buckets in a Countrey Quire
> Shall quench my rage.
> (5–7)[11]

To mark the anger even more strongly, Cleveland resorts to the ancient power of the curse:

> Before a *Scot* can properly be curst,
> I must (like *Hocus*) swallow daggers first.
> (25–26)

The poem concluded, Cleveland gets to the business of libeling the Scots. Since the structure of the poem is essentially demonstrative, that is, direct abuse, nearly everything is in the present tense, and what is not refers specifically to the present situation. To the satirist's overwrought mind, Scotland is

> A Land where one may pray with curst intent,
> O may they never suffer banishment!

Had *Cain* been *Scot,* God would have chang'd his doome,
Not forc'd him wander, but confin'd him home.
(61–64)

The "curst intent" and the curse of Cain fulfill Cleveland's desire to imple-
ment the force of magical incantation against a people whose rebellious
nature has fomented a full-scale civil war.

But even in this intrinsically demonstrative and simple series of couplet
incantations, the satirist is making some interesting additions. First of all,
there is a brief panegyrical segment, which emerges naturally from the general
vituperation:

Nature her selfe doth Scotch-men beasts confesse,
Making their Countrey such a wildernesse:
A Land that brings in question and suspense
Gods omnipresence, but that CHARLES came thence:
But that *Montrose* and *Crawfords* loyall Band
Atton'd their sins, and christ'ned halfe the Land.
Nor is it all the Nation hath these spots;
There is a Church, as well as *Kirk* of Scots . . .
(47–54)

This passage hardly qualifies as a vision of utopia, but it is clearly panegyric,
balancing somewhat the negative assessment of the Scots at large. As such it
is reminiscent of Dryden's technique in *Absalom and Achitophel,* when the
plotters are paralleled to Barzillai and the other supporters of the king, as well
as to the king himself.

Another aspect of the poem which might suggest something of Dryden's
strategy in *Absalom and Achitophel* is the prophetic or deliberative element
that Cleveland employs near the end of his poem. Unlike Dryden, however,
Cleveland calls for harsh measures against the rebels:

Nor gold, nor Acts of Grace; 'tis steel must tame
The stubborn *Scot:* A Prince that would reclaime
Rebells by yeelding, doth like him (or worse)
Who sadled his own back to shame his horse.
(91–94)

The satirist concludes with an apocalyptic vision of hell. Into the infernal
regions pour the souls of the executed Scots rebels.

Thus Cleveland uses an essentially demonstrative format, but he introduces brief panegyric and a deliberative element near the conclusion. There is a certain judicial tendency in the poem as well, but since the past actions of the Scots are not considered, the judicial element arises more by implication than by overt design. As in *Absalom and Achitophel*, no specific decision is reached. But here the king, like David in Dryden's poem, who has the power to conclude the conflict successfully, is given the benefit of Cleveland's bloody advice.

Demonstrative satire consists of most of the fundamental satiric utterances. From curse to lampoon to larger forms that never develop beyond the raw anger of the satirist, demonstrative satire encompasses direct attack in the present tense against individuals or specific groups. It is the most vituperative of satiric expressions, but the anger it imitates finds quite naturally the shape of demonstrative rhetoric.

But not all demonstrative satire is imprecatory. Erasmus's *Moriae Encomium* (1511) is rather mild satire when compared with other demonstrative works, but it follows an epideictic pattern more or less closely depending on which commentator you happen to be reading. Hoyt Hudson, for example, saw the *Moriae* as a manifestation of the Roman demonstrative oration and presented a detailed analytical table to support his contention.[12] Finding Quintilian's Roman paradigm inadequate to account for all parts of the *Moriae*, Walter Kaiser has compared the organization of the work to the Aphthonian scheme which Erasmus would have known through Lucian.[13] More recently, however, Clarence Miller has expressed doubts about Kaiser's proposal and has suggested the loosely structured *lalia* as a more likely model.[14]

It is not surprising that the *Moriae* can now be seen as imitating a less rigorously prescriptive oratorical model. In his careful study of the speeches in Vergil's *Aeneid*, Gilbert Highet could find no evidence of a formulary pattern.[15] Indeed, oratory itself was less strictly formulated than the handbooks often suggest. Imitated orations in literary works conform even less to the rules.

The *Moriae Encomium* is nonetheless an exemplary demonstrative structure within general limits. It fluctuates between ironic praise, mild invective, and, finally, encomium without obvious irony. In moving through all of these phases, the work shows the potential, at least, to become complex. At each point, Stultitia, or Folly, undergoes transformations which correspond to the modes in which she speaks.

Not only does Folly exhibit a protean identity, she is herself capable of effecting change in others. Her opening remarks about her audience are a case in point:

> when the sun first reveals his fair golden face to the earth, or when a harsh winter yields to the balmy breezes of early spring, everything suddenly takes on a new appearance, a new color, and a certain youthful freshness: so too, when you caught sight of me, your faces were transformed. Thus, what these eloquent orators can hardly accomplish in a long and carefully thought out speech—namely, to clear the mind of troubles and sorrows—that very goal I achieved in a flash simply by making an appearance.[16]

At the outset Folly's agenda would be daunting to anyone but a fool. It is to transform unhappiness into joy, pain into pleasure, disaccord into compatibility, and self-reproach to self-love. Through ironic sleight of hand, she makes the old young again:

> just as the gods of mythology help the dying by some metamorphosis, so I too bring those who already have one foot in the grave, back once more as close as possible to childhood. (20)

Although we are likely to resist Folly's logic that second childhood is a desirable state, she presses her argument to show that an old man who has lost contact with reality avoids thereby the "wretched worries that torment the wise man" (21). Stultitia, who has stressed her powers of change, analyzes them in greater detail:

> Now anyone who likes can go and compare this benefit of mine with the sort of metamorphosis bestowed by the other gods. No need to mention what they do when they are angry: those whom they favor most, they have a habit of turning into a tree, a bird, a locust, or even a snake—as if to become something else were not in itself a kind of death. But I, on the other hand, restore the same man to the happiest part of his life. In fact, if mortals would refrain completely from any contact with wisdom and live their entire lives with me, there would not be any old age at all. Instead, they would enjoy perpetual youth and live happily ever after. (22)

The specific reference to Ovid's *Metamorphoses* (early first century) proves that Folly's imagery of transformation has a direct literary antecedent. Here, though, we are taken further. Folly foreshadows her own transformation to come by speaking of the gods as if she is herself one of them. Indeed, by the end of the oration, with the transvaluation of values complete, all will receive invitations to metamorphose into Christians on a very different basis from what is offered by the present Church. At this stage Folly offers eternal youth in the ironic context of second childhood and the rejection of the seriousness associated with maturity. Later, however, the promise of eternal youth will translate into eternal salvation. Folly continues directly to assert her own divinity by arguing that only the contemptible and repulsive gods lack "a share of my divine afflatus" (24).

Folly's praise of self-love (*philautia*) is a particularly important stage of her design. First she blames Nature for implanting "a defect in the minds of mortals—especially those who have little more intelligence—namely, the tendency to be dissatisfied with what they have and to admire what belongs to others" (34). This defect, however, paradoxically leads to rejection of all one's natural qualities, exemplified by self-love. Since Folly wishes to provide us with happiness, self-love, being the chief point of happiness, leads to this result (35).

If, however, we are too much inclined to read all of Folly's praise as reversing accepted values, we shall be stymied by her assertion that foolishness is necessary in war. Here the reader must heartily agree that Folly has spoken the truth, but her praise of war puts her clearly on the wrong side of the question.

With the Sileni of Alcibiades, Erasmus introduces the central image of paradox, which serves as a representation of satire itself.[17] With the Sileni "what appears . . . to be death, will, if you examine it more closely, turn out to be life; conversely, life will turn out to be death . . ." (43). This is precisely the kernel of truth Erasmus has had waiting for us. Wisdom is folly; folly, wisdom. At the heart of satire, despite the playfulness and nonsense, lies the truth: that the expulsion of all human emotions, which the stoic wisemen take such pride in achieving, is a violation of human nature (45). To follow Folly's advice is to follow nature.

But if the groundwork for Erasmus's Christian-Epicurean position is laid down by Folly throughout the first part of her oration, she never permits us to read everything in this way. Gamblers, liars, flatterers, the superstitious are all praised, and so satirized by indirection. This inconsistency of presentation, however, disrupts the text and confounds the readers' expectations. Realizing that we are dealing with an ironic fiction of unusual subtlety, we, the readers, must give the work our undivided attention. But just as we become accustomed to the unexpected, Folly shifts gears into an overdrive of invective.

At the opening of part 2, this bold, unironic satire begins with the momentary intention of surveying society from top to bottom (76). Here Folly tries to abate her enthusiasm by making "the lives of outstanding personages" her focal point. But in spite of herself, she completes a relatively lengthy tirade against the common people, who all belong to her (76).

Grammarians, poets, rhetoricians, scholars, lawyers, dialecticians, philosophers, theologians, religious, kings and courtiers, popes, cardinals, and bishops are all inducted into Folly's company, but here without the mildness of the Erasmian satire in the first part of the book. Folly concludes with a bitter attack on priests, especially secular ones. But suddenly she utters a disclaimer:

> [I]t is no part of my present plan to rummage through the lives of popes and priests, lest I should seem to be composing a satire rather than delivering an encomium, or lest anyone should imagine I am reproaching good princes when I praise bad ones. (115)

In part 1 we moved fitfully between Folly's encomium (indirect satire) and an Erasmian attempt to set up nature as a standard of judgment. In the second part, Folly reveals the evils of the most powerful and influential members of society. The concluding disclaimer proves beyond question that the supposed encomium has been transformed to a satire. The instability of the persona, greater in the earlier editions than in later revisions, stops short of the admission that Erasmus is speaking in propria persona: "But I will stop *propounding apothegms* lest I seem to have rifled the commentaries of my friend Erasmus" (116).

Folly next observes how devoid wise men are either of friends or riches. She then employs the scholars' technique of citing authorities, commencing with the ancient authors. Recognizing the ancients' lack of authority among Christians, she then begins the process of justifying herself by reference to scripture. This she does by reinterpreting attacks on fools as support for them. She takes for her authority St. Paul himself, who interpreted a pagan inscription on an altar as "an argument for the Christian Faith" (124). Folly follows Paul in this, arriving at the conclusion "that the Christian religion taken all together has a certain affinity with some sort of folly and has little or nothing to do with wisdom" (132).

This new definition of fool, applied to those "with a burning devotion to Christian piety" (132) marks yet another change in the form and meaning of the *Moriae Encomium*. What was indirect satire, employing irony, became direct invective in the second part. Now, in the third section, Folly returns to encomium, but also establishes an Erasmian theology which was foreshadowed in the first part. Yet neither is the satiric function abandoned. The Pauline Christianity, as interpreted by Erasmus, becomes a standing reproach to the scholastic philosophy and contemporary religious practice satirized in part 2. Erasmus's form of piety focuses on spiritual things only, but the popes, cardinals, bishops, and priests attacked earlier wallow in material concerns:

> the pious man flees from whatever is related to the body and is carried away in the pursuit of the eternal and invisible things of the spirit. (136)

This spiritualism, which Folly calls madness, is a first step in a transformation that is even more profound after death:

> the spirit, stronger at last and victorious, will absorb the body. And it will do so all the more easily, partly because it is in its own kingdom now, partly because even in its former life it had purged and refined the body in preparation for such a transformation. Then the spirit will be absorbed by that highest mind of all, whose power is infinitely greater, in such a way that the whole man will be outside himself, and will be happy for no other reason than that he is located outside himself, and will receive unspeakable joy from that Highest Good which gathers all things to Himself. (136–37)

The oration ends with an adaptation of Erasmian spirituality to living individuals transported, for short periods, by "madness." This process makes the satiric point even sharper: the professions under attack in both parts 1 and 2 were characterized by their materialism, by their love of physical pleasures. Now such pleasures can be good if they lead to things of the spirit, but since as practiced they do not, that materialism is a perversion of nature. Erasmus's simple message is that worldly vanities lead us away from supreme spiritual values. Like so many satirists, Erasmus is something of a reactionary. He returns, as M. A. Screech has recently argued, "to the riches of the Greek Bible and of the early Greek fathers of the Church, as well as to the Christian insights of the great early Latins, especially Jerome, Ambrose, Augustine."[18]

But Erasmus has not chosen to state his viewpoint simply, partly because he understood what a controversy he was entering, and partly because what he was saying did not admit of simple statement. Natural pleasures, such as sex and drinking, have their place in the natural life that leads to God, Erasmus believes. It is a mistake to make life a denial of physical joy. Those who denounce such pleasures and deprive themselves of them turn instead to the complexities of theology, statecraft, and, ultimately, war. Here is the danger to man that satire denounces. These unnatural pursuits, capped by war, transform men into monsters incapable of grasping the simple piety requisite to natural spiritual transcendence.

The form of the *Moriae Encomium* seems appropriate to the paradoxical nature of its content. The work seems to be a demonstrative oration, although the person of Folly makes its fictiveness clear from the outset. But the quizzical letter to More at the beginning and Folly's stated unwillingness to conclude properly with a peroration (138) are only two of the more obvious aberrations. The movement from the indirect, ironic satire of part 1 presented as encomium to the open invective of part 2 and then back to real encomium, the praise of Christian folly, are textual disruptions that tell us this is a satire, an imitation of a demonstrative oration. Erasmus's unification of formal and thematic transformations provides a significant model for the practice of later satire.

3

DELIBERATIVE SATIRE

We shall have occasion to remark how many satires contain a deliberative element. As with demonstrative forms, this element is a likely survival of the close relationship between satire and rhetorical form. The deliberative oration, from which this form derives, is a speech before a council, legislative body, or even the general population. Deliberative speeches outline a program or recommend a course of action. For example, the Phillippics of Demosthenes (384–322 B.C.) deliberate the possible courses of action open to the Athenians in their struggles against Phillip of Macedon.

The act of deliberation gives form to a large number of satires, and of these the dialogue is one of the most numerous. Dialogue normally embodies a discussion of an issue leading to a course of action. Unlike demonstrative satire which focuses on the present, the dialogue and other deliberative forms look to the future.

Dialogues that are satires usually parody dialogues drawn from other genres. Drama, epic, philosophy, and history supply dialogues with nonsatiric purposes, although each of these forms can provide satiric dialogues as well. A dialogue becomes a satire when its primary purpose is satiric. Quite often dialogues that are satires make use of a narrative setting or frame.

The dialogue form in satire can be found as early as the works of Ennius (239–169 B.C.) and Lucilius (second century B.C.).[1] With few exceptions, the satires of Horace (first century B.C.), Persius (34–62), and Juvenal (early second century) make use of this same format. For example, Horace's First

Satire of the Second Book is a deliberation between the poet and the famed lawyer Trebatius over whether to continue writing satire. "Please advise me, Trebatius; what am I to do?" Horace queries his friend.[2] The resolution of the deliberation comes about when a trial is imagined for the offending satirist. Trebatius describes the danger: "if a party compose / foul verses to another's hurt, a hearing and trial / ensue" (81–83). Horace, however, arranges the trial in his own favor:

> Foul verses, yes; but what if a party compose
> fine verses which win a favourable verdict from Caesar?
> Or snarl at a public menace when he himself is blameless?
> (83–85)

Trebatius, brilliant lawyer that he is, foresees the only possible result: "The indictment will dissolve in laughter and you'll go scot free" (86).

Although a judicial element, quite appropriate in view of Trebatius's profession, emerges here, the poem remains essentially deliberative. What Horace will do in the future remains the primary focus. The trial scene merely confirms him in the profession of satirist.

Most of Horace's satires follow this deliberative procedure. After a central question is asked somewhere early in the poem, the remainder of the sermo is devoted to answering it. Examples are abundant. In 2:7 Davus asks "quid, si me stultior ipso / quingentis empto drachmis deprenderis?" ("What if you were found to be a greater fool than even I, who cost you five hundred drachmas?") (42–43).[3] In 2:3 Damasippus comments on Horace's inability to produce a substantial quantity of poetry, and quickly the deliberative question is raised: "quid fiet?" ("What will be the end?") (4).

Horace does vary his deliberative structure and even experiments with demonstrative forms (Satires 1:7, 1:8). But even so the deliberative question, directly posed or implied, tends to govern the logical order of the poem.

Persius seems to follow the textbook more closely than Horace, perhaps explaining in part why his often obscure satires were so highly valued by neoclassical critics. All six of them present deliberative questions early, and the remainder of the poem is dedicated to a full and often complex response. In Satire 2, for example, the attack on superstition, a favorite device among satirists, may be summed up in the following rhetorical question: "Heus age, responde (minimum est quod scire laboro): / de Jove quid sentis?" (Come now, answer me this question: it is a very little thing that I want to know; What is your opinion of Jupiter?) (17–18).[4] The real question which Persius presents is "How are we to pray to the gods?" But the seeming absurdity of the first construction carries the reader along into a series of equally absurd superstitions. When, at last, the gamut has been run, Persius produces his response to the deliberative question he posed:

> compositum ius fasque animo sanctosque recessus
> mentis et incoctum generoso pectus honesto.
> (a soul where human and divine commands are blended, a mind
> which is pure within, a heart steeped in fine old honour.)[5]
>
> (73–74)

In Satire 3 Persius is the object of a lecture on the evils of sloth and the virtues of Stoic philosophy. Again, the procedure is deliberative, since the advice points toward future action.

But not all of Persius' satires, deliberative though they be, take exactly the same structure. Satire 4, apparently influenced by the pseudo-Platonic dialogue "Alcibiades I," looks ahead to Lucian's dialogues of the dead. Although it preserves a fairly strict deliberative structure, Satire 6 is an epistle.

Juvenal's rhetorical regularity seems even more striking than Persius'. Like his predecessor, Juvenal presents a question or simple declaration early in the satire, which determines the action or focus of the poem.

Satire 1 is a good example of Juvenal's use of a leading question. In the opening hemistich ("Semper ego auditor tantum?") a series of questions is begun. Examples in response to those rhetorical questions follow. Sometimes the examples come first, as in this famous passage:

> When a limp eunuch gets wived, and women, breasts Amazon-
>   naked,
> Face wild boars at the games, or a fellow who once was a barber
> (I ought to know; he shaved me) grows richer than all the
>   patricians,
> When that spawn of the Nile, Curly the Cur of Canopus,
> Hitches his crimson cloak with a jerk of his idiot shoulder,
> Air-cools his summer ring, or tries to—his fingers are sweating—
> And is unable to stand the burden of one more carat,
> Then it is difficult NOT to write satire.[6]

The final declaration, probably the most famous hemistich in Juvenal, is really a declarative form of the dominant question: "How can I keep from writing satire? Am I to keep my mouth shut when I see such outrages taking place everywhere?" These questions set the deliberative tenor of the poem, and the examples of immoral and perverse conduct answer the questions in support of the satirist's position. Thus the satire is written as naturally as Juvenal pretends it can be: by presenting the evils of the day, with a minimum of comment, the satirist does his job.

Satire 2 asks several related questions of which "castigas turpia, cum sis / inter Socraticos notissima fossa cinaedos?" (You rail at foul practices, do you, / When you're the ditch where they dig, the Socratic buggering perverts?) (9–10)[7] is the most central. How indeed can the Romans set themselves up as moralists when they are immoral? This is the basic issue, and, once again, Juvenal's multitudinous examples provide evidence of Roman immorality.

Satire 3 is more dramatic than most of the others, with Umbricius the major character of the piece. Here again there is a central inquiry: "Quid Romae faciam?" (What should I do in Rome?) (41).[8] The format is essentially deliberative, turning on what Umbricius can do with his future life. Since the answer is that a moral man cannot survive in Rome, he has come to the conclusion that his only recourse is to leave.

Satire 6, for all its length, is also simply organized. Postumus, who is contemplating marriage, receives the satirist's candid advice: "Don't!" Plain rhetorical questions, such as "certe sanus eras; uxorem, Postume, ducis? / dic, qua Tisiphone, quibus exagitare colubris?" (Surely you used to be sane. Postumus are you taking a wife? / Tell me what Fury, what snakes, have driven you on to this madness?) (28–29)[9] prepare for the host of examples of women who make their husbands miserable by breaking their marriage vows or behaving in other unworthy ways.

Satire 7, on the poverty of poets, proceeds to an enthymeme:

> Only poets who receive adequate support can write good poetry.
> No poets receive support.
> ∴ No poets write good poetry.

The enthymeme appears in the form of a typical Juvenalian query: "neque enim cantare sub antro / Pierio thyrsumque potest contingere maesta / paupertas atque aeris inops . . .?" (But Poverty isn't a singer— / How can you sing in the grot when you haven't a cent in your pockets?) (59–61).[10] The plea for patronage extends to rhetoricians as well, adding an even more poignant personal touch.

Satire 9 has a simple dramatic structure. The speaker meets an acquaintance who looks the worse for wear. The man responds to inquiries by detailing
his sad fate as homosexual whore and general sexual factotum. The satire is
deliberative, since the speaker gives Naevolus advice and is in turn answered
by him. The conclusion of the deliberation is that the life devoted to pleasure
is thankless and wasteful:

> "What about my particular case, with so much time wasted,
> Disappointment, dismay? For our life is most short and unhappy,
> Fading away like a flower, and even while we are drinking,
> Calling for garlands and girls and perfumes, old age steals upon us,
> Always, before we know." [11]

Satire 10 has a very orderly structure. Knoche observes that it "resembles
a declamation in poetic form on the folly of human wishes." [12] Indeed the
opening of the poem takes the form of an enthymeme, which is basic to
many deliberative orations. With a slight adjustment, the syllogism may be
stated thus:

Prayers not governed by reason will be harmful.
Human prayers are not governed by reason.
∴ Human prayers will be harmful.

Early in the poem Juvenal briefly presents some of the categories of human
wishes with which he will deal later on: eloquence, physical prowess, and
love of riches. Riches take precedence, since more people have been ruined
by a passion for wealth than by any other. The poem, thus, immediately deals
with this important issue. Desire for wealth is so widespread that the satirist
wonders how Heraclitus could produce enough tears to weep as he did at the
follies of men (29–30).
The weeping philosopher, who is not named, merely serves in counter-
point to the more important figure of Democritus. Democritus, of course, is
the laughing philosopher who, by means of his laughter at the follies of mankind, refuses to make Fortune a goddess (52–53). To some degree also he represents the satirist, who, like Democritus, is a lonely outcast from his city by
virtue of his insight, if not in actuality.
Having mentioned physical strength earlier, the poet turns to power generally in the narration of the fall of Sejanus. Next, eloquence, also mentioned

earlier, is reintroduced. The disastrous ends of Demosthenes and Cicero are alluded to.

These falls from the high places of public life lead to the next category, military success. This recalls Juvenal's early observation that vain wishes are to be found in both civil and military settings: "nocitura toga, nocitura petuntur / militia . . ." (In peace, in war, in both, we ask for the things that will hurt us) (8–9).[13]

Next the prayer for long life is found to be specious and destructive. Finally, the bad effects of the beauty that parents wish for their children are catalogued in detail.

At the close of the satire, the philosophical motif of the early part becomes the means of resolution: "orandum est ut sit mens sana in corpore sano" (Pray for a healthy mind in a healthy body) (356).[14] Additional Stoic virtues may also be sought:

> Pray for . . . a spirit
> Unafraid of death, but reconciled to it, and able
> To bear up, to endure whatever troubles afflict it,
> Free from hate and desire, preferring Hercules' labors
> To the cushions and loves and feasts of Sardanapalus.[15]

Just as virtue was the only true source of nobility in Satire 8, it is the only road to the life of peace and tranquillity here in Satire 10 (363–64). In the concluding distich, the poet observes:

> If men had any sense, Fortune would not be a goddess.
> We are the ones who make her so, and give her a place in the
>   heavens.[16]

This conclusion brings Democritus, the aggressive philosopher of the early part of the poem, to mind again. We recall that

> cum Fortunae ipse minaci
> mandaret laqueum mediumque ostenderet unguem.
> (When Fortune threatened he told her to hang herself,
> and raised his middle finger in the air for good measure.)[17]
>   (52–53)

The resolution of this satire comes about through a rigorous but plain rhetorical organization. We begin with a subject for deliberation and conclude with a solution to the problem. In Satire 10, as in Juvenal's other poems, the deliberative rhetorical structure conveys a unity and clarity from beginning to end.

What I have tried to show by this short examination of the three major Roman satirists—Horace, Persius, and Juvenal—is that the form of their satires can be understood in relation to deliberative rhetoric. This is not to say that those satires are organized like model orations, but rather that the simple, logical format of a deliberation lies behind the more complex poetic and satiric strategies and effects. As in all satire, the transformation from the host form (in this case, rhetoric) to generic satire is the dynamic that makes these formal verse satires works of art.

Whether or not it fulfills all the requirements of a formal verse satire as outlined by later European authors and summed up by Dryden in his criticism, each satire can be understood in terms of a rhetorical form, usually deliberative, but sometimes demonstrative. This is true as well of verse satire in the later Elizabethan and early Jacobean periods, whether the essentially Juvenalian poems of John Marston and Joseph Hall, or the more Horatian satires of John Donne and Ben Jonson. Rochester's later *Satyr Against Reason and Mankind* (1679) possesses an even more rigorous deliberative structure. What is important to keep in mind, however, is that although formal verse satire demands treatment as a subgenre, it belongs as well to a much broader tradition of generic satire.

Another dialogue format used in satire is the dialogue of the dead. Like every other kind of dialogue, it is not necessarily used for satiric purposes. But it is often chosen for satire. This form, the earliest extant examples of which are by Lucian, is particularly attractive to satirists because it lends itself to parodic reinterpretations of history. Conversations between persons who could never have met and who represent different cultural and intellectual positions provide fresh perspectives on important ideas and events.[18]

In Lucian, the erroneous values of the wealthy and powerful can be seen for what they are in the context of hell. The dead, who no longer have use for wealth and status, nonetheless cling to their vain possessions. Where all men and women are brought to one dead level, only the Cynics, Diogenes and Menippus, behave creditably (See "Menippus and Cerberus") and possess an adequate philosophical grasp of the issues of life and death. In part 3 of *Gulliver's Travels* (1726), Gulliver interviews a number of significant figures from Homer on in a tongue-in-cheek revision of history. Henry Fielding also experimented with the form in *A Journey From this World to the Next* (1743), in which the classical judge of souls, Minos, plays an important role in some strongly judicial passages, as he decides who may enter Elysium.

A very important deliberative format is the symposium. This is, as Northrop Frye points out,[19] an elaboration of the dialogue form. Just as the dialogue of the dead exists in epic poetry (book 9 of the *Odyssey*, book 6 of the *Aeneid*), the symposium does as well. Telemachus dines with Menelaus and Helen, Odysseus with the Phaeacians, and the suitors, without the leave of Penelope or the absent Odysseus, appropriate the royal table in hopes of usurping even more. As Fielding noted, the *Odyssey* is an "eating poem."[20] Early in *Tom Jones* (1749), Fielding calls his book a feast and uses the banquet or a simple meal as touchstones of moral rectitude. The pigsty manners of a Parson Trulliber in *Joseph Andrews* (1742) appear most egregious at table.

Using Homer as a criterion, ancient commentators recognized the banquet as a central metaphor. Athenaeus, sometime after 280 A.D., composed an encyclopedic work on banquets in which he discussed the art and morality of the form. For example, in valuing Homer's banquets above all others, Athenaeus compares them with feasts of his own age: "his [Homer's] heroes sit at their banquets, and do not lie down. . . . But now we have come to such a pitch of effeminacy as to lie down while at our meals."[21]

After Homer, the great literary symposia of ancient Greece were philosophic in character. The banquets of Plato and Xenophon are best known, but Epicurus, among others, also composed a symposium. Another important example of the nonsatiric symposium is Macrobius's *Saturnalia* (fifth century?). An extended dialogue, it is an encyclopedic display of knowledge assembled for a pedagogical purpose. From this work Vergil emerges as the complete rhetorician and perfect model for emulation.

Indeed the symposium of antiquity tends toward either encyclopedic comprehensiveness or philosophic pointedness. In either case, however, the banquet is a metaphor representing the world at large. Dio Chrysostom (second century), for example, makes the banquet a microcosm of the world in his *Thirtieth Discourse*. Not all persons, Dio tells us, "enjoy the merrymaking and banqueting in the same way, but each according to his own nature."[22] The moral significance of the banquet continues to occupy thinkers through the Renaissance and into the eighteenth century. Petrarch, for example, in his *Letter to Posterity* (1373), troubles himself with the issue of luxury, particularly with regard to the taking of meals:

> I have always possessed an extreme contempt for wealth; not that riches are not desirable in themselves, but because I hate the anxiety and care which are invariably associated with them. I certainly do not long to be able to give gorgeous banquets. I have, on the contrary, led

a happier existence with plain living and ordinary fare than all the followers of Apicius, with their elaborate dainties. So-called "convivia", which are but vulgar bouts, sinning against sobriety and good manners, have always been repugnant to me. I have ever felt that it was irksome and profitless to invite others to such affairs, and not less so to be bidden to them myself. On the other hand, the pleasure of dining with one's friends is so great that nothing has ever given me more delight than their unexpected arrival, nor have I ever willingly sat down to table without a companion.[23]

Petrarch's ethical position is usually prominent in satiric symposia. It is such ethical commonplaces of the Western tradition that give generic satire a unified moral viewpoint transcending local culture. But it is not only an agreement in ethical principles that sustains satire. Just as important are the structural similarities which unite the earliest satires with those of the eighteenth century. Far from being the "farrago" implied by the term *satura*, satire has a rhetorical and ethical focus that is seldom approached in intensity by the other genres.

The earliest satiric banquets are to be found in Aristophanes (fifth century B.C.). *Knights* may be read as an extended parody of a symposium, and in *Ecclesiazusae* the disruption of the legal system culminates in dinner. The first banquets as satires, however, can be found in the work of Lucilius. In book 5, for example, there is an account of a rustic meal, book 13 probably contains a *cena* too, and book 20 describes a famous banquet given by the herald Granius. Lucilius is thought to have given yet another description of this last banquet in book 21. The fact that additional symposia could be found in books 28 and 30 indicates that Lucilius turned to that form so often as to make it a standard motif at the very initial stages of the formal verse satire.

Horace follows Lucilius with a description of an unsatisfactory banquet in Satire 2:8, the *Cena Nasidienus*. Here the banquet is presented in a dialogue between two persons, Horace and a friend, so that we have two structures: the normal verse satire conversation between the satirist speaker and his interlocutor; and the banquet itself within the dialogue frame.

Juvenal's Satire 5 is also a banquet, although as usual Juvenal keeps his poem much closer to a sharply defined rhetorical organization than Horace does. Nevertheless, Trebius is a friend and, for purposes of this poem, an adversary, who is chastised for attending dinners like the one described, where humiliation rather than satisfaction is the reward. Juvenal's Satire 11 is reminiscent of Horace's 2:2. Both poets compare the sumptuous banquet with the simple life and fare of rural districts. As in much satire, the banquet in both poems serves as a symbol of excess and disharmony. As in bad art, a bad banquet has no unity of theme, purpose, or action. Everything is in poor taste. In the satire, on the other hand, although excess and disunity provide the major themes under scrutiny, the satirist's attitude toward his material provides an equable balance. Further, the introduction of a utopian vision, in these cases, one of rural health, establishes a sense of proportion. Panegyric emerges to counterbalance satire. Generic difference creates harmony in a *concordia discors.*

If the satirist risks madness in his vocation, he rights that imbalance by presenting an idealized vision. And even if that ideal is not specifically evoked, where satire is most intense, its opposite, panegyric, is always implied. To condemn is always to imply that something better is possible, just as panegyric always constitutes satire against those who fall short of the praiseworthy virtues. This does not mean that amendment is always possible. Some objects of satire may be beyond such hope. But to say something is bad is also to say that things can be better or at least should be. Thus satire always contains an antidote to its own poison, whether in theme or form. When chaos is viewed in satire, the perspective is that of a civilized expectation structuring the disunity it perceives and denigrates. In one sense satire destroys the subject matter to which it applies its sting, but even as it does that, it recreates the material in an essentially humane structure of human proportions, which is the satire itself. Satire does not transcend human existence as epic and tragedy tend to do. Although satire becomes the microscope under which all that is wrong with humanity can be seen at its worst, it is nonetheless an instrument of human proportions and human making. Its forms are those most intimately associated with human expression and social need: the letter, the banquet, the discourse, the court at law. These are relatively homely structures to be sure, but they are primary structures too, where the chaos of human experience can be made tractable on a human scale.

The full range of worldly desires emerges in Petronius' *Cena Trimalchionis* (first century), the first satiric banquet in prose. Trimalchio is a modern success story. He has risen from slavery to enormous wealth and prestige. But his rise has come through corruption, not out of it, and his origins and ignorance dog his every attempt to recreate his image. Having become a vile master, he remains always a slave. Thus he represents Roman society from top to bottom in its love of money, its superstition and bad taste.

Lucian's "Symposium, or the Lapiths" (second century) is a banquet set in a framing dialogue between Philo and his friend Lycinus. The satire is primarily an attack on the incivility of philosophers expressed, finally, in a vulgar brawl. The Stoics are the worst behaved, and, as is usual in Lucian, the Epicureans are the best. A heated philosophical debate destroys the concord of a wedding banquet and turns the hall into a shambles when a complete disrespect for rational debate leads to physical violence.

Horace's Satire 2:8, the *Cena Nasidienus*, provides the primary model for three important symposia in formal verse satire: Mathurin Régnier's Eleventh Satire (1608), Nicholas Boileau's Third Satire (1665), and John Wilmot, Earl of Rochester's "Timon" (1680). David Farley-Hills makes a valuable comparison of these symposia, but attributes the dispute on literary matters and subsequent donnybrook in each of the poems to Régnier's invention and imitation by his two successors.[24] A more likely possibility is that, although using Horace as his main source, Régnier is borrowing the idea for the dispute and brawl from Lucian's symposium. Régnier, witness to a more brutal and irrational world than Horace, evidently found Lucian's conclusion more to his liking, and had no reservations about introducing it into his Horatian imitation. Although Boileau and Rochester probably knew Lucian's satire, Dustin Griffin is likely correct in asserting that Rochester knew Régnier's work and relied on it for significant details.[25]

This pattern of borrowing is particularly interesting because it marks yet another example of Ovidian influence. Lucian's "Symposium, or the Lapiths" is directly influenced by one of the most brutal banquets ever imagined, Ovid's tale of the centaurs and the Lapiths in book 12 of the *Metamorphoses*. As in Lucian, the scene is a marriage feast. One of the guests, the centaur Eurytus, hot with wine, attacks the bride herself in a fit of lust. The other centaurs join in and wreak havoc until Theseus leads the Lapiths in a bloody counterattack against them. The battle is described at length and in heroic (perhaps mock-heroic) terms. Finally, true to Ovid's central theme of metamorphosis, the Lapith hero Caenus (if the account be true) turns into a golden bird which takes wing to heaven. Lucian, Régnier, Boileau, and Rochester, however, dispense with the divine transformation. They have as their respective focal points the more mundane transformations of supposedly civilized men and institutions into savagery approximating that of Ovid's centaurs.

Transformations, some explicitly Ovidian, are very common in formal satires. Swift's *Baucis and Philemon* (1709) is a direct imitation of Ovid which transforms itself into a satire as the homely couple experiences a series of metamorphoses. The translations of Shadwell to the throne of dullness, of Belinda into termagant, and of Gulliver to Houyhnhnm postulant are just a few of the transmutations that satire records. Formal social occasions, such as a coronation, a trip to Hampton Court, or a symposium, provide appropriate settings in which to chronicle the human kaleidoscope.

The symposium survives as a satiric format in later fiction. There are elaborate banquets in Thomas Love Peacock's *Headlong Hall* (1816), *Nightmare Abbey* (1818), *Crotchet Castle* (1831), and *Gryll Grange* (1860). These parodies of philosophical symposia, in which ideas, not food, are the primary fare, are more comic than satiric; but the influence of generic satire on the novels that contain them should not be underestimated. Like complex satire, Peacock's work makes use of many genres, but parody is the usual mode. Comic plots and comic resolutions in these novels may reinforce a satiric point against gothic novels and other romantic excesses. But the tendency to assimilate novelistic closure takes Peacock's work away from the open-endedness normal to generic satire.

A novel strongly influenced in form by Peacock's novels of ideas is Aldous Huxley's *Crome Yellow* (1922). Specific borrowings from such satires as *Absalom and Achitophel* and *Gulliver's Travels* make it probable that the secret banquets of the Lapith sisters were influenced more by Lucian's *Symposium* than by Ovid. Indeed, the characteristically Lucianic attack on false intellectuality is the modus operandi of Huxley's novel.

Yet another deliberative form borrowed for purposes of satire is the epistle. Epistolary satires normally deliberate over an issue or an action. The recipient of the epistle may be an important factor or largely ignored. In more complex epistolary structures, there is an exchange of letters and irony is heightened from either side of a correspondence.

The verse epistles of Horace are in many ways a further development of the *sermo*.[26] Unlike the satires, however, the epistles stress philosophical questions and moderate direct satire. Although Renaissance criticism held that the epistle was different from verse satire, it was nonetheless to be classified as satire.[27] Conventional wisdom held that satires were chiefly to attack vice and drive it out; epistles, on the other hand, had the function of inculcating virtue.

Although there is some truth in this division of responsibility, it is to be expected that theory will seldom be an exact description of practice, and this is no exception. It is difficult to divide Horace's satires and epistles into precise categories. His satires are not nearly as circumscribed in their attacks on vice as most Renaissance critics would have them, and the epistles do not always refrain from sharp satire. If there is a difference to be noted, it is that the epistle is an even freer form than the satire. The epistle, with its greater emphasis on virtue, tends more toward panegyric, helping to create a highly mixed form that increasingly becomes the model for most satire. Indeed, the verse epistle, more than the verse satire, was to become the model for a great deal of prose satire throughout the Renaissance and eighteenth century.

There were, of course, verse epistles in vague imitation of Horace, but before Boileau's regularization of the epistle, they were mainly satires in epistolary form. Making small distinction between satire and epistle, Ariosto called his seven epistolary poems satires. Ben Jonson, in England, was also fond of putting his satiric poems in the form of verse letters.

It was in prose, however, that epistolary satire became really significant. Two of Lucian's most brilliant "biographical" works are in this form: *Alexander the False Prophet* and *The Death of Peregrinus*. Sententious epistles by Cicero, Seneca, and Pliny the Younger, although not satiric, imparted prestige to the letter format and so indirectly influenced the development of epistolary satire.

The letters of the great humanists of the Renaissance, modeled on those of ancient Rome, led directly to the first major satiric masterpiece in letter form of the period. Ulrich von Hutten and his German collaborators composed *The Letters of Obscure Men* (1516), an exchange of imaginary letters directed against anti-Semitism in the sixteenth-century Church.

The prose letter as a weapon in religious dispute rose to new heights in Pascal's *Provincial Letters* (1656–7). Many of these letters, and perhaps the most effective of them, are narrative accounts of conversations between the speaker and the Jesuit opponents of the Jansenists. Although having no direct connection with the English tradition of anti-Jesuit satire, the *Provincial Letters* is the most brilliant among such remarkable works as Donne's *Ignatius His Conclave* (1611) and John Oldham's *Satires Upon the Jesuits* (1678–81). Donne's prose work, however, is a predominantly judicial structure, and Oldham's poems, while mainly deliberative (the fourth satire is demonstrative), may together be taken as a complex satire.

Perhaps the first attempt to present modern Europe from an exotic viewpoint is a series of ironic letters, the first volume of which was published in French by Giovanni Marana in 1684. Succeeding volumes appeared in English as *Letters Writ By a Turkish Spy*. Supposedly written by one Mahmut, residing in Paris, to a number of correspondents in the Muslim world, the *Letters* satirize self-righteousness and complacency in religion by showing the

Muslims to be as sure of the truth of their beliefs as their counterparts in the Christian world. The antagonism toward religion and the tendency to regard it as mere superstition reflect a strong enlightenment point of view.

Influenced by Marana's work, Montesquieu's classic exchange of letters, *The Persian Letters* (1721), comments on French politics, customs, and literature from the perspective of a Persian residing in Paris. The exemplary model of Montesquieu was followed later in the eighteenth century by Oliver Goldsmith in his "Chinese Letters," later named *The Citizen of the World* (1760–61). The influence of such works on the epistolary novel is not within the scope of this book; but in such an elaborate form, the letter exchange begins to move into artistic areas claimed by the novel.

Another important example of deliberative satiric structure is the discourse. In antiquity the discourse was an oration, and therefore meant to be delivered orally. But by the seventeenth century, deliberative discourses were often destined to appear only in print. Some well-known examples of such satires are Nathaniel Ward's *Simple Cobbler of Agawam* (1647), Defoe's *The Shortest Way With Dissenters* (1702), and Swift's *Argument Against Abolishing Christianity* (1708) and *A Modest Proposal* (1729). In these works the organization is clear. A basic project is espoused or opposed. The projector goes on to prove his point as he would in a deliberative oration, and, indeed, the structure is similar to the rhetorical form. The examples cited above are all parodies of real discourses, either because of the use of irony, the assumption of a persona, or by reason of a madcap procedure. The organization and structure of the satire are similar to those of a real oration, but the premises or logic does not conform to the norms of rhetoric. In short, satire achieves a freedom from usual rhetorical procedure. One reason why it is such a difficult mode to define is its protean individuality. Nevertheless, as we have seen, it possesses certain norms, at least in its basic attachment to traditional structures. The very essence of satire is its freedom from restraint, but the movement toward that freedom always implies a circumscribed starting point and boundaries to violate. Satire achieves its freedom by finding its way in a pattern of traditional forms. Once all such restraint is thrown off, the effectiveness of satire tends to diminish.

Nathaniel Ward assumes the role of a poor American cobbler to present in an imaginative, neologizing style an unimaginative argument against the principles of toleration. There is a semblance of a logical procedure, although the work often gives way to a cranky enthusiasm untempered by irony.

Andrew Marvell's *The Rehearsal Transpros'd* (1672), an attack on Samuel

Parker, is both a controversial work and a parody of such a work. Like Ward's satire, it affects anger and a madcap style. Marvell explains his intention in his concluding remarks:

> And now I have done. And shall think my self largely recompensed for this trouble, if any one that hath been formerly of another mind, shall learn by this Example, that it is not impossible to be merry and angry as long time as I have been writing, without profaning and violating those things which are and ought to be most sacred.[28]

James Sutherland has called *The Rehearsal Transpros'd* a "rambling, shapeless, and often trivial and irrelevant" piece of writing.[29] But such a bantering style was widely appreciated in the later seventeenth century. A manner linked to satire commanded respect.

Very much the same kind of banter brought John Eachard's work into prominence. *The Grounds and Occasions of the Contempt of the Clergy* (1670) and *Mr. Hobb's State of Nature Considered* (1672) are mild satire, if indeed we can call what is mostly droll comedy satire at all.[30] Yet what is important to note here is that the deliberative structure of Eachard's controversial discourses is unmistakable.

Daniel Defoe's "The Shortest Way with Dissenters" is a remarkable example of the deliberative discourse. The major difficulty in reading it as a satire is that it relies, perhaps too heavily, on a single exaggerated proposal: i.e., a call for the execution of dissenters who refuse to submit to the Church of England. Once this proposal is countenanced as plausible, there are no significant disruptions in the text to signal the existence of satire.

Swift's "Against Abolishing Christianity" and "A Modest Proposal" are much more obviously satire than "The Shortest Way." In both of these magnificent deliberative structures the text is sufficiently distorted to leave no doubt about the object of attack and the fact that these are imitations of deliberative discourses. Both parody serious discourses and employ a devastating irony to condemn the mind that puts economic considerations ahead of religion and humanity.

Yet another class of deliberative satires is based on Edmund Waller's "Instructions to a Painter" (1665) and an Italian tradition of pictorial poetry of which Waller's panegyric is an imitation. Andrew Marvell invented the satiric version of these "painter poems" with his "Second Advice to a Painter" (1666). In the subsequent exchange with various antagonists, he contributed three additional satires: "Third Advice to a Painter" (1666), *The Last Instructions to a Painter* (1667), and "Further Advice to a Painter" (1671). *The Last Instructions*, by far the most remarkable of the painter satires, is a combination of satire and partisan history. Its striking combination of portraits, satiric and elegiac pastoral, and historical and epic scope carry it quite beyond simple satire. *The Last Instructions* is a good example of how a poem of real quality can emerge from a sub-genre.

Instructions to a painter poems continued to appear until roughly the middle of the nineteenth century.[31] Such persistence gives them serious claim to be regarded as a minor genre.

Every commentator on Thomas More's *Utopia* (1516) must come to terms with its generic status. Is it a satire? Or is it a serious contribution on government couched in an imaginary politeia? The answer is not an easy one, but the generic approach to satire outlined thus far can provide some help.

What we know of the composition of the *Utopia* will prove relevant. If we accept J. H. Hexter's analysis of the order of composition, the introductory portion of book 1 up to the beginning of the dialogue of counsel and the major portion of book 2 were written by More during his stay in the Netherlands from May to late October 1515.[32] The dialogue of counsel, including the extended symposium at Cardinal Morton's residence and the exordium, in part 1 and the peroration and conclusion of part 2 were composed after More's return to England and before he sent the manuscript to Erasmus in September 1516.[33] These facts suggest that More began with the intention of writing an imaginary politeia, since the introductory parts of book 1 and the bulk of book 2 compose precisely such a work. Even assuming that all the satiric material, explicit and implied, in book 2 was written while More was in the Netherlands, the preponderance of the contents suggests an intended politeia.

With the addition of the dialogue of counsel and the subsequent contents of part 1, the peroration and conclusion to part 2, and the extensive prolegomenal and suffixal material, the *Utopia*, from a structural standpoint, is a formal satire. Since it assumes several rhetorical forms, it is technically a complex satire. But its retention of a deliberative pattern throughout makes it an ideal example of a work in transition between simple and complex satire.

The extensive prefatory material, consisting of letters from Erasmus, Budé, Giles, Desmarais, Busleyden, and, of course, More himself, matter on the Utopian alphabet, poems, and maps of Utopia, must all be taken as part of the final structure. In addition to providing a sense of verisimilitude, it unveils immediately the *via diversa* associated with mixed satire.[34] The letters to and from real persons, with explicit and implicit acceptance of the truth of Hythlodaeus and his utopian experience, present both a trap to the unwary and a clear warning to practiced readers. The anecdote by Beatus Rhenanus about the man who could not understand why More received such praise for his *Utopia,* when all he did was copy out what Raphael Hythlodaeus had told him, suggests that the perils of an unsophisticated reading were very much in the minds of More and his friends. The immoderate addition of prefatory materials to successive editions is an early example of what was to become common in later deliberative satire.

More's letter to Giles represents an epitome of the intended effect. The fiction that Raphael is the source of knowledge about Utopia is maintained in the same breath as other factual observations, such as More's lack of leisure because of his professional duties and his family responsibilities (39–41).[35] The supposed disagreement between More and his pupil, John Clement (who was present to hear Raphael's narrative), over the length of the bridge that spans the river Anydrus and the expectation that Giles will resolve it expands both the verisimilitude and multiple ironies which govern the entire work. More's proposal to resolve the discrepancies focuses the irony:

> If you do not remember, I shall put down, as I have actually done, what I myself seem to remember. Just as I shall take great pains to have nothing incorrect in the book, so, if there is doubt about anything, I shall rather tell an objective falsehood than an intentional lie—for I would rather be honest than wise. (41)

The nearly full page of nonsense that follows, Raphael's hopes of becoming bishop to the Utopians and More's willingness to withdraw his work if Raphael wished to write his own adventures, must strike the alert reader as precisely that. Our author is simply too scrupulous—too overtly honest—to be true. Further, his strong admonition to those who fear satirical wit (45) persuades us that he is either totally inept or up to some mischief.

The banquet simile in the penultimate paragraph of the letter to Giles establishes a central image for the book in keeping with its deliberative structure. The letter introduces the book as factual report and symposium, but expresses fear of a readership of limited perception. A partial resolution of this difficulty will come in part 1 when John Cardinal Morton's attitude toward the fool and regard for Hythlodaeus mark him as an exemplar of taste and tolerance. Such a man, it goes without saying, would make a fit audience for the *Utopia.*

The book's satiric utility is enhanced by the fact that Raphael's knowledge of strange lands is never valued for its own sake. He looks at everything with the eye of a moralist:

> just as he called attention to many ill-advised customs among these new nations, so he rehearsed not a few points from which our own cities, nations, races, and kingdoms may take example for the correction of their errors. (55)

But Raphael declines to put that skill at the service of a king, and he uses More's suggestion that he do so as a pretext for a vigorous attack on courtiers.

When this is completed, Raphael shifts the scene to a symposium presided over by the former Lord Chancellor of England, Cardinal Morton. Here we see the open-mindedness of Morton as he responds with interest to the radical critiques by Hythlodaeus of capital punishment for theft, the laws of inclosure, and the monopolies of wealth (65–71). But when a lawyer prepares to counter these points in tedious detail, Morton adjourns the debate and requests additional facts from Raphael (71).

Proving again his knack for applying a knowledge of foreign customs to insoluble local problems, Hythlodaeus gives us a foretaste of his technique in part 2 by drawing cogent examples from his travels (75). The courtiers, as expected, unite in disapproving of his advice to substitute slavery for the death penalty. But when Morton detects merit in the plan, chameleonlike, they praise what they had just condemned (81).

Next the foolish parasite, a figure out of Roman comedy or Horatian satire, contributes an attack on secular religious. But when a friar seeks to make use of this for his own advantage and that of his order, the parasite insults the monastic orders by proposing that beggars be distributed among the Benedictine monasteries and convents (83). In the exchange that follows, the friar displays both his temper and his ignorance of Latin, despite the Cardinal's attempts to restore peace. With the friar at his highest pitch of anger, Morton counsels wise moderation:

> "Maybe," said the Cardinal, "you behave with proper feeling, but I think that you would act, if not more holily, at any rate more wisely, if you would not set your wits against those of a silly fellow and provoke a foolish duel with a fool." (85)

It bears repeating in this context that Morton's respect for Hythlodaeus's suggestions and his tolerance of the fool's insults provide us with a model response to the *Utopia* as a whole. Morton's enlightened view is that rejection of Raphael's proposals is premature and inappropriate since present policies are manifestly unsuccessful. Further, the implementation of Raphael's recommendations would entail no risk. Finally, when remarks like the fool's are made a serious response is uncalled for. To the *Utopia*, a mixture of serious and foolish propositions, we should have a complex reaction.

Another aspect of this indirect method appears in the disagreement between More and Raphael on the subject of statecraft. More speaks for a tactful approach to erroneous opinions:

> by the indirect approach you must seek and strive to the best of your power to handle matters tactfully. What you cannot turn to good you must make as little bad as you can. (99–101)

Hythlodaeus, of course, responds in vigorous opposition:

> By this approach . . . I should accomplish nothing else than to share the madness of others as I tried to cure their lunacy. If I would stick to the truth, I must needs speak in the manner I have described. To speak falsehoods, for all I know, may be the part of a philosopher, but it is certainly not for me. (101)

Raphael will have full opportunity to speak out in part 2, indeed, as he does in part 1. But More's method of indirection prevails. In his role as outspoken man, without regard for the consequences of his speech, Hythlodaeus contrasts with the cautious More, whose very presence and expression of reservations temper the views of the bluff old seacaptain, even as they provide a foil to them. Moreover, such indirection is the method of satire. It is clearly related to the *spoudegeloion*, the wise-fooling of the Socratic dialogues and Horatian satire.[36] Raphael's plain speaking is thus qualified by the complex of formal strategies which the book itself represents.

This method creates obvious difficulties for the interpretation of the *Utopia* as a politeia. The repetition of certain basic proposals, e.g., the abolition of private property, may provide us with a sense of which propositions are most important. But whatever the status of the *Utopia* as politeia, the work is much less ambiguous when interpreted as a satire. The strange institutions of the Utopians need not be evaluated literally as social proposals. Rather they serve the function of calling attention to the pride and ignorance which cripple European institutions. Even more they show how far Europe had deviated from the basic principles of the early Christians. And, like Erasmus, More associated those principles with the natural law.[37] We need not believe that More felt a society based on the natural law was possible to understand that a closer approximation of that law would improve any society. Indeed, the qualifications the character More places on Raphael's proposals suggest that accepting them literally will only cloud the real issues the book raises. Those issues are satiric ones: the failure of modern institutions because of their deviation from the natural law. Since, for More, the early Christians' rites reflected the keeping of the natural law, modern practices may be seen as deviations from pristine Christianity as well.

Since the natural law concerns itself only with necessities, the Utopians, with no concern for money, value only what is needed for healthful subsistence. With everyone, or nearly everyone, employed, labor can be limited to six hours a day. Nature, therefore, sets a limit to toil. On the other hand, Europeans, who use money, are addicted to luxury. Devoting themselves to the acquisition of wealth, they trade tranquillity for the pride of riches. Since pride "counts it a personal glory to excel others by superfluous display of possessions," it cannot exist in a society that has excluded personal ownership of any kind whatsoever (139).

Although the Utopians have not, for the most part, been introduced to Christianity, some of their actions illustrate early Christian principles. For example, the Utopians associate gold and silver with ill fame (153) and bind prisoners and slaves with those metals. Precious stones they use to adorn little children (153). This information prepares us to interpret the episode of the Anemolian ambassadors' ill-conceived attempt to impress the Utopians. When the citizens see them in their "splendid adornment" of gold and jewels (155), the ambassadors are the recipients of scorn and laughter instead of the admiration they expect. What More very likely has in mind here is St. Paul's reflection that when he was a child, he spake as a child and thought as a child, but since becoming a man, he has put those things away (1 Cor. 13:11). The ambassadors, unlike the Utopians, have failed to heed Paul's injunction. Also, since the natural properties of gold and jewels entitle them to no special status (151), it is a violation of the natural law to ascribe significance to them. That the Anemolians stand for Europeans in their overestimation of such baubles is implicit in the Utopians' bewilderment at such behavior:

> They wonder, too, that gold, which by its very nature is so useless, is now everywhere in the world valued so highly that man himself, through whose agency and for whose use it got this value, is priced much cheaper than gold itself. This is true to such an extent that a blockhead who has no more intelligence than a log and who is as dishonest as he is foolish keeps in bondage many wise men and good men merely for the reason that a great heap of gold coins happens to be his. (157)

Here again is a violation of the natural law. Even the humblest of men should be ranked above mere things. And yet Europe is witness daily to the sacrifice of human lives to the getting of money.

Hythlodaeus's consistent application of Utopian "facts" to European foibles disrupts the rhetorical stability of the politeia of part 2. But the peroration and conclusion, added later in London, make the satiric point even clearer. After surveying the injustice of the European system, Raphael launches into a tirade against pride:

> Pride measures prosperity not by her own advantages but by others' disadvantages. Pride would not consent to be made even a goddess if no poor wretches were left for her to domineer over and scoff at, if her good fortune might not dazzle by comparison with their miseries, if the display of her riches did not torment and intensify their poverty. This serpent from hell entwines itself around the hearts of men and acts like the suckfish in preventing and hindering them from entering on a better way of life. (243–45)

Reflecting on the fact that "Pride is too deeply fixed in men to be easily plucked out" (245), Raphael goes on to rejoice in the good fortune of the Utopians who "At home . . . have extirpated the roots of ambition and factionalism along with all the other vices" (245). Even in the unfettered expression of an honest sea captain there is no sense that the Europeans can accomplish a utopian renovation. Even more important it is clear that they will have no will to do so.

The character More, clearly siding with popular opinion, takes issue, in the conclusion, with the centerpiece of Utopian civilization, what he describes as "very absurdly established in the customs and laws of the people described" (245). This is "their common life and subsistence—without any exchange of money" (245). "This latter alone," More judges, "utterly over-throws all the nobility, magnificence, splendor, and majesty which are, in the estimation of the common people, the true glories and ornaments of the com-monwealth" (245). This judgment returns us to Raphael's interpretation of pride. If the pride of the rich is the golden calf of the common people, as the character More affirms, then Hythlodaeus is right to imply that Utopian re-forms will never be seen in Europe. Utopian ideals remain merely as part of an imaginary politeia. But they provide form and substance to an effective satire against the primary evils of the modern world.

More's *Utopia*, then, consists of several deliberative rhetorical structures: epistle, dialogue, symposium, and politeia. Although identifiable as separate entities for the purpose of analysis, these constructions lose their formal iden-tities by becoming part of the dynamic of generic satire. Such deformation is a necessary first stage in the transformation of deliberative rhetoric to delibera-tive satire. Also, by imitating a variety of deliberative structures, More has demonstrated a command of some of the more subtle operations of complex satire. For example, by employing an imaginary politeia within a framework of competing constructions and rhetorical entropy, he has intensified his sa-tiric effect. Correlative to this generic transformation, More has manipulated a thematic one. By revealing in detail the norms of Utopian society under the natural law, he limns a probable metamorphosis of Europe to its present state of corruption. Like so many satires within the paramount tradition, the *Uto-pia* reveals a contempt for the modern world and a reactionary confidence in an earlier, undegenerate system of institutions.

4
JUDICIAL SATIRE

Few have read Byron's *The Vision of Judgment* (1821) without a keen awareness that the poem is built upon a tradition. Byron's own prefatory material refers us to Quevedo's *Visions* (1627), Fielding's *A Journey From this World to the Next* (1743), Chaucer's "Wife of Bath's Tale" (fourteenth century), Pulci's *Morgante Maggiore* (1482), Swift's *A Tale of a Tub* (1704), and last (and certainly least), Southey's *A Vision of Judgment* (1821), both subject and object of Byron's parody. Curiously, Byron fails to mention some of the most important works that compose the tradition in which he is writing and of which he was doubtless aware.

The visionary aspects of Byron's poem connect it with the middle ages and, more specifically, with the best and worst visionary poetry of his contemporaries. The medieval connection is relevant, since in a poem such as *Piers Plowman* (fourteenth century) vision and satire are united. Among the English poets of the early nineteenth century, on the other hand, it was left to Byron to turn vision to the uses of satire once again. The result was to be a scathing but comic critique of the excessively sober visionary poetry of the Romantic period, of which Southey's poem is one of the most egregious examples.

In addition to drawing on the tradition of dream visions, *The Vision of Judgment* makes use of a little noticed category of satire. When George III, "an old man / With an old soul, and both extremely blind" (181–82),[1] arrives at heaven's gate with an angelic company, we realize that a judicial procedure of sorts is imminent. The satire will proceed, more or less, along legal lines as in a court of law. Indeed, the use of explicit judicial settings for satire was a tradition of long standing by Byron's time.

We have to return to ancient Greece to find the earliest judicial settings. Aristophanes, for example, shows a substantial interest in the law courts and legal processes of Athens. In the *Wasps* Philocleon is "a law-court lover, like no one else. He loves judging, and groans if he's not in the front row."[2] In the *Frogs* there is a judgment of dramatic poets in Hades, in which Euripides, the butt of satire, loses out to Aeschylus. Again, in parody, the procedures and language of the law courts play a significant role.

Although the Old Comedy bears a resemblance to satire and major satiric themes in many respects, classical scholarship remains reluctant to link Aristophanes to the history of satire. Indeed, it seems more likely that Old Comedy and satire seem similar on a thematic basis because they are both related to rhetoric. In short, satire and Old Comedy share certain themes and structural patterns found in oratorical forms, and one of the principal oratorical forms is, of course, judicial rhetoric.

In Byron's *The Vision of Judgment* and earlier satires in the same mode, there is a narrative element which is not to be found in judicial orations. This includes a judicial setting and the parody of judicial procedure.

The ancient Athenian fixation with law courts and legal procedures marks the rise of rhetoric as the art of persuasion with a decidedly nonliterary function. Of course, rhetoric had always been associated with literature, and the Homeric poems contain speeches which are brilliant examples of oratory. These became models for the speeches of the later epics of Apollonius Rhodius, Vergil, and, of course, such Renaissance practitioners as Tasso and Milton. But Aristophanic comedy remains the best example of a literary use of specifically judicial forms.

After Aristophanes the most thoroughgoing critique of Athenian judicial procedure is to be found in Plato's early dialogue, the *Apology*. Along with the trial of Jesus, Socrates' trial stands as an embarrassing reminder of the injustice of which human beings are capable. But the trial of Socrates, unlike that of Jesus, contains no elements of a providential design to muddy the waters. Socrates' unjust condemnation is an unsullied example of an ingrained human preference for injustice.

The *Apology* is Socrates' defense against the charges brought against him over the years and those which provide the immediate occasion for the trial itself. First: "There is a wise man called Socrates who has theories about the heavens and has investigated everything below the earth, and can make the weaker argument defeat the stronger."[3] The new deposition, which, Socrates argues, is hardly a fresh prosecution, is this: "Socrates is guilty of corrupting the minds of the young, and of believing in deities of his own invention instead of the gods recognized by the state."[4]

One of the most remarkable achievements of Plato's early dialogues is, as F. M. Cornford pointed out many years ago,

> the way in which Plato, writing philosophy in dialogue form under the influence of the Sicilian Mime as practised by Sophron, exactly reversed the role of Socrates, and spent his early life as a man of letters in setting his master before us in the opposite character of the *eiron*.[5]

Thus Socrates, who had been the butt of comedy in Aristophanes' *The Clouds* and, apparently, other works as well, becomes the prototype for all philosophers who follow. In doing this, it is relevant to add that Socrates employs many of the ironic procedures later to be identified with satire.

After the oracle at Delphi had proclaimed him wisest of men, Socrates understood his life as "a sort of pilgrimage undertaken to establish the truth of the oracle once for all."[6] If his life was a search for truth, his trial is the culmination and justification of that life. But since the quest after truth led Socrates to discredit those who pretended to knowledge rather than to establish a body of knowledge on his own, his role is analogous to that of a satirist:

> It seemed to me, as I pursued my investigation at the god's command, that the people with the greatest reputations were almost entirely deficient, while others who were supposed to be their inferiors were much better qualified in practical intelligence.[7]

Since Socrates believes "that real wisdom is the property of God, and this oracle is his way of telling us that human wisdom has little or no value,"[8] he assists the cause of God by proving that anyone who claims to be wise is really not so at all.[9] Socrates' chief method of doing this is his dialectic, that irritating habit of cross-examination, which was largely responsible for his getting into trouble with the state and its citizens in the first place.

So it is the method employed by Socrates the gadfly that has brought the wrath of Athens upon him. Since Socrates' position is eminently just, the Athenians must pervert their system of justice in order to condemn the philosopher, just as the earlier oligarchy had ignored justice to take the property and life of Leon of Salamis. In this judicial murder Socrates refused to assist, and his own murder, under similar circumstances, was later performed by the democracy that had succeeded the oligarchy.

The death of Socrates will always be a strong indictment against the kind of justice humankind administers. Socrates, however, recognized the possibility of justice beyond the jurisdiction of human beings when he reflected on a blessing which death may bring:

> If on arrival in the other world, beyond the reach of our so-called justice, one will find there the true judges who are said to preside in those courts, Minos and Rhadamanthus and Aeacus and Triptolemus and all those other half-divinities who were upright in their earthly life, would that be an unrewarding journey?[10]

Unable to find justice in the real world, Socrates resorts to the imaginative power of Greek myth to discover a more hospitable judicial setting. This vision he lends to the satirists who follow him. They, in their turn, parody and critique the legal system and the process of judgment at every level, from the lowest district court presided over by an illiterate justice to the gates of heaven or hell.

Judicial satire comprises a large number of varied approaches. It is possible, however, to classify them according to the setting. First of all, there is the contemporary court situation, usually a parody of court practice in use at the time of writing. Second, there is the court scene in an historical setting. A third category consists of judgment pieces known as sessions poems. And the fourth and final category comprises those satires that depict the judgment of souls at the gates of heaven or hell.

Lucilius, the first writer of formal verse satires, seems to have led the way in judicial satire too. The first and only satire of his Second Book was apparently a parody of the trial of the jurist Quintus Mucius Scaevola. Of the other Roman satirists, Juvenal focused specifically on a courtroom trial in the Thirteenth Satire.

With Lucian the fantastic and allegorical are introduced in "The Dead Come to Life" and "The Double Indictment," wherein the satirist presents himself on trial for his opinions and the direction of his career.

Influential satiric "courts at law" scenes can be found in works that are not essentially satires. For example, in Rabelais' *Tiers Livre* (1546), the old judge Bridoye admits to using dice to reach a verdict. Although, at first glance, the scene would seem to be an indictment of judges, issues of divine guidance emerge to take the meaning far beyond the satiric. Pantagruel's eloquent plea for mercy in behalf of Bridoye leads us to some serious religious questions and some positive meanings for Bridoye's absurd procedure.[11] In *Don Quixote* (1605–15), Sancho's rendering of Solomonic justice as governor of the island is satiric insofar as it ridicules real judges, who, with more learning than Sancho, are not so wise. Like Rabelais, however, Cervantes refuses to restrict his meaning. Sancho also exemplifies the wise fool.[12] Both *Gargantua and Pantagruel* and *Don Quixote* are examples of the paradoxical literature of the Renaissance, under the strong influence of Erasmus' *Praise of Folly*. In these works, even satiric ironies are turned into comic affirmation.

A work with religious import strictly subordinated to satire is John Caryll's *Naboth's Vinyard* (1679). As in I Kings, Ahab covets Naboth's vineyard, but its owner refuses to sell it to the king. In order to secure the vineyard Ahab orders the judicial murder of Naboth. Here the biblical allegory becomes a vehicle to satirize royal interference in the system of justice. There is no trial, however, in the biblical source. It is Caryll's invention entirely. In fact, with the inclusion of the satiric trial, the very brief tale of Naboth is extended by Caryll to a poem of nearly five hundred lines.

The injustice of King Ahab is the opposite of the just administration of the laws promised by David of Dryden's great poem *Absalom and Achitophel*. Although no trial of plotters against the king is enacted in the poem, the rigor of the law is poised for imminent implementation:

> Must I at length the Sword of Justice draw?
> Oh curst Effects of necessary Law!
> How ill my Fear they by my Mercy scan,
> Beware the Fury of a Patient Man.
> Law they require, let Law then shew her Face;
> They coud not be content to look on Grace
> (1002–7)[13]
> . . . .
> By their own arts 'tis Righteously decreed,
> Those dire Artificers of Death shall bleed.
> Against themselves their Witnesses will Swear,
> Till Viper-like their Mother Plot they tear:
> And suck for Nutriment that bloody gore
> Which was their Principle of Life before.
> (1010–15)

Here the Old Testament setting points up, through the use of allegory, the serious challenge to law and stability which Shaftesbury and Monmouth, the principal conspirators pose. The poem cites the relevant evidence to be used by the prosecution if a trial of the plotters should become necessary.

The best known of the so-called sessions poems is Sir John Suckling's "The Wits," also called "A Sessions of the Poets" (1637). This is a "trial for the bays," in the tradition of the "judgment of Paris," in which Apollo proposes to award the laurel to the most deserving of Suckling's contemporaries. In quatrains set in a version of the "bob and wheel," Suckling disposes of the wits of his time:

> The first that broke silence was good old *Ben,*
> Prepar'd before with Canary wine,
> And he told them plainly he deserv'd the Bayes,
> For his were call'd Works, where others were but Plaies;
>   And
> Bid them remember how he had purg'd the Stage
> Of errors, that had lasted many an Age,
> And he hop'd they did think the *silent Woman,*
> *The Fox,* and the *Alchymist* out done by no man.
>   (17–24)[14]

At the conclusion no poet receives the bays. Rather the poets are ridiculed for their poverty and, in the same figure, the politicians, for their graft:

> At length who but an Alderman did appear,
> At which *Will. Davenant* began to swear;
> But wiser *Apollo* bid him draw nigher,
> And when he was mounted a little higher
>   He
> Openly declared that 'twas the best signe
> Of good store of wit to have good store of coyn,
> And without a Syllable more or lesse said,
> He put the Laurel on the Aldermans head.
>   (103–10)

The sessions poems depict trials in which the formalities of the court are not observed, and where a prize, not punishment, is the reward. In *A Session of the Poets* (1676) Apollo awards the bays to Tom Betterton, the player, thereby angering the poets. In *The Lover's Session* (1687) Venus presides and in *The Session of Ladies* (1688) Cupid is present to judge the ladies who compete for the favors of a decrepit Adonis.

The final group of judgment pieces, and the ones that come closest in format to Byron's *The Vision of Judgment*, depict judgment in the other world. The most venerable of this kind is the *Apocolocyntosis* (first century), a prose work, possibly by Seneca, in which the emperor Claudius, recently deceased, is imagined being refused admittance to heaven and accepting a menial position in hades. The emperor Julian's "Symposium, or Kronia" (fourth century) combines banquet motifs with a council of the gods, but it is clearly a judgment piece and a judicial satire. The allegorical figure Dike passes judgment on the Caesars who attempt to join the banquet of the gods. The gods cross-examine and judge the great rulers and conquerors who come before them.

A work clearly dependent on the *Apocolocyntosis* is Erasmus' *Julius Exclusus* (1517), in which the bellicose Pope Julius, like Claudius before him, is denied entrance to heaven after a full review of the crimes he committed during his life. Both Lucianic and Erasmian is John Donne's *Ignatius His Conclave* (1611). In this judicial satire the setting is hell. Ignatius of Loyola argues for his right to the place of honor beside Lucifer's throne by proving his own evil greater than that of his modern competitors. Functioning as "kings Atturney," Ignatius conducts quasi-judicial proceedings against a succession of adversaries. Copernicus and Paracelsus succumb rather easily; Machiavelli proves more resistant. But at last Ignatius triumphs by hurling Pope Boniface from the seat of honor. Lucifer cooperates out of fear of being deposed himself, presumably by one of even greater evil. Like *Ignatius*, the *Suennos* (1627) of Quevedo are satires framed by a dream vision. These "visions" contain many variations on the judgment theme as it reflects on morality in society at large. Quevedo's concern is typical rather than topical, and his ethical review cuts through all social strata. The range of social concern in the *Suennos* is similar to that in the author's celebrated picaresque novel, *La Vida del Buscón* (1626).

Close to the Lucianic spirit of Quevedo is Fielding's *A Journey From this World to the Next* (1743), especially chapter 7. Excluding the powerful, pretentious, and uncharitable, Minos admits the poor, humble, and repentant to Elysium. Fielding's emphasis on sentiment, character, and plot, however, look ahead to his novels. Nonetheless, the satiric provenance of this work is unmistakable. The justice meted out at the gates of Elysium is in stark contrast with the unjust proceedings of the world. Even allowing for the comic tone of much of these works, most satirists imply a certain confidence in eternal justice.

Byron, however, is an exception. Indeed, his sharp rejection of many traditional values, coupled with a high respect for traditional literary forms, makes *The Vision of Judgment* a remarkably original poem. Yet even here

Byron makes his own way. Following directly in the line of the *Apocolocyntosis* and *Julius Exclusus,* although neither of those works is a poem, Byron sets up a loosely organized judicial structure—a trial—to determine the fitness of George III, newly deceased, to enter the kingdom of heaven.

The poem is first of all a parody of "A Vision of Judgment," Robert Southey's bathetic rendering, in classical hexameters, of the king's apotheosis. Byron begins by setting the record straight, in ottava rima, as antidote to Southey's heroic view of George:

> In the first year of freedom's second dawn
>   Died George the Third; although no tyrant, one
> Who shielded tyrants, till each sense withdrawn
>   Left him nor mental nor external sun:
> A better farmer ne'er brush'd dew from lawn,
>   A worse king never left a realm undone!
>   (57–62)

In Southey's poem we witness the beatification of this same king:

> Thither the King drew nigh, and kneeling he drank of the water.
> Oh, what a change was wrought! In the semblance of age he had
>   risen,
> Such as at last he appeared, with the traces of time and affliction
> Deep on his faded form, when the burden of years was upon him.
> Oh, what a change was wrought! For now the corruptible put on
> Incorruption; the mortal put off mortality. Rising
> Rejuvenescent, he stood in a glorified body obnoxious
> Never again to change, nor to evil and trouble and sorrow,
> But for eternity formed, and to bliss everlasting appointed.[15]

But for Byron there is no transformation from corruption:

> It seem'd the mockery of hell to fold
> The rottenness of eighty years in gold.
>
> So mix his body with the dust! It might
>   Return to what it *must* far sooner, were
> The natural compound left alone to fight
>   Its way back into earth, and fire, and air;
> But the unnatural balsams merely blight
>   What nature made him at his birth, as bare

As the mere million's base unmummied clay—
Yet all his spices but prolong decay.
                                    (79–88)

Also, quite unlike Southey's version, Byron's King George is forced to undergo
a trial before he can enter heaven to determine if Satan has a better claim to
his company in hell. Neither of George's predecessors in this judicial procedure was successful in gaining admittance to heaven. Claudius was denied
apotheosis and at last punished by being made a legal clerk. Pope Julius,
in Erasmus' brilliant judicial satire, discovered that his actions merited
only hell.

In *The Vision of Judgment*, Satan, playing the role of prosecuting attorney,
subpoenas witnesses, such as Wilkes and Junius, who are sworn political enemies of the king. Their testimony, however, is inconclusive since they have
mellowed somewhat and are loath to pursue George after his death. Wilkes,
ever the politician, mistakes the dead assembled for freeholders and even so-
licits Saint Peter's vote. Junius, the unidentified satirist, appears successively
in all his protean shapes, like satire itself.

With Satan preparing to call George Washington, John Horne Tooke, and
Benjamin Franklin to the stand, Asmodeus suddenly appears carrying the
living Southey whom he accuses of having written libels on both history and
scripture. The point is that Southey, by describing George's translation to
heaven, has insulted divine wisdom by anticipating its decisions. Southey argues his case by revealing in detail his changeable nature:

> He had written praises of a regicide;
>   He had written praises of all kings whatever;
> He had written for republics far and wide,
>   And then against them bitterer than ever;
> For pantisocracy he once had cried
>   Aloud, a scheme less moral than 't was clever;
> Then grew a hearty anti-jacobin—
> Had turn'd his coat—and would have turn'd his skin.
>   (769–76)

His turncoat nature is reflected further in his willingness to place his talents at
the service of Satan:

> He had written Wesley's life:—here turning round
>   To Satan, 'Sir, I'm ready to write yours,

In two octavo volumes, nicely bound,
    With notes and preface, all that most allures
The pious purchaser; and there's no ground
    For fear, for I can choose my own reviewers:
So let me have the proper documents,
    That I may add you to my other saints.'
                                              (785–92)

Here, of course, Byron is turning the tables on the man who had accused him of belonging to the "Satanic School" of poetry.

After Satan declines the honor of Southey's attentions, Saint Michael receives the same offer. But without waiting for the archangel's reply, the visionary Lake poet offers his "A Vision of Judgment" as a paradigm of divine judgment:

                                here's my Vision!
    Now you shall judge, all people; yes, you shall
Judge with my judgment, and by my decision
    Be guided who shall enter heaven or fall.
                                              (801–4)

The torrent of his reading drives the devils back to hell and causes the angels to stop their ears. But at the fifth line Saint Peter manages to knock the poet down and out of heaven, not to the underworld, but into his lake, where, appropriately:

He first sank to the bottom—like his works,
    But soon rose to the surface—like himself;
For all corrupted things are buoy'd like corks,
    By their own rottenness. . . .
                                              (833–36)

After disposing of Southey, Byron's narrator promptly concludes his poem:

As for the rest, to come to the conclusion
    Of this true dream, the telescope is gone
Which kept my optics free from all delusion,
    And show'd me what I in my turn have shown;
All I saw farther, in the last confusion,
    Was, that King George slipp'd into heaven for one;

And when the tumult dwindled to a calm,
I left him practising the hundredth psalm.
(841–48)

The disposal of Southey and the entry by stealth of George, despite the satire, are not unlike the actions in a Mack Sennett comedy. Byron attributes no particular dignity to divine beings and even less to a poet like Southey who treats them with servility. Heaven operates with a certain commonsense, perhaps; but as a repository of justice, it falls far short. Hell, as Bernard Shaw was later to assert, is likely to be a far more interesting place than heaven.

As a parody, *The Vision of Judgment* transforms all aspects of the Southey poem. The replacement of the indefinite article in Southey's title with the more emphatic definite article suggests that *The Vision of Judgment* is *the* definitive account of what transpired in heaven. Southey's ponderous hexameters become comic ottava rima. Byron transforms a sentimental and obsequious treatment of George to withering satire. And the satiric structure transforms the rhetoric of the judicial setting as is usual in simple satire. But the use of metamorphosis, in the manner of Swift and Pope, for the presentation of King George, Junius, and Southey himself creates a thematic unity in addition to the formal one. Southey's final corklike rottenness recalls George's rottenness in death earlier in the poem. Transformation from the human form to something else is a kind of death, as Stultitia reminded us in the *Moriae Encomium*. Since George is dead, Byron would prefer that his putrescence were left ungilded by dishonesty and self-interest. But Southey alive transmutes his own human form to an image of death even as he resurrects George's carcass in eternity. By perverting truth and justice, he degrades and demeans all human values, and thus becomes an appropriate object of satire. By reversing the value system implied in Southey's poem, Byron's *The Vision of Judgment* reasserts the commitment to truth which the satiric tradition stands for.

Byron's apparent disbelief in justice in our world or the hereafter leads to some serious implications for satire. It places a grave responsibility with the satirist who must discover a basis for satire and then, himself, become the chief dispenser of justice. For Byron the idea of personal and political freedom was coupled with a strong regard for literary tradition. Such individualistic world views, however, do not seem to sort well with the traditional grasp of forms required for generic satire. Byron was able to overcome this contradiction, but his success with his audience was increasingly dependent on his personal wit. If the satirist is able to reconstruct an adequate sense of genre, his audience is unwilling or unable to do so. The appeals to tradition which Byron makes and depends on can no longer be expected to have an effect.[16] Satire as a genre is on the wane.

This decline of judicial satire suggests an hypothesis for the early development and progress of satire as a genre. The fact that all satire is judicial or judgmental to some degree and its affinity for a judicial format make it highly probable that satire and the rhetoric of the law courts provided inspiration and sustenance to one another as they grew up together, sometimes in an adversary relationship, from the rise of Athenian democracy to the end of the eighteenth century. The anonymous author of the anti-Whig broadside *The Cabal* (1680) argued briefly for a strict relationship between satire and the law:

> To correct vice keen satire may prevail
> Beyond the law when preaching blockheads fail;
> For law and satire from one fountain flow
> (Were not men vicious there would be no law). . . .
>   (4–7)[17]

In 1687, in a prefatory poem to Higden's translation of Juvenal's Tenth Satire, Dryden linked satire and law in a similar way: "*Satyr* is our *Court of Chancery*" (13).[18] That the connection between satire and law remained established seems to be supported by some minor verses by George Crabbe, written in 1818:

> I love not the satiric Muse,
> No man on earth would I abuse;
> Nor with empoison'd verses grieve
> The most offending son of Eve;
> Leave him to law, if he have done
> What injures any other son.[19]

What is interesting here, too, is Crabbe's rejection of the role of satirist. Instead of taking up where the law leaves off, Crabbe shuns the prospect of inflicting punishment. Sympathy overwhelms the satiric motive.

Finally, as Byron's *The Vision of Judgment* shows, the excesses of Romanticism provided what some thought to be an easier and more direct road to truth, without even an overnight stop at a court of justice. As the legal and ethical foundations upon which satire had been built began to decay from disuse, the traditional forms by which it had flourished also gave way. Satire would continue to exist, of course, even as it does today; but the forms that had given it a generic strength were no longer bound to it as they had once been. The fragmentation of a great tradition continued apace.

Yet while satire remained a popular genre, judicial setting played an important role. If evildoers cannot be brought before a real bar of justice, they can be tried in the court of satire where they have little chance of escape. Since, as Aristotle pointed out, judicial oratory deals with past actions, all satire is, in a sense, judicial: i.e., a judgment is rendered. But the court of law format, with defendants, accusers, and judges, has a special status in generic satire. Like the symposium, the court of law is a touchstone of any society. To show the corrupters of the law at trial in a fictional courtroom or at the bar of an eternal and incorruptible justice is one of the satirist's most satisfying tasks. The court of law setting provides the essential structure for judicial satire and serves as an important component in complex satires and more complicated dramatic and fictional forms.

PART 2
THE COMPLEX
STRUCTURES OF
SATIRE

5

DRYDEN

Mac Flecknoe

Dryden's *Mac Flecknoe* is a remarkable poem. Although much of its satire is personal, i.e., directed against Thomas Shadwell, its strongest satirical thrust has more general, cultural significance. The dynamic of the poem is activated by a profound paradox: although Shadwell is an essentially comic figure in the poem, who, despite his rotund materiality, amounts to nothing, the threat he poses to culture and art in particular cannot be so easily dismissed.

The satire consists in two closely related emphases: first, the personal, comic ridicule directed at Shadwell; and second, the assessment of the impact on culture and art by Shadwell and his kind. The mock-heroic qualities of the poem thus have a double significance. Mac Flecknoe (Shadwell) is reduced in stature by implied comparison with the heroes of epic. But also the maintenance of the heroic style and manner imparts, paradoxically, some significance to Mac Flecknoe and thus to what he represents. This requires us to take him more seriously than even Father Flecknoe himself might seem to do.

The deliberative form of the poem is apparent at the outset. The poem opens on the conclusion of a deliberation to determine Flecknoe's successor. True also to epic requirements, the poem begins in medias res, not at the beginning of the deliberation, but somewhat later at the point where the resolution of it is to be explained. This enables Flecknoe to announce his decision and present his reasons for it. Although the question has already been settled, we are to consider the evidence as if the deliberation were still in progress.

Yet the particularly judicial quality of this deliberation may lead us to the realization that *Mac Flecknoe* is the recapitulation of a sessions poem.[1] There was, however, no real selection process. With Shadwell the obvious and necessary choice, the sessions structure is only the merest formality. But this is true as well of every genre that contributes to the poem. Each one reveals its momentary relevance to satire and promptly yields to yet another formal strategy. The ultimate structure is the sum of these diverse parts.

Unusual to a sessions poem or more general judicial and deliberative structures is the unmistakable heroic sound of the opening six lines. The disquieting "Non-sense" in line six, however, abruptly changes our sense of the preceding five verses:

> All humane things are subject to decay,
> And, when Fate summons, Monarchs must obey:
> This *Fleckno* found, who, like Augustus, young
> Was call'd to Empire, and had govern'd long:
> In Prose and Verse, was own'd, without dispute
> Through all the Realms of *Non-sense,* absolute.
>
> (1–6)

The word "Non-sense" is the axle on which the poem turns from the impression of heroic poetry to its countergenre, mock-heroic. Thus, right at the outset, the issue of generic identity becomes important to our understanding of *Mac Flecknoe.* By line 6 we have begun to realize that one kind of literature is being played consciously against another. Also, "Non-sense" stresses a departure from sense; i.e., it is less a negative quality than the absence of any quality at all. Shadwell's peculiar kind of nonsense proceeds from his inability to achieve any generic integrity. The generic transformation to satire has begun.

If the opening lines have a heroic sound to them, they also masquerade as history. Flecknoe is compared to Augustus (3) and a rough outline of his reign is sketched (4–10). Once the setting is given, Flecknoe begins to describe his deliberations, interrupting the historical narration like one of Thucydides' movers and shakers.[2] The words that follow are in the heightened language of panegyric; but, of course, only Flecknoe and his attendants can regard them as words of praise.

Dryden's introduction of kinds continues apace. The allusion to Augustus sets the action in classical history, but soon biblical history and dramatic history are fused:

> Heywood and Shirley were but Types of thee,
> Thou last great Prophet of Tautology:
> Even I, a dunce of more renown than they,
> Was sent before but to prepare thy way. . . .
>   (29–32)

Here begins the process of extracting Shadwell from the tradition of Ben Jonson, with which he had aligned himself, and placing him among the lightly regarded Heywoods and Shirleys. To accomplish this Dryden draws an analogy with a typological reading of biblical history. On the one hand, Shadwell is the antitype of two inferior earlier dramatists and, on the other, he is the Christ to whom Flecknoe has been John the Baptist. Paul J. Korshin identifies this as "typological satire" and points out the importance of yet another structure, the prophecy, in the composition of *Mac Flecknoe*.[3]

Already major demands are being placed on the reader to disentangle levels of style and a series of integrated literary kinds which follow one another with rapidity. But even more difficulty is to come. Flecknoe's Portuguese recital is only a prelude to Shadwell's English success:

> My warbling Lute, the Lute I whilom strung
> When to King *John* of *Portugal* I sung,
> Was but the prelude to that glorious day,
> When thou on silver *Thames* did'st cut thy way. . . .
>   (35–38)

Here we reach a central question of genre. The "warbling Lute" suggests lyrical poetry, or more precisely the popular songs that Flecknoe supposedly sang to his own accompaniment at the court of King John (Catherine of Braganza, Charles's queen, was John's daughter). The use of "whilom" suggests a medieval, perhaps gothic, quality, as though Flecknoe were a wandering minstrel or troubador, a lutanist of a more romantic and lyrical time. But although "whilom" ("whylom") appears often in Chaucer, it is to be found in Spenser as well. So the passage is by no means restricted to a medieval locus, for the "silver *Thames*" and the lines that follow, "With well tim'd Oars before the Royal Barge, / Swell'd with the Pride of thy Celestial charge . . ." (39–40), are probable echoes of panegyric by Edmund Waller,[4] and also recall more generally the language of Spenser in his *Prothalamion* (1596) and Shakespeare in Enobarbus's great description of Cleopatra upon the river Cydnus. The Spenser and Shakespeare allusions stress the bondage of love. The insistence upon the lute in succeeding lines (44, 58, 210) underscores the ineffectual romantic lyricism with which both father and son are identified. The lute may also suggest the unripe sexual loves of Shadwell satirized later in the poem (122–25). When in book 4 of the *Dunciad* Pope imagines realms to which Dulness directs her children, he includes "Love-whisp'ring woods, and lute-resounding waves" (4:306). Pope undoubtedly follows Dryden in linking and disparaging lutany and love.

But the old poet's lute playing in Portugal is also a typological prefiguration of Shadwell's far more extensive musical career. With the lute still in his hand, the heir apparent rivals the "Morning Toast" for the attention of the "little Fishes" (49–50) and, like a thresher translated from field to podium, rises into sway over a consort of musicians:

> Sometimes as Prince of thy Harmonious band
> Thou weild'st thy Papers in thy threshing hand.
> (51–52)

Such an assembly, Dryden suggests, is all that Shadwell can aspire to be prince of—unless he become prince of dullness as well. The crudity of his musical understanding, however, is indicated by his "threshing hand," hardly expressive of grace and indicative of a profession to which Shadwell might better have aspired. The chief point throughout this complex pattern of accusations is that Shadwell has improperly assumed the roles of playwright and satirist, for neither of which nature has fitted him. A corollary of this is that comedy and satire are genres requiring consummate artistic skill. Shadwell would do better to confine his efforts to less demanding forms.

Unfortunately, however, Flecknoe's son has not been content to play his lute and lead his band. He has, first and foremost, attempted to write plays, and such has been his success that

> All arguments, but most this Plays, perswade,
> That for anointed dullness he was made.
> (62–63)

Next Dryden describes in some detail the milieu from which Shadwell's plays spring. Again, a sense of the past, with a Spenserian flavor, is evoked:

> An ancient fabrick, rais'd t'inform the sight,
> There stood of yore, and *Barbican* it hight. . . .
>   (66–67)

A faint hint of the glorious Elizabethan past may have been given earlier in Flecknoe's account of Shadwell's musical success: "When thou on silver *Thames* did'st cut thy way . . ." (38). The absurdity of the immense lutanist

> Swell'd with the Pride of thy Celestial charge;
> And big with Hymn, Commander of an Host . . .
>   (40–41)

is underscored in the implicit comparison with the white swans and "silver streaming Themmes" of Spenser's *Prothalamion*. Here, too, Shadwell, pregnant with pride and hymn, is seen as unnaturally bisexual. The images suggest his association with religious dissent as well, pride and hymn singing being ordinary charges in anti-Puritan satire. The introduction of Spenserian diction also provides a comparison with the vulgar "suburbian" language of Shadwell's plays. In the neighborhood around the Barbican, a place associated with low pleasures, Mac Flecknoe's plays find a good reception:

> Pure Clinches, the suburbian Muse affords;
> And *Panton* waging harmless War with words.
> Here *Fleckno*, as a place to Fame well known,
> Ambitiously design'd his *Sh*—'s Throne.
>   (83–86)

The passage ends with a flow of Shadwellian titles and character names. But the setting is by no means complete. Shadwell's territory, from Bun-Hill to Watling Street, is evoked in all its crowded and irrelevant chaos, leading up to the parody of Vergilian majesty represented by Flecknoe and his son.

The essential dramatic quality of this coronation scene and of the poem generally has been pointed out.[5] But it is also important to underscore how deliberately Dryden employs certain aspects of Shadwell's dramatic style for purposes of satire. Just as the title of Flecknoe's play, *Love's Kingdom* (1664), has set a precedent for his son's self-indulgence in ale and opium, and the youthful practice of sex, it has provided the inspiration to his art as well. Thus Shadwell's opera *Psyche* (1674)—and, by implication, his mind—have sprung from his loins. By these images unnatural qualities and practices are attributed to Shadwell. He can now be seen as a bit more dangerous than Flecknoe's comic account may seem to make him.

Next begins a series of events, some of which are drawn from stylistic oddities in Shadwell's plays. In *The Sullen Lovers* (1668), the term "owl" is used a number of times to denote stupidity or foolishness.[6] Dryden introduces his owls just as the coronation is complete, when Shadwell's brains are entirely opiated:

> His Temples last with Poppies were o'erspread,
> That nodding seem'd to consecrate his head:
> Just at that point of time, if Fame not lye,
> On his left hand twelve reverend *Owls* did fly.
> (126–29)[7]

In Flecknoe's panegyric on his son which follows, explicit references to *The Virtuoso* (1676), *Epsom Wells* (1673), and *Psyche* are included in unfavorable comparison with the estimable art of Etherege. But when Jonson's name is introduced, Dryden employs direct parody of Shadwell's style, utilizing language from *The Virtuoso*. What relation can we possibly have to Jonson? Flecknoe asks:

> Where sold he Bargains, Whip-stitch, kiss my Arse,
> Promis'd a Play and dwindled to a Farce?
> (181–82)

In *The Virtuoso* Sir Samuel Hearty responds to Longvil: "Prithee Longvil, hold thy peace with a whipstitch, your nose in my breech."[8] This locution is evidently one of Hearty's favorites, for he repeats it three times in the course of the play.[9]

The second line of this couplet is also of interest. In it Dryden sums up his objections to Shadwell: he is incapable of achieving his purposes. In attempting to be witty, he succeeds only in being dull. The insight is developed in a parody of lines from the epilogue to Shadwell's *The Humorists* (1671). Here, first, are Shadwell's lines:

> A Humor is the Byas of the Mind,
> By which with violence 'tis one way inclin'd:
> It makes our Actions lean on one side still,
> And in all Changes that way bends the Will.
> (15–18)[10]

Flecknoe's praise emphasizes his son's originality or innovation, always a negative in Dryden's view:

> This is thy Province, this thy wondrous way,
> New Humours to invent for each new Play. . . .
> (187–88)

The invention of new humors is totally perverse, an unnatural parody of true creativity. This is followed by a direct parody of Shadwell's lines:

> This is that boasted Byas of thy mind,
> By which one way, to dullness, 'tis inclin'd;
> Which makes thy writings lean on one side still,
> And in all changes that way bends thy will.
> (189–92)

Shadwell, then, is condemned by his own works. Jonson promises a play and delivers one. Shadwell, on the other hand, aborts. The promise he tenders is never realized in performance. If Shadwell is portly, like Jonson, and that bulk pledges a Jonsonian performance (similar to Pope's "I cough like Horace, and, though lean, am short"), there the resemblance ends:

> Nor let thy mountain belly make pretence
> Of likeness; thine's a tympany of sense.
> A Tun of Man in thy Large bulk is writ,
> But sure thou'rt but a Kilderkin of wit.
> (193–96)

The word "tympany" is a brilliant choice, uniting percussion with pregnancy, tumor, and bombast. Again and again, but always in surprising variation, Flecknoe's panegyric repeats the major attack of Dryden's satire: Shadwell is never in control of his own ends. Whatever he intends, the opposite is always realized:

> Like mine thy gentle numbers feebly creep,
> Thy Tragick Muse gives smiles, thy Comick sleep.
> With whate'er gall thou sett'st thy self to write,
> Thy inoffensive Satyrs never bite.
> (197–200)

It is clear from all of this that Shadwell has missed his calling. His abilities do not permit him to aspire to tragedy, comedy, or satire. Instead he should turn his energies to lesser forms:

> Thy Genius calls thee not to purchase fame
> In keen Iambicks, but mild Anagram:
> Leave writing Plays, and chuse for thy command
> Some peacefull Province in Acrostick Land.
> There thou maist wings display and Altars raise,
> And torture one poor word Ten thousand ways.
> (203–8)

The province of anagrams and acrostics reminds Flecknoe of his son's other talent as musical director and lutanist:

> Or if thou would'st thy diff'rent talents suit,
> Set thy own Songs, and sing them to thy lute.
> (209–10)

Surely anagram, acrostic, and song do not argue for much difference in talent. Shadwell's ineffectuality is mirrored in whatever form or genre he endeavors to work with. It stands to reason, then, that he should choose the least effectual genres available.

Flecknoe's oration, like his son's plays, would go on forever were it not for the introduction of a deus ex machina or some other contrivance. The contrivance in *Mac Flecknoe*, as in *The Virtuoso*, is a trap door. Shadwell's own characters work that door by which the action is brought to sudden conclusion, and the poet is left above as reigning king of dullness. Once again, Dryden effectively parodies Shadwell's dramatic technique, just as earlier in the poem, he parodies his language and dramatic theory. To a certain extent, *Mac Flecknoe* assumes the form of a Shadwell comedy.

Thus, in *Mac Flecknoe*, Dryden employs a very subtle interplay of genres, both as form and theme. The hierarchy of genres provides a basis for comic ridicule leveled against Shadwell, since he is relegated to the inferior forms for lack of poetic talent. But the form of Dryden's poem is precisely compatible with his subject matter in another important way. Just as Shadwell "Promis'd a Play and dwindled to a Farce . . ." (182), Dryden, by the heroic style of his opening lines "promises" a heroic poem. Of course, the promise was never meant to be kept, but true to its parody of a Shadwell play, *Mac Flecknoe* "dwindles" to a farce.

The poem begins like a heroic poem, but promptly establishes its dramatic affinities by use of elaborate theatrical metaphors. Within the dramatic structure, the speeches of Flecknoe can be seen as deliberative oratory first and then demonstrative oratory or panegyric. There are brief suggestions of medieval and Renaissance lyricism, culminating in the advice to Shadwell to confine his efforts to insignificant forms. Tragedy, comedy, and satire reign supreme, far beyond the grasp of the prince of dullness; but even as Mac Flecknoe falls ludicrously short of artistic success in those forms, the reader glimpses real achievement on the inevitable utopian or panegyrical side of the satiric coin. Jonson, Fletcher, and Etherege stand out as model playwrights, compared with whose achievements Shadwell's failures seem even more pathetic. Indeed, *Mac Flecknoe* itself emerges as an exemplar against which the "inoffensive Satyrs" of the prince of dullness can be measured and found wanting.

But if comic ridicule as it emerges from parody unifies subject and form, the poem becomes a satire as Shadwell's perversity and the harmful impact of his failed ethics and aesthetics are recognized. He is "a scourge of Wit, and flayle of Sense" (89). Though insignificant by comparison, he is nonetheless like Hannibal "a mortal Foe to *Rome*" (113). Intemperate drinking, unripe sexuality, and papaveraceous indulgence unite with dissenter enthusiasm to create something of a monster. Shadwell is only inoffensive when he chooses to be offensive; though it cannot gain access to his pen, venom does indeed lie in his "fellonious heart" (201). What is evil about Mac Flecknoe and what makes him a proper butt of satire is his unnatural influence on everything he touches. If he were merely ineffectual, he would be a comic figure, not a satiric one. Of course, he is a comic figure and a brilliant one, but the darker hints which Dryden inserts for us edge him into a more serious context. As Harry Levin tells us, "When comedy becomes more purposeful than playful, then it is satire."[11]

But finally what makes Mac Flecknoe dangerous is not his intentions, since they, we have seen, are never realized. The poem itself does not turn from playful to purposeful at a single turning point. Rather the poem becomes a satire as Shadwell's perversity in life and art emerge in antithesis to classical and traditional values. *Mac Flecknoe* can be read largely as comedy. But as we contemplate the failure of ethical and artistic values which Shadwell represents, his accession to the throne of dullness becomes less of a laughing matter.

Absalom and Achitophel

The genre of *Absalom and Achitophel* has proved controversial for generations of critics. Some regard it as satire, but they seldom do so without serious reservations. Epic or epyllion is another possibility, and Verrall in 1914 decided it was a combination of satire and epic.[12] Perhaps Paul Ramsey, tongue in cheek, has expressed the problem best when, after reviewing the generic uncertainties of the poem, he writes: "Hence we can say that the poem is an occasional, polemical, historical, satirical, panegyrical, truncated, narrative, allegorical poem."[13]

But even Ramsey has not included all the possibilities, as the following essay will show. *Absalom and Achitophel,* as is typical of complex satires, makes use of many belletristic forms. Characteristic of satire, too, it employs rhetorical forms as essential parts of its structure.

The poem begins as biblical history, but an attentive reader will promptly realize that the "pious times, e'r Priest-craft did begin" (1) are equivalent to an imagined Agapemone or Cloudcuckooland. The most notable pious time without priests was in the Garden of Eden itself. But if such a utopia existed at a later date, it was surely before the time of David.[14]

But Dryden's purpose in alluding to such a time is to show us that it occurred mainly in David's bed, where the king, perhaps, "inspir'd by some diviner Lust" (19), begets the ill-fated Absalom. The point is that Absalom is a child of nature; i.e., a natural child or bastard and fruit of love "When Nature prompted, and no law deny'd / Promiscuous use of Concubine and Bride . . ." (5–6). As a natural man, "What e'r he did was done with so much ease, / In him alone, 'twas Natural to please . . ." (27–28). Absalom, indeed, representing nature, unites that same nature with a second key term in the poem, "grace": "His motions all accompanied with grace; / And *Paradise* was open'd in his face" (29–30). Here "grace" means merely gracefulness, but the term will come to represent a complex of meanings as the poem proceeds. It is enough to note, for the time being, that Absalom is associated with it at an early stage.

In his salad days David had indulged in love freely, prompted by nature; but it is important to note that no law had denied him his amours. For

Absalom there are excesses as well; but for these the law is manipulated some-what, even to the point of exonerating him from murder:

> Some warm excesses, which the Law forbore,
> Were constru'd Youth that purg'd by boyling o'er:
> And *Amnon's* Murther, by a specious Name,
> Was call'd a Just Revenge for injur'd Fame.
> (37–40)

The "nature" and "grace" of Absalom, we shall see, attracts similar qualities in the Jews.

The Jews in the poem are equivalent to the English, as any modern edition of the poem makes abundantly clear. But not every Englishman is included among them. Rather they are a particularly enthusiastic breed, with marked dissenter qualities:

> The *Jews,* a Headstrong, Moody, Murmuring race,
> As ever try'd th'extent and stretch of grace;
> God's pamper'd people whom, debauch'd with ease,
> No King could govern, nor no God could please. . . .
> (45–48)

This grace is God's and David's both. As God's, the theological concept is introduced, and a comment is made on the Calvinist position. "As ever try'd th'extent and stretch of grace" suggests that having God's grace may be contingent upon one's behavior. This, of course, was an Arminian position, rejected by the majority of dissenting Protestants. For them grace was a free gift of God's, which placed its possessors among the elect. Dryden, as we shall see, is taking the Arminian position: grace is under God's control and its transmission contingent upon good behavior. But the populace behaves as though its behavior is not at issue.

If the people, in their passion for grace, as opposed to good works, find Absalom attractive, his natural qualities make him suitable to their ends as well. Just as Absalom had "*Paradise* . . . open'd in his face," the people are represented in an Edenic setting produced by their own wild imaginations:

> These *Adam*-wits, too fortunately free,
> Began to dream they wanted libertie;
> And when no rule, no president was found

Of men, by Laws less circumscrib'd and bound,
They led their wild desires to Woods and Caves,
And thought that all but Savages were Slaves.
                                        (51–56)

By choosing a natural life they become, in effect, savages, making Absalom, the natural man, their leader. Dryden will make all of this clear in due course. For the time being it is enough to identify the exponents of "the Good Old Cause" with a kind of lawless self-indulgence. The only problem is that

when to Sin our byast Nature leans,
The carefull Devil is still at hand with means;
And providently Pimps for ill desires:
The Good Old Cause reviv'd, a Plot requires.
                                        (79–82)

It is not the plot, however, that causes concern. Dryden drops any pretense to suspense by informing us promptly: "This Plot . . . fail'd for want of common Sense . . ." (134). But the effects of the plot are much more dire, leading to a serious attack on lawful monarchy. It is this larger uprising that Dryden will dissect throughout the remainder of the poem.

At this point there is also an adjustment of form. With the introduction of the magnificent Theophrastan character of Achitophel, Dryden brings his full satiric powers to bear. Earlier, the mood of the rabble had been presented with skill, but a general assessment was the outcome. Here we get down to specifics; the characterization brings to light information pro and con; but the final result is disastrous to Shaftesbury. He is clearly on trial. Indeed, the poem has moved from what Earl Miner calls "partisan history" to a quasi-judicial setting. The judicial aspect of the portrait is made clear about halfway through:

So easie still it proves in Factious Times,
With publick Zeal to cancel private Crimes.
                                        (180–81)

Achitophel's late criminal behavior is contrasted with his earlier judicial temperament:

Yet, Fame deserv'd, no Enemy can grudge;
The Statesman we abhor, but praise the Judge.

> In *Israels* Courts ne'er sat an *Abbethdin*
> With more discerning Eyes, or Hands more clean:
> Unbrib'd, unsought, the Wretched to redress;
> Swift of Dispatch, and easie of Access.
> (186–91)

Here also the narrator establishes his own essential fairness in presenting the evidence with restraint and exactitude.

More important, Achitophel, who before upheld the law, now violates and abuses it. His earlier dedication may be cited to prove that even the worst among us recognizes at some time the inherent value of legal probity. But now,

> *Achitophel*, grown weary to possess
> A lawfull Fame, and lazy Happiness;
> Disdain'd the Golden fruit to gather free,
> And lent the Croud his Arm to shake the Tree.
> Now, manifest of Crimes, contriv'd long since,
> He stood at bold Defiance with his Prince:
> Held up the Buckler of the Peoples Cause,
> Against the Crown; and sculk'd behind the Laws.
> (200–207)

Legal issues become paramount as the evidence against Achitophel piles up. His arguments are presented and will be presented in greater detail as the temptation of Absalom is overheard in its entirety.

Achitophel's speech marks another stylistic shift, as Miltonic diction introduces the elaborate temptation:

> Him he attempts, with studied Arts to please,
> And sheds his Venome, in such words as these. . . .
> (228–29)

Since Milton's language and imagery were invented to capture the grandeur of a biblical subject, the shift is by no means abrupt. Indeed in most effective satire the seams between stylistic shifts are usually not easily apparent. But the Miltonic diction here is unmistakable, and so a sense of Satanic evil on the grand scale is evoked. Mixed with biblical language (the "Young-mens Vision, and the Old mens Dream!"), the Miltonic effects set off Achitophel's rhetorical speech from the rest of the poem in a particularly striking way.

The satirist undertakes the apparently contradictory task of both separating out genres and integrating them. Since every satire is a collection of more or fewer different genres, the essential task is to integrate them into a focused satire. Nonetheless, the various generic identities contribute to meaning in diverse ways, depending on how satiric intention and related artistic purposes are to be combined.

In this case, the brilliant shift to a Satanic temptation contrasts Achitophel unfavorably with the mild David. The shift from narrative to rhetorical form also sets off this passage from the remainder of the poem. This use of rhetorical forms, specifically persuasive in their intention, also underscores the judicial theme, which will emerge as even more important as the poem proceeds. But at the same time that the speech becomes a brilliant setpiece and tour de force in its generic identity, it may be found to have a strong thematic unity with the poem as a whole.

Achitophel's temptation of Absalom, like Satan's directed to Eve, is perfectly adjusted to its object. Absalom, as we have seen, is the natural man from several points of view. As such he is also love's minion who "seem'd as he were only born for love" (26). Recognizing this attribute, Achitophel presses his argument in precisely the right direction. Barely muted sexual imagery begins the attack as the tempter calls Absalom "Thy longing Countries Darling and Desire . . ." (232). The sexuality, however, is never explicit, since the stress is more completely on vague and visionary associations. He is "The Young-mens Vision, and the Old mens Dream!" (239). And even more explicitly, Absalom is something higher than an object of sense; he is a veritable god and Christ-figure:

> Thee, *Saviour*, Thee, the Nations Vows confess;
> And, never satisfi'd with seeing, bless. . . .
> (240–41)

The emphasis next returns to Absalom's natural qualities as his failure to assert himself as ruler by right of nature (not natural right, except in the perverse sense of his bastardy) is seen as depriving the people of joy, sustenance, and what is rightly theirs by natural law:

> How long wilt thou the general Joy detain;
> Starve, and defraud the People of thy Reign?
> (244–45)

The significance of the word "starve" is brought into brilliant relief by the Miltonic imagery to follow:

Believe me, Royal Youth, thy Fruit must be,
Or gather'd Ripe, or rot upon the Tree.
(250–51)

We see by this that what the people starve for is the forbidden fruit of Eden. If Absalom agrees to supply their needs, we understand just what they will be getting. The people do not hunger after truth and righteousness, but rather after the sweet fruits of sin.

Next, as Achitophel launches upon a catalogue of David's weaknesses, he points to another naturalistic reason for Absalom's right by nature: David is now in his declining years. Early in the temptation Absalom's "dawning day" was noted. Now Absalom is told to shun David's

example of Declining Age:
Behold him setting in his Western Skies,
The Shadows lengthning as the Vapours rise.
(267–69)

As Achitophel concludes the first effort at temptation, he recurs to Absalom's chief characteristic, his love of love. Here the tempter speaks of the special value of whatever rule is "Giv'n by the Love of all your Native Land . . ." (300). Thus Absalom, the love-child, is seduced by love to assert his right by nature to the throne. Of course, his natural debt to his father and the fact that he has no legal right to the kingship are conveniently ignored. Youth, vigor, and love, it would seem, entitle Absalom to rule. It is, of course, a romantic and totally fallacious assumption. In fact, Absalom's shaky answer to Achitophel's arguments stresses David's lawful and just rule: "My Father Governs with unquestion'd Right" (317). David is "Good, Gracious, Just, observant of the Laws" (319). "Who sues for Justice to his Throne in Vain?" (322) The crown "Is Justly Destin'd for a Worthier Head" (348) and "His Lawfull Issue shall the Throne ascend" (351). It is clear from all this that Absalom recognizes that law and justice are against his claim; but his natural gifts and status cry out for dominion: "Desire of Greatness is a Godlike Sin" (372).

In Achitophel's second try at a weakening Absalom, the tempter asserts his ability to manipulate money to his own political advantage. David, who is characterized as generous, is always in need of money. Achitophel will therefore be able to govern him by Parliamentary control of the royal purse strings:

Let him give on till he can give no more,
The Thrifty Sanhedrin shall keep him poor:

> And every Sheckle which he can receive,
> Shall cost a Limb of his Prerogative.
> (389–92)

The parsimony and concomitant love of money of the Parliamentary forces will become a significant point of attack for Dryden's satire as the poem continues. But here Achitophel makes one more appeal to the natural law. In trying to make Absalom suspicious and fearful of his father's motives, the tempter exhorts the young man to resort to "Self-defence [which] is Natures Eldest Law" (458).

Finally Achitophel, saving the best for last, presents an argument perfectly suited to Absalom's character:

> And who can sound the depth of *David's* Soul?
> Perhaps his fear, his kindness may Controul.
> He fears his Brother, though he loves his Son,
> For plighted Vows too late to be undone.
> If so, by Force he wishes to be gain'd,
> Like womens Leachery, to seem Constrain'd:
> Doubt not, but when he most affects the Frown,
> Commit a pleasing Rape upon the Crown.
> (467–74)

This is a tissue of bad suppositions, but ones carefully calculated to prevail. David's mildness does indeed suggest to his enemies that he is fearful, and so why should he not fear his brother (James) who is, after all, consistently portrayed as an ogre by Achitophel and his partisans? The simile, rightfully distressing to feminists, is nonetheless perfect to capture the hot-blooded youth. He is a would-be rapist, if not a confirmed one, and his lust after the crown would make it seem an appropriate object of his advances. The perverse sexuality of Absalom thus comes to the fore as his essential characteristic. This tainted sexuality colors even the lines that follow:

> Secure his [David's] Person to secure your Cause;
> They who possess the Prince, possess the Laws.
> (475–76)

Aside from the shocking suggestion that David can be susceptible to Absalom's sex appeal, these lines communicate the view that personal influence, however demeaned and demeaning, is superior to the law. That, of course, is

Achitophel's perverse belief. As equivocal in sex as Absalom is lusty, Achitophel always looks to pervert whatever challenges his power. Since to him nothing is sacred and everything is manipulable, his temptation speeches embody these monstrous assumptions. The idea of possessing the crown by means of sex (Absalom identifies rape with love) "With *Absalom's* Mild nature suited best" (478). If we take the meaning of these lines seriously, fail to overlook his "warm excesses" (37), and believe that "*Amnon's* Murther" (39) refers to something in Monmouth's past as well as in Absalom's, the two lines which follow cannot be read literally:

> Unblam'd of Life, (Ambition set aside,)
> Not stain'd with Cruelty, nor puft with Pride. . . .
> (479–80)

Perhaps there is some irony here, but the tendency to overlook sexual transgressions in David probably extends to his son as well. Absalom has the overt sexual nature of his father, and as the son of his father likewise enjoys the indulgence of David's supporters.

After adding a further explanation of Absalom's character and a call to lament his transgression rather than accuse (486), more details of the rebels are presented. Here the buying and selling motif, mentioned earlier, is developed further. Here also the outworn anti-Semitic identification of the Jews with usury and mercantilism is used to satirize the enemies of David:

> The next for Interest sought t'embroil the State,
> To sell their Duty at a dearer rate;
> And make their *Jewish* Markets of the Throne,
> Pretending publick Good, to serve their own.
> Others thought Kings an useless heavy Load,
> Who Cost too much, and did too little Good.
> These were for laying Honest *David* by,
> On Principles of pure good Husbandry.
> (501–8)

Puritans and dissenters, united in their opposition to David, reduce everything to thrift. Duty, which should be freely and willingly done, is sold to the highest bidder. These are the ancestors of the contemporary weapons manufacturers who encourage wars, the better to sell their merchandise.

Anti-Puritan satire continues as the rabblement

> Resum'd their Cant, and with a Zealous Cry,
> Pursu'd their old belov'd Theocracy:
> Where Sanhedrin and Priest inslav'd the Nation,
> And justifi'd their Spoils by Inspiration;
> For who so fit for Reign as *Aaron's* Race,
> If once Dominion they could found in Grace?
> (521–26)

"Cant," "Zealous cry," "Theocracy," "Inspiration," and "Grace" are all contemptuous references to the dissenter tendencies of David's opponents. The final term, "Grace," picks up a significant theme mentioned earlier. Grace, in various forms, from Absalom's grace of motion and David's kingly grace to the strictly theological concept, has thematic significance in the poem. Here the dissenters seek to rule under the aegis of their idea of grace. Already we have seen that Absalom is attracted to the kingship because of his natural qualities. It is clear at this point in the poem that Absalom seeks to rule by right of nature; the dissenting mob, by right of grace.

Dryden goes on to score a direct hit by characterizing the Puritan concept of predestination and free grace. In doing this he facetiously unites the concepts of nature and grace:

> These, out of meer instinct, they knew not why,
> Ador'd their fathers God and Property:
> And, by the same blind benefit of Fate,
> The Devil and the *Jebusite* did hate:
> Born to be sav'd, even in their own despight;
> Because they could not help believing right.
> (535–40)

Thus grace comes naturally to the rabble whether deserved or not. With them everything comes and goes by instinct, including grace. We may recall that "By natural Instinct they change their Lord" (219).

Interesting and effective as this part of the poem may be, it is inevitable that we think of it as a narrative transition between the remarkable temptation of Absalom and the brilliant character-portraits of Zimri, Shimei, and Corah. At this point it becomes clear just how important it is to note the generic shifts in the poem. First, there is the narrative or historical account by which the essential themes are set. This includes establishing the relationship between Absalom and David as well as limited characterizations of both. The mob is presented in historical relief so that its tendencies and character can be evaluated.

This combination of narrative and characterization leads us directly into the first of the great character-portraits: that of Achitophel himself. Once we understand his character, we are ready to see him in action, and the dialogue (consisting mainly of long rhetorical speeches) between him and Absalom, the key to Absalom's resolution to act, is presented.

The portrait of Zimri embodies its essential theme in two discrete concepts. The first is that Zimri is so mercurial that his character is in constant transition, never static, and therefore practically indescribable. A figure in perpetual movement can never focus on a single end. Although he is unlike the other plotters in his incapacity for plot, he reflects the instability of the mob. This inability to effect evil makes him essentially harmless:

> A man so various, that he seem'd to be
> Not one, but all Mankinds Epitome.
> (545–46)

By running through the diapason of human characteristics, Zimri retains a certain humanity which the other plotters manage to dispense with. Nonetheless, governed by the changeable moon, Zimri eludes definition as he assumes the roles of "Chymist, Fidler, States-Man, and Buffoon" (549–50). In a constant state of metamorphosis, by assuming all roles, he defines himself in none. This mercurial quality he shares with the satirist-panegyrist:

> Rayling and praising were his usual Theams;
> And both (to shew his Judgment) in Extreams . . .
> (555–56)

This inclination toward excess (which strongly marks the plot itself, 110), however, is precisely what the judicious narrator of the poem seeks to avoid. Like Mac Flecknoe, Zimri lacks the ability to accomplish his ends. This makes him essentially a comic figure whom laughter follows everywhere:

> Begger'd by Fools, whom still he found too late:
> He had his Jest, and they had his Estate.
> He laught himself from Court . . .
> (561–63)

But also, like Mac Flecknoe, Zimri possesses a second trait. Contrasting with his comic ineffectuality is his felonious heart. He is "wicked but in will, of means bereft" (567). As such he remains a curiously amphibean creature who lives for evil but can never achieve it.

That Zimri is evil and therefore perverse, Dryden leaves no doubt. But his role as satiric butt arises more from his association with the plot than from any success as a plotter. As inconsequential traitor, he seems as giddy and volatile as the Jews of the poem. And he is like them in yet another respect: By his variousness he becomes a one-man crowd.

With the portrait of Shimei, Dryden focuses on a much more dangerous opponent of the king. Shimei is presented as a miser in both public life and private. He is therefore the opposite of the generous David. Much worse is his activity in the law where he perverts justice in his role as judge:

> His Hand a Vare of Justice did uphold;
> His Neck was loaded with a Chain of Gold.
> During his Office, Treason was no Crime;
> The sons of *Belial* had a glorious Time. . . .
> (595–98)

His badges of justice reflect only his love of wealth and a desire to turn public office into private aggrandizement. His perversion of the legal system includes anything that will serve his "higher law":

> If any durst his Factious Friends accuse,
> He pact a Jury of dissenting *Jews:*
> Whose fellow-feeling in the godly Cause,
> Would free the suff'ring Saint from Humane Laws.
> For Laws are only made to Punish those,
> Who serve the King, and to protect his Foes.
> (606–11)

Thus, in their supposed state of grace, the dissenter plotters can ignore the law. But the end they have in view is never religious; it always involves the filling of their coffers:

> His business was, by Writing, to Persuade,
> That Kings were Useless, and a Clog to Trade. . . .
> (614–15)

Shimei's miserliness is further reflected in his inhospitality. The demonstration of this gives Dryden an opportunity to present a brief symposium:

> And, that his noble Stile he might refine,
> No *Rechabite* more shund the fumes of Wine.
> Chast were his Cellars, and his Shrieval Board
> The Grossness of a City Feast abhor'd:
> His Cooks, with long disuse, their Trade forgot;
> Cool was his Kitchen, tho his Brains were hot.
> (616–21)

Thus the dinner never really comes off. The only cooking is in Shimei's brains, overheated with rebellion.

To sum up, Dryden unites the two major indictments against Shimei: his perversion of the law and his niggardliness:

> And *Moses's* Laws he held in more account,
> For forty days of Fasting in the Mount.
> (628–29)

In his account of Shimei Dryden stresses two major themes of the poem. As in the portrait of Zimri, Shimei epitomizes traits of the populace at large: venality and loudmouthed dissatisfaction with a lawful king.

With Corah we reach the nadir of the conspiracy and a high point of Dryden's satiric effort. The poetry communicates the paradox which Corah represents: lowborn, but "High as the Serpent of thy mettall made . . ." (634). Like the character-portrait of Shimei, the one of Corah develops two major themes: the perversion of the law and the Puritan tendencies of the plotters. Again, these two themes are united.

Corah's role as false witness is begun early and developed to a climax. He is, first, the "Arch-Attestor for the Publick Good" (640). False testimony ironically dignifies his entire lineage:

> Who ever ask'd the Witnesses high race,
> Whose Oath with Martyrdom did *Stephen* grace?
> (642–43)

The use of "grace" introduces yet another meaning of that word. It attests to the uses to which false oaths may be put and recalls with irony the theological concept of grace with which the dissenter plotters identify. This, indeed, is their achievement. No doubt the mention of the first martyr, Stephen, suggested to many a later martyr, King Charles I, whose decollation some prototypes of Oates were responsible for.

That Oates is identified with Puritans and dissenters is readily apparent. His is a "Saintlike Grace" (648), the word "Saint" referring, of course, to the dissenter opponents of the Church of England. He also speaks as a prophet (655) and is taken with visions (656). The perversion of judgment and law by lust after profit is made clear in the following lines:

> Let *Israels* foes suspect his heav'nly call,
> And rashly judge his writ Apocryphal;
> Our Laws for such affronts have forfeits made:
> He takes his life, who takes away his trade.
>
> (664–67)

By identifying once again the Puritan vision with the perversion of law and the advancement of mercenary motives, Dryden intensifies his satire. The vulgarity and obscenity of false witness and unjust denunciation emanate directly from Corah's perverse religious principles:

> His Zeal to heav'n, made him his Prince despise,
> And load his person with indignities:
> But Zeal peculiar priviledg affords;
> Indulging latitude to deeds and words.
> And *Corah* might for *Agag's* murther call,
> In terms as course as *Samuel* us'd to *Saul.*
>
> (672–76)

Corah, then, stands erect, the monumental brass who perverts deeds and words totally. But most important, as a perjurer he stands as a living rebuke to justice itself. The stinging final line of Corah's character-portrait, "For *witness* is a Common Name to all" (681), sums up his contribution. He has transformed the name of witness, whether to an alleged crime or the truth of God's word, to a reproach. In doing so, he has erected a monument of himself to all that is evil in human affairs. He has truly become a monumental brass. Corah's judicial record, as well as that of Shimei, serves as a foil to the concluding judicial resolution of the poem.

Dryden takes us next from character-portrait to Absalom's rhetorical foray. True to his mild nature, the natural son of David speaks "with a kind compassionating look, / And sighs, bespeaking pity" (694–95). His short speech is framed to elicit sympathy, and so it does, but not entirely on its own merits:

> Youth, Beauty, Graceful Action, seldom fail:
> But Common Interest always will prevail:
> And pity never Ceases to be shown
> To him who makes the peoples wrongs his own.
> (723–26)

After a short account of Monmouth's success with the people, the narrator delivers a warning, followed by a closely reasoned argument denying the right of the people to decide who their king should be. The argument is that laws must have precedence over the will of the people and the arbitrary sway of any monarch:

> And Laws are vain, by which we Right enjoy,
> If Kings unquestiond can those laws destroy.
> (763–64)

If such a disregard for law is allowed, only one outcome is possible:

> . . . Government it self at length must fall
> To Natures state; where all have Right to all.
> (793–94)

Here Dryden expresses horror at a Hobbesian state of nature; but the use of the word nature also recalls the association of Absalom and the dissenting rebels with that concept. Thus the point is made that if Absalom, Achitophel, and their accomplices are successful, there will be a return to nature in the Hobbesian sense. That is, all distinctions of right and property will give way to the primitive struggle for survival. The speaker in the poem contemplates the destruction of society's fabric:

> To change Foundations, cast the Frame anew,
> Is work for Rebels who base Ends pursue:
> At once Divine and Humane Laws controul;
> And mend the Parts by ruine of the Whole.
> (805–8)

The important word "base" is resonant with many aspects of the evil of conspiracy. Rebellion's new foundation and frame are tempered, so to speak, with the baseness of Absalom's birth and the even baser metal of Corah. Each conspirator pursues his own base end to the destruction of the whole. At this, the lowest point of the narrative, David seems impotent and, paradoxically, ineffectually mired in his own goodness:

> Now what Relief can Righteous *David* bring?
> How Fatall 'tis to be too good a King!
> (811–12)

But at this moment there is a formal shift in the poem to a new voice, not heard clearly until now. It is the voice of panegyric which is to give an account of those who support David and the monarchical cause: "Some let me name, and Naming is to praise" (816).

The litany of praise begins with Barzillai. Since this is the only fully developed portrait of praise, Dryden might well have been tempted to establish some parallels with the earlier character-portrait of Achitophel. This would seem to be the case. Achitophel was presented in an extended maritime metaphor:

> A daring Pilot in extremity;
> Pleas'd with the Danger, when the Waves went high
> He sought the Storms; but for a Calm unfit,
> Would Steer too nigh the Sands, to boast his Wit.
> (159–62)

Barzillai is presented with relation to some water imagery too, but with an entirely different result:

> Long since, the rising Rebells he withstood
> In Regions Waste, beyond the *Jordans* Flood:
> Unfortunately Brave to buoy the State;
> But sinking underneath his Masters Fate. . . .
> (819–22)

More striking is the comparison of sons. Achitophel's son is alive, but barely so. The boy is

> . . . that unfeather'd, two Leg'd thing, a Son:
> Got, while his Soul did hudled Notions try;
> And born a shapeless Lump, like Anarchy.
> (170–72)

Barzillai's son is unfortunately dead, but he lives in Dryden's elegiac offering:

> His Eldest Hope, with every Grace adorn'd,
> By me (so Heav'n will have it) always Mourn'd,
> And always honour'd, snatcht in Manhoods prime
> By'unequal Fates, and Providences crime:
> Yet not before the Goal of Honour won,
> All parts fulfill'd of Subject and of Son;
> Swift was the Race, but short the Time to run.
> Oh Narrow Circle, but of Pow'r Divine,
> Scanted in Space, but perfect in thy Line!
>   (831–39)

Unlike Achitophel's boy, Barzillai's son is adorned with grace, yet an additional meaning for that key word in this poem, but one that resonates with the other meanings. Unlike the shapeless lump, Barzillai's child fulfills all aspects of being subject and son. He is "perfect" in his line. Another extraordinary irony is that Achitophel's living son, who may endure the anarchy of his life for years to come, is treated in a mere three lines. Barzillai's son, on the other hand, who lived a scanted life, is immortalized in a full twenty-three lines, by which Dryden offsets, in traditional elegiac form, the "crime" of Providence:

> By Sea, by Land, thy Matchless Worth was known;
> Arms thy Delight, and War was all thy Own:
> Thy force, Infus'd, the fainting *Tyrians* prop'd:
> And Haughty *Pharaoh* found his Fortune stop'd.
> Oh Ancient Honour, Oh Unconquer'd Hand,
> Whom Foes unpunish'd never coud withstand!
> But *Israel* was unworthy of thy Name;
> Short is the date of all Immoderate Fame.
> It looks as Heaven our Ruine had design'd,
> And durst not trust thy Fortune and thy Mind.
> Now, free from Earth, thy disencumbred Soul
> Mounts up, and leaves behind the Clouds and Starry Pole:
> From thence thy kindred legions mayst thou bring
> To aid the guardian Angel of thy King.
>   (840–53)

The elegant ascendance of the alexandrine (851) may suggest, with only a slight adjustment of the basic iambic pentameter, the line variation of classical elegiacs. In this part of the poem, Dryden moves easily from panegyric to elegy, and back to panegyric again.

The next panegyrical character-portraits are of Zadoc the priest and the Sagan of Jerusalem. The first parallels certain aspects of Shimei's portrait earlier in the poem. Unlike Shimei, who accepts high office as a reward for his hatred to Charles, Zadoc shuns both power and position. The Sagan of Jerusalem's "hospitable Soul" (867) may remind us of Shimei's inhospitable kitchen. The "heavenly eloquence" (869) of John Dolben, "Him of the Western dome," (868) is the antithesis of Shimei's foul curses. In general the cultural attitudes of David's supporters are the opposite of those belonging to Achitophel's followers. By such deliberate patterning, the structure of the poem is strengthened.

David's party is characterized by "Pillars of the Laws, / Who best cou'd plead and best can judge a Cause" (874–75). Jotham embodies the powers of deliberation in public assemblies (884) and Amiel ruled with reason the deliberations of the Sanhedrin (902–3). These details once again show the importance that Dryden attributes to rhetorically related skills.

The climax and conclusion of the poem comes with David's speech, which Godfrey Davies, many years ago, proved was based on Charles' "Declaration."[15] Although the incorporation of some principal elements of Charles' speech in the poem had obvious political utility, the conclusion has been condemned for lack of artistry, by critics from Johnson on.[16] These objections can be dismissed, I believe, when the relationship of David's speech to the key terms we have been examining is made clear.

In the course of the poem, we have seen a trend toward disregard for law emerge. Those who defend the rights of a lawful king have seemed to fall from power along with their master. Nature and grace, both perversely misinterpreted, have taken the place of law, and, as a result, a catastrophe impends. The deliberative efforts of the plotters have also seemed to advance their cause despite the arguments of the narrator.

But true to the tradition of satire in which speech usually counts for more than action, David delivers a declaration that changes the probable course of action and resolves the central problem of the poem.

First David displays nature, rightly understood, by expressing his feelings for his son, Absalom. Even after Absalom's pretensions David shows fatherly affection by offering his son the opportunity of a pardon:

> With how few Tears a Pardon might be won
> From Nature, pleading for a Darling Son!
> (959–60)

The king, however, makes it clear that his natural feelings are not to be mistaken for weakness. He is prepared to act with severity, and will do so if the circumstances require it. In specifying the source of Absalom's aberration, David points to the two remaining key concepts in the poem:

> Whence comes it that Religion and the Laws
> Should more be *Absalom's* than *David's* Cause?
> His old Instructor, e're he lost his Place,
> Was never thought indu'd with so much Grace.
> (969–72)

Absalom's attempt, under the guidance of Achitophel, to make a case for his own succession is an obvious perversion of the law. In addition, another meaning of "grace" is put forward in line 972. The significance of this is that only the grace which is properly David's is sufficient to uphold religion and law. Since Achitophel was manifestly inadequate, from the point of view of grace, to uphold religion and law, it is clear that his pupil will fare no better. The concept of insufficiency of grace refers also to the theological meaning discussed earlier. David possesses grace of every kind, whether it be that which comes from God or that which informs his kingly bearing. The plotters, on the other hand, lack all grace, theological or social.

Finally, therefore, it is the law that comes to the fore. David puts aside his natural feelings and, like the judge he becomes in the passage, prepares to pass sentence on the criminals before him:

> Must I at length the Sword of Justice draw?
> Oh curst Effects of necessary Law!
> (1002–3)

> Law they require, let Law then shew her Face;
> They coud not be content to look on Grace,
> Her hinder parts, but with a daring Eye
> To tempt the terror of her Front, and Dye.
> (1006–10)

This passage, which most commentators have found difficult, makes sense within the thematic pattern I have been describing. The image here is of Law as a gorgon. Those who rely on David's God-given grace, that is, who obey and accept the king as mediator, will never have to suffer the penalty of Law, i.e., look it directly in the face as they suffer the supreme penalty. David's grace consisted in his generosity and moderation of the laws. Those who were not content with David's mediating role, having willed to thrust the king aside, must now confront the reality of law without the protection of that gracious mediator. Such grace as David has comes from God, of course, but it is real grace, not the false concept to which the dissenters make pretense. In David true grace is personal, social, and theological. It has a comprehensiveness extending to all aspects of human existence and far beyond the narrow ideology of the plotters.

What is important to see is that in this final speech David has emerged as judge, representing the will of God. The sword of justice is poised above the plotters' heads, and with the iteration of the word "law," the fact that we have been witnesses to a trial becomes abundantly clear.[17] The arguments of the narrator have been those of a prosecuting attorney. The treacherous dialogue between Absalom and Achitophel has been presented to condemn them. We have been allowed to look into the motives of the plotters to assess their religious, political, and, indeed, their cultural deficiencies. As jurymen and women, we are forced to render a guilty verdict. The deliberations of the early part of the poem have become increasingly judicial as the question of law emerges into prominence. Dryden, as he has done so often, turns upside down whatever biblical pattern may be found in the narrative. Grace is found inadequate to the plotters, who make their claim to be especially entitled to grace. Saint Paul claimed that with Christ the covenant of law—the old Hebrew law—had been replaced by the new covenant of grace. But Dryden reverses the process. Finding the dissenting populace and its plotting leaders unworthy of grace, and therefore unworthy of the very Christianity they profess, Dryden, in an extraordinary tour de force, returns the covenant of law to the place of preeminence it held among the ancient Hebrews. Since the English dissenters have, like the Jews, made their own calf of gold—Monmouth—and rejected God's lawful representative—David—they are entitled to the same harsh punishment that an angry Old Testament God often meted out. In that sense, then, if in no other, the parallel between England and ancient Israel holds good. The English who have denied their king have turned themselves into Jews and as such merit the harsh penalties of Hebrew Law.

Even as the covenants are reversed, however, there remains the hope that penalties will not have to be exacted. In that hope, a retiring David transforms to the assertive Charles, a Christian king, who stresses repentance and forgiveness. Although judge and jury have returned a verdict, the sentence cannot as yet be carried out. Thus *Absalom and Achitophel* poises on the edge of final judgment, holding back, as it were, the full force of the covenant of law until all pleas for repentance have gone unheeded.

If repentance does come to the plotters, it will signal a transformation which has been an important theme in the poem from the beginning. The giddy Jews, misguided by Puritan enthusiasm, wish for a world governed by natural law. Achitophel, by means of Miltonic allusion, becomes Satan; Absalom, convinced by specious arguments from nature, abandons filial duty for treasonous intrigue; Zimri, becoming everything, remains nothing; and Oates variously assumes the shapes of "monumental brass," serpent, comet, and—quintessentially—false witness.

The multiplicity of genres, the threat of destruction to the state, and the transformations of the main characters under the influence of ridicule or panegyric are evidence for the poem's identity as a generic satire. The elaborate thematic pattern of nature, grace, and law reveals not just an immediate political purpose, but a strong cultural bias. Dryden's "panegyrical imagination" shapes a tradition as well as an apology for the Stuarts and the royalist cause. Against the background of this ancient order, the grasping, hypocritical, and perverse modernity of the dissenters is seen as a direct threat to a major value system:

> 'Gainst Form and Order they their Power employ;
> Nothing to Build and all things to Destroy.
> (531–32)

Their deforming might, bent on destruction, can only be neutralized by an even stronger commitment to tradition on the part of Charles and his retainers. *Absalom and Achitophel*, a satire of epic scope, by a demonstrated dedication to tradition, transforms instability to peace in a comprehensive interpretation of history, human nature, and the role of civilization.

6

POPE

The Rape of the Lock

The title of *The Rape of the Lock* reveals the major contrast in the poem. Although a rape is an unnatural and violent act, the actual object of that passion is only a lock of hair. Thus the seriousness of satire and the triviality of comedy are linked from the outset.

Although not everyone agrees that *The Rape of the Lock* is a satire, few would deny its containing important satiric elements. The satire is mild, however, and the question of harm needs to be addressed. The harm that Pope identifies is clearly not the rape. That act is excused by a combination of male bias and extenuating circumstances. Aware that perversions of nature may result in more easily perceptible changes of physique or personality, Pope focuses on one major metamorphosis that reveals the denial of essential nature: the transformation of a girl, not to woman, but to coquette. In rendering perversion concrete by comic means, Pope manages to move *The Rape of the Lock* in the direction of satire.

Although epic conventions dominate the opening of the poem and much of what follows, a rhetorical pattern closer to that of satire than of epic is introduced by line 7:

> Say what strange Motive, Goddess! cou'd compel
> A well-bred *Lord* t'assault a gentle *Belle?*

> Oh say what stranger Cause, yet unexplor'd,
> Cou'd make a gentle *Belle* reject a *Lord?*
>
> (1.7–10)[1]

Why indeed does the Baron resort to rape, even if it is only a harmless, symbolic one? The answer, I believe, is that Belinda dwells in a world of fantasy, which, though it may seem harmless enough, is an unnatural state for a woman. The perversity of her condition is underscored by the fact that her commitment to ephemera makes her oblivious to the advantages of accepting a desirable suitor.

In her morning dream, engineered by Ariel the guardian sylph, Belinda is told of visions, elves, and Angel-powers, hardly the stuff of reality. This world, appropriately presided over by the airy sylphs, is juxtaposed with the real world to which it is feared Belinda may awake. To avoid this occurrence, Ariel, through the medium of the dream, admonishes Belinda not to bound her "narrow Views to Things below" (1.36). She is further exhorted to "Think what an Equipage thou hast in Air, / And view with scorn *Two Pages* and a *Chair*" (1.45–46). Things below, of course, are those of the sublunary world, sexual and otherwise, and two pages and a chair are presumably the modest material benefits an earthly lover and husband might provide her with. Belinda, however, seduced by the promise of a real equipage, is content for the time being with an airy one, and is convinced not to trade it in for a mere sedan chair and the married state. Thus to scorn the things of the world is to remain a maid, addicted to the childish occupations encouraged by the nurse and the priest. The activities of belles and beaux are merely childish occupations, though indulged in by adults. They are also calculated to keep love at bay. Even more significant is the teaching that Belinda know her own importance (1.35). Our heroine learns this so well that no entreaty to love or marriage can have any effect upon her.

This behavior we are to see as unnatural. A young woman of Belinda's status should be susceptible to masculine charms, and her failure to be so inclined requires an explanation. As is clear from the beginning, the sylphs minister effectively to Belinda's violent addiction to chastity. They are former coquettes and the gnomes erstwhile prudes. Since both coquettes and prudes are by their natures averse to sexual activity, they are effective guardians of Belinda's virginity.

Like the sylphs and gnomes, Belinda undergoes a change, a metamorphosis, reminiscent of the Ovidian kind. For example, her toilet transforms her into an amazon of sorts, prepared to resist sexual advances. Even the artifacts of that toilet have themselves been transformed:

> The Tortoise here and Elephant unite,
> Transform'd to *Combs*, the speckled and the white.
> (1.135–36)

As the puffs, powders, and patches assume their roles, Belinda emerges metamorphosed:

> Now awful Beauty puts on all its Arms;
> The Fair each moment rises in her Charms,
> Repairs her Smiles, awakens ev'ry Grace,
> And calls forth all the Wonders of her Face;
> Sees by Degrees a purer Blush arise,
> And keener Lightnings quicken in her Eyes.
> (1.139–44)

Although this metamorphosis makes Belinda more formidable, it also increases her sex appeal. Indeed, her attractions are such that the Baron is made a desperate man. Since his suit has no chance of success, he undertakes to have his way by guile and force.

Now if we place on one side this female sense of self-importance and all the equipages of upper air and fairyland, which sustain that self-conceit, and on the other hand we set the attractions of being a woman well-married, we see a pattern of contrasts begun in the lyric poetry of the ancient world and become commonplace in poetry of the Elizabethan period and the earlier seventeenth century.

This pattern culminates in what Earl Miner has called the cavalier mode.[2] The particular topos typical of this mode and functioning most prominently in *The Rape of the Lock* will be understood most readily by a quotation from Horace's Odes, I, xi:

> dum loquimur, fugerit invida
> aetas: carpe diem, quam minimum credula postero. . . .
> (7–8)[3]

The phrase *carpe diem* is recognizable to all as an important topos in lyric poetry. It is a specific aspect of a broader theme which Earl Miner felicitously calls *memento temporis*.[4]

What I intend to show here is that a significant meaning of *The Rape of the Lock* is communicated in Pope's version of the carpe diem topos, and that this essentially lyric theme functions in the poem in a complex set of harmonies with the broader memento temporis of epic and other genres. But before we trace in detail Pope's representation of the carpe diem theme, an example of the way he employs lyric motifs in the poem may be in order.

Let us compare two couplets of similar import, the first from *The Rape of the Lock* and the second from Thomas Carew's "To A. L. Perswasions to love" (1640):

> Fair Tresses Man's Imperial Race insnare,
> And Beauty draws us with a single Hair.
> (2.27–28)

and

> These curious locks so aptly twind,
> Whose every haire a soule doth bind. . . .
> (37–38)[5]

A late classical use of the same conceit may serve to illuminate the modifications Pope has introduced. Here is a translation of an epigram from *The Greek Anthology*:

> Doris pulled one thread from her golden hair and bound my hands with it, as if I were her prisoner. At first I laughed, thinking it easy to shake off charming Doris' fetters. But finding I had not strength to break them, I presently began to moan, as one held tight by galling irons. And now most ill-fated of men, I am hung on a hair and must ever follow where my mistress chooses to drag me.[6]

Carew uses the image in his much longer poem in couplets, but the poem is still a love lyric. Pope, on the other hand, adapts the image to the demands of his heroi-comical poem, as he calls it. He begins the verse paragraph in which the image is contained with a specific woman, Belinda, but he proceeds to a series of more general observations. The phrase "Imperial Race" seems to be an ironic concession to the supreme status of epic protagonists. In *The Greek Anthology* and Carew, the locks always belong to an individual lady. Pope, however, heightens our sense of generic distinction, even as he seems to ignore the differences between our expectations in lyric and epic. The inappropriateness of the heightened language to the lyric motif underscores the impotence of heroical muscle in the toils of a single lyrical hair. If this be mock-heroic, it is also mock-lyric. We laugh at the hyperbole of the heroes, but we laugh as well at the hyperbole of the hair. In other words, in this disruption of contexts, neither world, of heroes or lovers, can be taken seriously. Each generic context acts as a distorting mirror to the other.

Pope prepares us for this at the very opening of *The Rape of the Lock* with his revised quotation from one of Martial's epigrams. By that epigraph Pope makes clear to us that the subject of the lock is essentially an amorous and therefore lyrical theme. His reference in line 2 to "trivial things" and his assertion that his subject is slight (5) make explicit the discrepancy between the heroic aspect of the poem and this more lyrical-comical dimension. Other generic abnormalities at the very outset, like the epistolary address to Caryll (3) and the suggestion of panegyric to come (5), should provide more than a hint that we have before us no exercise in conventional genre.

As I indicated earlier, Belinda is as much victim as she is coquette. The teachings of the nurse and priest and the vigilance, not to mention the deceit, of the sylphs determine her negative response to any suitor. By this distinction Pope the narrator hopes to persuade Belinda and her prototype, Arabella Fermor, to yield to love.

The failure of Belinda to be the feminine complement to the Baron's masculinity is seen in the imagery of childhood which surrounds her. Ariel treats her like a child, not like the woman she ought to be, when he speaks of her "infant Thought" (1.29). In evoking the fantasy world he represents, he refers to "Some secret Truths from Learned Pride conceal'd, / To Maids alone and Children are reveal'd . . ." (1.37–38). Thus sylphs preserve maidens from their natural progress toward maturity, a maturity marked by sexual surrender and the assumption of the name of woman. The moving toyship of a maiden's heart is appropriate to Belinda's childish state, one totally manipulated by outside forces.

That Belinda is not irremediably hard-hearted we see only moments before the rape of the lock, when the power of the sylphs disappears. After entering Belinda's thought, Ariel sees "in spite of all her Art, / An Earthly Lover lurking at her Heart. / Amaz'd, confus'd, he found his Pow'r expir'd, / Resign'd to Fate, and with a Sigh retir'd" (3.143–46). But invariably the sylphs, Thalestris, and Umbriel reassert their disruptive power to ensure that there will be no conciliation.

Umbriel's journey to the Cave of Spleen to ensure that Belinda's heart remains hardened against the Baron is more an adaptation of the Cave of Morpheus in Chaucer's *The Book of the Duchess* (1369), perhaps by way of Spenser, than it is an epic descent. Umbriel is a gnome, a former prude, who, like the sylphs, is designated as male, but was a female in his mortal state. The confusion of gender is another result of metamorphosis that terminates in unnatural sexlessness. In the cave itself

> Unnumber'd Throngs on ev'ry side are seen
> Of Bodies chang'd to various Forms by *Spleen.*
> Here living *Teapots* stand, one Arm held out,
> One bent; the Handle this, and that the Spout:
> A Pipkin there like *Homer's Tripod* walks;
> Here sighs a Jar, and there a Goose-pye talks;
> Men prove with Child, as pow'rful Fancy works,
> And Maids turn'd Bottels, call aloud for Corks.
>   (4.47–54)

When the gnome begs the goddess to "touch *Belinda* with Chagrin; / That single Act gives half the World the Spleen" (4.77–78), his prayer is granted. From then on any reconciliation of Belinda with the Baron becomes impossible.

If there were any question about the poem's tending toward the carpe diem topos in its early editions, the inclusion in 1717 of Clarissa's speech should settle the matter. The major adjustment that Pope made in Sarpedon's address to Glaucus in the *Iliad* exactly reflects his intention in *The Rape of the Lock*. Sarpedon's speech is a memento mori utterance and exhortation to valor, but it is in no way an argument for sexual surrender. Clarissa's speech substitutes the carpe diem theme for the heroic motif:

> But since, alas! frail Beauty must decay,
> Curl'd or uncurl'd, since Locks will turn to grey,
> Since painted, or not painted, all shall fade,
> And she who scorns a Man, must die a Maid;
> What then remains, but well our Pow'r to use,
> And keep good Humour still whate'er we lose?
>   (5.25–30)

Although Clarissa substitutes the loss of maidenhead for the loss of life stressed by Sarpedon, in bringing virtue and merit into prominence, Pope follows Spenser and the cavaliers. Recommending marriage along with love, Herrick counsels the virgins in a well-known quatrain (1648):

> Then be not coy, but use your time;
> And while ye may, goe marry:
> For having lost but once your prime,
> You may for ever tarry.
>   (13–16)[7]

Although it is unlikely that Pope is recalling Herrick specifically, what he has done with Clarissa's speech is adapt a strictly epic utterance to the requirements of an essentially lyrical carpe diem topos.

The splenetic influence, however, leads to the final stage of Belinda's transformation to asexual amazon warrior. The mock-heroic battle that ensues is thus viewed triumphantly by Umbriel (5.53). With all its sexual innuendoes, the struggle between beaux and belles is a reproach to normal sexuality. The coquettes and prudes have won the day.

Another aspect of Pope's memento temporis in *The Rape of the Lock* is the much acclaimed sun imagery. It first appears as Belinda awakes, only to be eclipsed by her bright eyes: "*Sol* thro' white Curtains shot a tim'rous Ray, / And op'd those Eyes that must eclipse the Day . . ." (1.13–14). In canto 2, as Belinda sets out on her voyage up the Thames, she shines forth, a cynosure among celestial objects: "Bright as the Sun, her Eyes the Gazers strike, / And, like the Sun, they shine on all alike" (2.13–14). In the third canto, however, we have the first hint of the meaning the sun will later assume:

> Mean while declining from the Noon of Day,
> The Sun obliquely shoots his burning Ray;
> The hungry Judges soon the Sentence sign,
> And Wretches hang that Jury-men may Dine. . . .
>   (3.19–22)

With the sun declining from its apogee, the memento temporis asserts itself in the reminder of the death sentence that wretches are under. Herrick's lyric may serve as a gloss to Pope's epic:

> The glorious Lamp of Heaven, the Sun,
>   The higher he's a getting;

The sooner will his Race be run,
And neerer he's to Setting.
                                    (5–8)[8]

After the rape in canto 3, canto 4 appropriately descends with Umbriel
into the darkness of the Cave of Spleen. During this canto as well, Belinda's
eyes are "half-drown'd in Tears . . ." (4.144), making it clear that she rejects
the solution prescribed in Marvell's "To His Coy Mistress": "Thus though we
cannot make our Sun / Stand still, yet we will make him run" (45–46).[9]

If we have missed the fact that even in the opening canto, Belinda, by
arising from bed at noon, has lost half her day, we cannot overlook the memento temporis at the conclusion of the poem. Here Belinda's eventual death
and the setting of the sun become one and the same thing:

> For, after all the Murders of your Eye,
> When, after Millions slain, your self shall die;
> When those fair Suns shall sett, as sett they must,
> And all those Tresses shall be laid in Dust. . . .
>   (5.145–48)

If she maintains her present status, Belinda will grow old and die without
having anything to show for it. But if the conceit is metaphysical, the tone is
elegiac: "*This Lock*, the Muse shall consecrate to Fame, / And mid'st the Stars
inscribe *Belinda's* Name!" (5.149–50) Elegy, which is often epigrammatic,
especially in the epitaph, can be found in English in many forms other
than classical elegiac verse. Here is a passage from the octosyllabic "On the
Death of Mistress Elizabeth Filmer: An Elegiac Epitaph" (1649) by Richard
Lovelace:

> Thus, although this marble must,
> As all things, crumble into dust,
> And though you finde this faire-built Tombe
> Ashes, as what lyes in it's Wombe;
> Yet her Saint-like name shall shine
> A living Glory to this Shrine,
> And her eternal Fame be read,
> When all, but *very Vertue's dead.* [10]

From this we can see that, despite the difference in versification, Pope has
caught the lyrical elegiac tone precisely. Once again he has combined elegy

appropriate to epic with the accents and verbal contours of the cavalier mode. From all of this we must conclude that, from a generic standpoint, *The Rape of the Lock* is more heterogeneous than studies of the poem up to now have led us to believe. The juxtaposition of lyric and mock-heroic modes creates comic ridicule directed chiefly against Belinda as representative of all the hard-hearted fair. The Baron is implicated too, however, and so the satire is mild. Yet satire emerges because of the stress laid on Belinda's rejection of her natural role. The use of metamorphosis to point up her perversity introduces the Ovidian epic as still another counter in Pope's generic sleight of hand.

Such mixing of genres should lead to a structure as perverse as Belinda's splenetic tirade, but by some more mysterious metamorphosis, all disparate generic elements fall into place. The poet proves that he can harmonize the discordant parts of the poem. Whether or not he can turn a quarrel into similar concord remains to be seen.

But the resolution of the poem is only an illusion. By taking the lock and turning it into a constellation, Pope has removed from earth the object of contention. But this is only a poetic legerdemain, a belletristic metamorphosis. The conflict between Belinda and the Baron can only be resolved by the real persons themselves, Arabella Fermor and Lord Petre. Just as in *Absalom and Achitophel* action is halted and a solution is prescribed. But there is no certainty that the poet's solution will be accepted.

Indeed, for all its brilliance, the deus ex machina at the end resolves nothing. Belinda and the Baron, we may expect, will remain committed to their own perversities. As in so many satires, nothing really occurs. The Baron's rape has left Belinda a virgin. That is precisely the point. All the transformations we have seen lead away from nature to a kind of negation. If Belinda is to become the woman the poet wants her to be, something more positive must happen. And with the help of the carpe diem topos we are left with no doubt as to what that something ought to be.

The Dunciad

As in *The Rape of the Lock,* the satiric emphasis in *The Dunciad* emerges from a series of metamorphoses. The metamorphoses we witness in *The Dunciad* are always perverse, but, as in Ovid, they have much to do with form. Thus a central cluster of images in Pope's satire involves genre. As Pope's poetic vision draws us ineluctably toward uncreation, one of the prominent signals of the decline is the alteration of genre.[11] But other perversions are contributory, too, and they gradually add up to the dissolution of civilization. *The Dunciad* is Pope's anatomy of the changes that will lead to disaster.

Since "the Action of *The Dunciad* is the Removal of the imperial seat of Dulness from the City to the polite world,"[12] it is the poets who embody the transformation from nature to perversity:

> Hence Bards, like Proteus long in vain ty'd down,
> Escape in Monsters, and amaze the town.
> (1.37–38)[13]

With the return of Chaos, generic integrity, one of the highest achievements of civilization, faces utter dissolution. A self-congratulating Dulness looks on with approval:

> She sees a Mob of Metaphors advance,
> Pleas'd with the madness of the mazy dance:
> How Tragedy and Comedy embrace;
> How Farce and Epic get a jumbled race;
> How Time himself stands still at her command,
> Realms shift their place, and Ocean turns to land.
> (1.67–72)

The goddess herself has undergone a transformation:

> Dulness with transport eyes the lively Dunce,
> Remembring she herself was Pertness once.
> (1.111–12)

But since, for Pope, the chief trait of debased modern literature is departure from nature, the producers and their products personify the unnatural. Indeed, the grotesque transformations to which modern works are subject suggest that they possess no substantial form whatsoever. They suck their mercurial insubstantiality from their goddess mother, Dulness:

> She, tinsel'd o'er in robes of varying hues,
> With self-applause her wild creation views;
> Sees momentary monsters rise and fall,
> And with her own fools-colours gilds them all.
> (1.81–84)

With the advent of the antihero, Cibber, the focus on literature takes a more personal direction. Like Mac Flecknoe in Dryden's poem, Cibber is constantly trying to produce a literary work. The outcome, however, never accords with his intention. After blaspheming, the poet

> Then gnaw'd his pen, then dash'd it on the ground,
> Sinking from thought to thought, a vast profound!
> Plung'd for his sense, but found no bottom there,
> Yet wrote and flounder'd on, in mere despair.
> Round him much Embryo, much Abortion lay,
> Much future Ode, and abdicated Play. . . .
> (1.117–22)

A future ode, of course, is nothing at all, and an abdicated play is one its author dare not claim. Both are embryos and abortions, neither fulfilling the requirement of classical genre. What accompanies these unrealized forms is even less determinate: "Nonsense precipitate" (1.123) and "Fruits of dull Heat, and Sooterkins of Wit" (1.126). Amidst debased books of various size, Cibber's altar is crowned with "unsully'd lays" (1.158) and "A twisted Birthday Ode" at the top of the spire (1.162).

Again, Pope follows Dryden by turning a writer's own language against him. Cibber's account of himself contains direct allusions to the *Apology*. For example, "The brisk Example never fail'd to move" (1.194) may be a reference to Cibber's description of himself in his youth as "a brisk blockhead."[14] That Cibber's father intended him for a clergyman accounts for another line, "Take up the Bible, once my better guide . . ." (1.200).[15] References to "Fiddle" (1.224) and "christian progeny" (1.228) point to other eccentricities of Cibber's expression.[16] The "smutty sisters" (1.230) may be an allusion to the scandalous life of Cibber's daughter, Mrs. Charlotte Charke.[17]

When Dulness next shows her works to her "Chosen," the generic variation and uncertainty are again paramount: "Prose swell'd to verse, verse loit'ring into prose" (1.274). She further discloses

> How Prologues into Prefaces decay,
> And these to Notes are fritter'd quite away . . .
> (1.277–78)

The verse of a prologue presumably becomes the prose of a preface, and finally all presumption to organization and generic integrity is dissipated in mere notes.

Next amphibious categories, neither one thing nor the other, emerge to create the modern author:

> Small thanks to France, and none to Rome or Greece,
> A past, vamp'd, future, old, reviv'd, new piece,
> 'Twixt Plautus, Fletcher, Shakespear, and Corneille,
> Can make a Cibber, Tibbald, or Ozell.
>
> (1.283–86)

The new categories listed here violate every generic requirement. Just what a "future" piece might be is left to the reader's imagination, although it is probably one that has yet to be composed. The other classifications seem to refer to adaptations and "new" suggests originality, in its negative sense. For Pope a Plautus, Fletcher, Shakespeare, or Corneille is a known quality. Each is identifiable with stylistic and generic integrity. But something grotesque emerges between the boundaries of these familiar territories. This is the shapeless miscellany called Cibber, Theobald, or Ozell.

To underscore the hybrid nature of the dunces' literature, the goddess' bird, "Something betwixt a Heideggre and owl" (1.290), perched on Cibber's crown. Next all pretense to generic integrity dissipates in crude contrivances, as in the writing of Hervey:

> And thou! his Aid de camp, lead on my sons,
> Light-arm'd with Points, Antitheses, and Puns.
> Let Bawdry, Billingsgate, my daughters dear,
> Support his front, and Oaths bring up the rear. . . .
>
> (1.305–8)

Finally the writing degenerates into obscenity and blasphemy. Bawdry, billingsgate, and oaths are the genres by which Hervey's writings are to be understood.

Still another subliterary genre is introduced as Dulness exerts yet one more impulse to motherhood:

> "O! when shall rise a Monarch all our own,
> And I, a Nursing-mother, rock the throne,
> 'Twixt Prince and People close the Curtain draw,
> Shade him from Light, and cover him from Law;
> Fatten the Courtier, starve the learned band,
> And suckle Armies, and dry-nurse the land:

'Till Senates nod to Lullabies divine,
And all be sleep, as at an Ode of thine."
(1.311–18)

The lines drowse with the rhythms of the lullaby as the poem prepares us for a profounder sleep to come. In addition, the curtain between prince and people foreshadows the portentous curtain to be dropped at the end of book 4.

From somniferous lullaby Pope takes us without warning to a chorus of popular shouts. Here all pretense to form is dropped. Cibber is acclaimed as king of dullness from White's to Drury Lane. Allusions to *Mac Flecknoe* multiply with the acclamations from the less fashionable parts of town and the reiteration of Ogilby's name (1.328).[18] The final line, "And the hoarse nation croak'd, 'God save King Log!'" (1.330) drops us abruptly into the world of Aesop's fables. Thus, throughout book 1, we continue to mount and fall in a diapason of generic fluctuations.[19]

Generic confusion continues apace in book 2.[20] The funeral games, in addition to being mock-heroic, introduce a mock-pastoral element. Despite the obvious scatology of the following lines, the setting is unmistakably pastoral:

> Full in the middle way there stood a lake,
> Which Curl's Corinna chanc'd that morn to make. . . .
> (2.69–70)

The rustic name, Corinna, helps to establish a mock-pastoralism which emerges later in the extended swimming episode. This is all similar, especially for its dirt, to Swift's "Description of the Morning" (1709) and "Description of a City Shower" (1710).

When Curl seizes the papers of the phantom More, the issue of genre is raised again in another context:

> To seize his papers, Curl, was next thy care;
> His papers light, fly diverse, tost in air;
> Songs, sonnets, epigrams the winds uplift,
> And whisk 'em back to Evans, Young, and Swift.
> (2.113–16)

Throughout all of this, however, the omnipresent theme is metamorphosis. Dulness decks out members of Grub Street to represent Congreve, Addison, and Prior (2.122–24). The phantom More, who is equivalent to nothing,

pulled an earlier disappearing act (2.110–12) or shape-shifting ploy. Now
with false Congreves and Addisons in Dulness' train, Curl plays the role of an
unsuccessful Menelaus:

> Curl stretches after Gay, but Gay is gone,
> He grasps an empty Joseph for a John:
> So Proteus, hunted in a nobler shape,
> Became, when seiz'd, a puppy, or an ape.
> (2.127–30)

The modern world is seen as a place where everything is false. Seizing or
grasping anything is an impossibility, for nothing is truly substantial. The protean quality of identity continues to characterize Dulness' realm:

> Be thine, my stationer! this magic gift;
> Cook shall be Prior, and Concanen, Swift:
> So shall each hostile name become our own,
> And we too boast our Garth and Addison.
> (2.137–40)

It is clear that such protean imagery had a strongly censorious meaning in the
eighteenth century. Richardson's Lovelace, for example, is thoroughly protean. Clarissa writes to Anna Howe of her abductor's changeable qualities: "I
am strangely at a loss what to think of this man. He is a perfect Proteus. I can
but write according to the shape he assumes at the time."[21]

Mock-pastoral is emphasized again when the mud-covered form rises up to
tell of subterranean love:

> First he relates, how sinking to the chin,
> Smit with his mien, the Mud-nymphs suck'd him in:
> How young Lutetia, softer than the down,
> Nigrina black, and Merdamante brown,
> Vy'd for his love in jetty bow'rs below,
> As Hylas fair was ravish'd long ago.
> Then sung, how shown him by the Nut-brown maids
> A branch of Styx here rises from the Shades,
> That tinctur'd as it runs with Lethe's streams,
> And wafting Vapours from the Land of dreams,
> (As under seas Alphaeus' secret sluice
> Bears Pisa's off'rings to his Arethuse)
> Pours into Thames: and hence the mingled wave

Intoxicates the pert, and lulls the grave:
Here brisker vapours o'er the Temple creep,
There, all from Paul's to Aldgate drink and sleep.
                                        (2.331–46)

Just before the conclusion of the games, the army of clerical authors, marching along Fleet Street, is inundated with the kinds of literary works they write:

'Till show'rs of Sermons, Characters, Essays,
In circling fleeces whiten all the ways. . . .
                                        (2.361–62)

The contrast between the black clerical garb and the veritable storm of white paper is stressed in Pope's application of an epic simile to the spectacle:

So clouds replenish'd from some bog below,
Mount in dark volumes, and descend in snow.
                                        (2.363–64)

The felicity of the metaphor is intensified by the double application of the word "volumes," which applies both to a quantity of clouds (always insubstantial) and the books produced by this class of duncs. As he has done so often in the first two books of the *Dunciad*, Pope fits the disparate material of satire to the mock-epic design and so organizes everything into a unified vision. By presenting the material of modern life as though it might be understood within a coherent frame, the poet shows just how chaotic and degenerate it all is. Again, that ridiculous comparison produces the irony inherent in every attempt to measure the real by the ideal. Throughout the *Dunciad* the ideal genre—epic—is measured against the trivial attempts in genre of the duncs. The discrepancy is meant to show us how far short the modern concept of genre falls when measured against ancient practice. What was real for the ancients has become for the moderns an ideal grasped only in the parodic genre of satire. Modern materials lend themselves to little else, except in the works of those few authors who have escaped the trend toward dullness.

At the conclusion of book 2 a universal sleep overtakes the duncs. This transformation from pointless movement to motionless slumber is yet another metamorphosis which marks the transition to the modern world. This prepares the way for Cibber's dream vision of the future in book 3.

Book 3 opens with a pietà grouping of Dulness and her Cibberian son. Sexuality fairly oozes from Pope's descriptive language:

> But in her Temple's last recess inclos'd,
> On Dulness' lap th'Anointed head repos'd.
> Him close she curtains round with Vapours blue,
> And soft besprinkles with Cimmerian dew.
> Then raptures high the seat of Sense o'erflow,
> Which only heads refin'd from Reason know.
> (3.1–6)

Another curtaining effect hides the incestuous relationship between Dulness and her child.[22] The perversity of the relationship is underscored by the mixing of Vergilian, Miltonic, and "Tubbian" motifs. Indeed the world of *A Tale of a Tub* dominates *The Dunciad* throughout:

> Hence, from the straw where Bedlam's Prophet nods,
> He hears loud Oracles, and talks with Gods:
> Hence the Fool's Paradise, the Statesman's Scheme,
> The air-built Castle, and the golden Dream,
> The Maid's romantic wish, the Chemist's flame,
> And Poet's vision of eternal Fame.
> (3.7–12)

In this passage Pope follows the view expressed in *A Tale of a Tub* that all visionary experience originates in sensuality. With Cibber's anointed head reposed in the penetralium of Dulness' lap, incest becomes the incentive to inspiration. Thus an infantile, if grossly perverse, sexuality leads to a series of visionary and childlike desires. Although far less delicate, this process is reminiscent of the perverse infantilism which leads to Belinda's denial of womanhood.

As a series of fantastic, illogical events unravels, Cibber makes an epic descent to the underworld "on Fancy's easy wing convey'd" (3.13). There the "King" observes another kind of transformation of the souls of those newly arrived:

> Here, in a dusky vale where Lethe rolls,
> Old Bavius sits, to dip poetic souls,
> And blunt the sense, and fit it for a skull
> Of solid proof, impenetrably dull:

> Instant, when dipt, away they wing their flight,
> Where Brown and Mears unbar the gates of Light,
> Demand new bodies, and in Calf's array,
> Rush to the world, impatient for the day.
>   (3.23–30)

In the vision of father Settle and his prophecies of Dulness' future, the most important metamorphoses of book 3 reside. After the present world is imagined, "one wide Conflagration swallows all" (3.240), a new world, both perversion and parody of the old one, rises up:

> Thence a new world, to Nature's laws unknown,
> Breaks out refulgent, with a heav'n its own:
> Another Cynthia her new journey runs,
> And other planets circle other suns. . . .
>   (3.241–44)

That metamorphosis implies perversion becomes clear in the next lines:

> The forests dance, the rivers upward rise,
> Whales sport in woods, and dolphins in the skies,
> And last, to give the whole creation grace,
> Lo! one vast Egg produces human race.
>   (3.245–48)

The unnatural transformation of the world finds its symbol in a vast egg; the mode of birth characteristic of nonmammalian creatures becomes the new producer of humanity. It will not surprise us to consider that the new human race will fall far short of quintessential humanity.

Book 3 of the 1728 edition of *The Dunciad* provides an insight into Pope's procedure of mixing genres, which the introduction of book 4 into the final text might tend to obscure. In the A text Pope uses his notes to call attention to a peculiar generic mix. Father Settle addresses his son Theobald:

> And are these Wonders, Son, to thee unknown?
> Unknown to thee? These wonders are thy own.
> For works like these let deathless Journals tell,
> 'None but Thy self can be thy parallel.'
>   (A.3.269–72)

The concluding line of this passage is from *Double Falshood,* a play of indeterminate authorship. Pope claims in his note that the play was Theobald's, but Theobold insisted that it was by Shakespeare. It was certainly not by Shakespeare; but whatever its provenance, it was published by Theobald and reached a second edition by March 1728.[23]

Here again Pope turns an author's own language against him, and that language is from a play, a different genre. Many additional passages from the play are given in the long annotations that follow as Pope attempts to discredit *Double Falshood.* Both notes and quotations stress the generic uncertainty of the poem as a whole. In misrepresenting lines from the play in the new context of the poem's text and the notes, Pope is ridiculing Theobald. The mixing of genres, prose and verse, in the annotations creates the comic ridicule directed against the dunces, whose own works are indeterminate in any number of ways.

As Dulness progresses "from Booths to Theatre, to Court" (A.3.301), that is, from the world of the subliterary to the place where taste is expected to be the best, the theater becomes a primary vehicle as well as object:

> Already, Opera prepares the way,
> The sure fore-runner of her gentle sway.
> (A.3.303–5)

Opera, preeminently a mixed genre—music and drama in combination—seemed to Pope an unnatural violation of generic integrity, an Italian blemish on the English artistic scene. But the king of dunces in both A and B versions of *The Dunciad* were dramatists of some pretensions, and Cibber, of course, was an actor as well as a playwright. Even in the A version, Cibber is the "Lord-Chancellor of Plays" (A.3.320).

Indeed all the dramatic images and motifs veer toward a suitably dramatic conclusion of the A text. As each art, in its turn, goes out, the hand of Dulness

> lets the curtain fall,
> And universal Darkness covers all.
> (A.3.355–56)

That Pope intended the dramatic imagery throughout to lead up to the curtain's descent seems certain, since when he added book 4, he moved Dulness' curtain from book 3 to the conclusion of the poem. For Pope, as the world becomes increasingly a stage, art becomes more popular and corrupt. In the metamorphosis of serious drama to the indeterminacies of Theobald, Cibber, and Italian opera, the decline and destruction of all value is mirrored. As Ian Jack has pointed out, it was Pope's "mixture of styles that [Joseph] Warton was censuring when he called *The Dunciad* 'one of the most motley compositions . . . in the works of so exact a writer.'"[24] What Warton seems not to have realized is that mixed genre is a norm in satire and that it is particularly appropriate in *The Dunciad,* a work which seeks to locate cultural indisposition in generic chaos.

With book 4 the mixture of styles continues in some new combinations. As the pattern of metamorphosis moves from the comic to a more completely satiric effect, the long-range implications of Dulness' reign will become apparent.

Aubrey L. Williams has identified the extended dramatic metaphor which ends with the fall of the curtain at the conclusion of book 4. In addition he has argued persuasively that two lesser forms contribute to the structure of the book. One of these is the "Tablet of Cebes," an allegorical work mentioned by Pope in his notes, and the other is the sessions poem,[25] which I considered briefly as judicial satire, in Chapter 4. Still another model on which book 4, as well as the rest of *The Dunciad,* is formed is the progress poem, exemplified by Sir John Denham's, "The Progress of Learning."[26]

In the opening allegorical tableau, we find both a mixture of genres and, as we have come to expect from the earlier three books, genre as the subject of concern. In the area of Dulness' immediate rule, the Muses lie bound. The traditional forms express their frustration and distress at the new rule that restricts them:

> There to her heart sad Tragedy addrest
> The dagger wont to pierce the Tyrant's breast;
> But sober History restrain'd her rage,
> And promis'd Vengeance on a barb'rous age.
> There sunk Thalia, nerveless, cold, and dead,
> Had not her Sister Satyr held her head. . . .
> (4.37–42)

The final line of this passage reveals Pope's idea of satire's function in a corrupt age. Besides recording and condemning the evils done to the kinds of literature, satire preserves contact with the classical tradition and offers sustenance to generic integrity.

Italian opera, a symbol of the decline of genre and English culture throughout the first three books, steps forth as a personification in the allegorical pageant:

> When lo! a Harlot form soft sliding by,
> With mincing step, small voice, and languid eye;
> Foreign her air, her robe's discordant pride
> In patch-work flutt'ring, and her head aside:
> By singing Peers up-held on either hand,
> She tripp'd and laugh'd, too pretty much to stand. . . .
>   (4.45–50)

As a "patch-work" form opera represents the perversion of both drama and music. Like satire it is a mixed form, but its mixture is the result of a disunity of intellect and sensibility. For Pope, opera reflects a decline in the seriousness of art. Satire's mixed form is adapted to point out the kind of perversion represented by opera and other modern forms.

For Pope the bad use of the mind is to be seen not only among literary poseurs, but also among the politicians and government officials. Dulness sees wits and politicians complementing one another:

> So by each Bard an Alderman shall sit,   •
> A heavy Lord shall hang at ev'ry Wit. . . .
>   (4.131–32)

The reference to a poet's tomb, pointed out in the notes, communicates a foreboding of a bad end to come. The serious harm associated with satire emerges in greater force as book 4 proceeds.

With the appearance of Busby, to introduce the pedants, and the emergence of Bentley, the greatest pedant of all, the tone of book 4 changes abruptly. For some two hundred lines, the language of verse epistle, not epic parody, becomes dominant. As Pope himself pointed out to Joseph Spence, he originally composed these lines as part of a projected "Epistle on Education," but found another use for them when the project was abandoned.[27] The structure of generic satire, of course, lends itself to this sort of intercalation. But the shift in style is completely functional: it serves to call attention to the issue of education and to trace its sorry role in the decline of modern culture. The sad state of education is revealed by the major theme of transformation.

One of the benefits of education is the intellectual and moral growth of the student from callow youngster to mature adult. In schools presided over by Bentley, however, a metamorphosis takes place in the opposite direction. The scholar on the grand tour underwent an unfortunate alteration as he "gather'd ev'ry Vice on Christian ground" (4.312). Further, the young man visited courts where Dulness had already taken up residence:

> Saw ev'ry Court, heard ev'ry King declare
> His royal Sense, of Op'ra's or the Fair;
> The Stews and Palace equally explor'd,
> Intrigu'd with glory, and with spirit whor'd. . . .
>   (4.313–16)

The young scholar's loss of language, prepared for by the narrow focus on words alone in his earlier education, brings about another degenerative metamorphosis. After drinking and dining to surfeit, he

> Dropt the dull lumber of the Latin store,
> Spoil'd his own language, and acquir'd no more;
> All Classic learning lost on Classic ground;
> And last turn'd *Air*, the Echo of a Sound!
>   (4.319–22)

Thus language turns to mere nothing like the air of Jack's Aeolists in *A Tale of a Tub*.[28]

The descent to nothing began in a narrowing curriculum as expressed by Busby:

> "Since Man from beast by Words is known,
> Words are Man's province, Words we teach alone.
> When Reason doubtful, like the Samian letter,
> Points him two ways, the narrower is the better."
>   (4.149–52)

After the process of narrowing reaches its logical nadir, the argument is summed up in the words of Silenus to his goddess dam:

"From Priest-craft happily set free,
Lo! ev'ry finish'd Son returns to thee:
First slave to Words, then vassal to a Name,
Then dupe to Party; child and man the same;
Bounded by Nature, narrow'd still by Art,
A trifling head, and a contracted heart."
(4.499–504)

The note to this passage is an attack on the authority of systems and the delusion of party distinctions.[29] Both in the text of the poem and the notes, Pope is attempting the opposite of what the pedants, virtuosi, or a priori philosophers achieve by all their activity. Although he was unable to complete the magnum opus that he had projected,[30] Pope succeeds in developing a broad interpretation of his culture throughout the four books of *The Dunciad.*

But even as Pope takes his philosophical stand, the transformation to Dulness' kingdom continues unabated. Just as the touring youth lost both his Latin and his native tongue, the court flatterer gives everything in exchange for royal favor:

Lost is his God, his Country, ev'ry thing;
And nothing left but Homage to a King!
(4.523–24)

Again, the implication is that homage to a king is equivalent to nothing. The metamorphosis is from something substantial to total nonentity.

Next the wizard, a Circean figure, begins another round of metamorphoses. Here there is a curious twist, however, for the human form divine remains as a reproach to subhuman antics:

The vulgar herd turn off to roll with Hogs,
To run with Horses, or to hunt with Dogs;
But, sad example! never to escape
Their Infamy, still keep the human shape.
(4.525–28)

By this Dulness' power is nearly absolute. Only the satirist and perhaps a few others can see the change that has really taken place.

Even so, transformations continue apace. In the quest for status, the changes come with droll rapidity:

> How quick Ambition hastes to ridicule!
> The Sire is made a Peer, the Son a Fool.
> (4.547–48)

The Circean process continues into a perverse symposium of French luxury set under the auspices of Dulness: [31]

> On some, a Priest succinct in amice white
> Attends; all flesh is nothing in his sight!
> Beeves, at his touch, at once to jelly turn,
> And the huge Boar is shrunk into an Urn:
> The board with specious miracles he loads,
> Turns Hares to Larks, and Pigeons into Toads.
> (4.549–54)

The procedure is one of perverting, narrowing, and reducing, occasionally, to nothing.

Metamorphosis by title or degree is the next to take place:

> Next bidding all draw near on bended knees,
> The Queen confers her *Titles* and *Degrees.*
> Her children first of more distinguish'd sort,
> Who study Shakespeare at the Inns of Court,
> Impale a Glow-worm, or Vertù profess,
> Shine in the dignity of F.R.S.
> (4.565–70)

The entire *Dunciad* moves toward dehumanizing and denaturizing metamorphosis. At its conclusion book 4 reverts to the allegory with which it began. With Dulness' reign the restoration of Chaos will be complete and personified values extinguished, not by sleep, but by death:

> Thus at her felt approach, and secret might,
> *Art* after *Art* goes out, and all is Night.
> See skulking *Truth* to her old Cavern fled,
> Mountains of Casuistry heap'd o'er her head!
> *Philosophy* that lean'd on Heav'n before,
> Shrinks to her second cause, and is no more.
> *Physic* of *Metaphysic* begs defence,
> And *Metaphysic* calls for aid on *Sense!*
> See *Mystery* to *Mathematics* fly!

> In vain! they gaze, turn giddy, rave, and die.
> *Religion* blushing veils her sacred fires,
> And unawares *Morality* expires.
>
>   (4.639–50)

In every instance the personification dies or suffers some nearly equivalent eclipse. But the insistence on death in so many cases shows that Pope intended to alarm. He can imagine no greater harm than the destruction of the values by which society and culture have their being. By showing these values expire before our eyes, he gives a sharp edge to the comic techniques that dominate the first three books of *The Dunciad*. In the final six lines, light itself—a traditional symbol of God—dies, and everything else, presumably also dead or dying, is buried in darkness:

> Nor *public* Flame, nor *private*, dares to shine;
> Nor *human* Spark is left, nor Glimpse *divine!*
> Lo! thy dread Empire, CHAOS! is restor'd;
> Light dies before thy uncreating word:
> Thy hand, great Anarch! lets the curtain fall;
> And Universal Darkness buries All.
>
>   (4.651–56)

In the 1729 text, *The Dunciad Variorum*, most of these allegorical deaths took place at the end of book 3, but with some variations and in a slightly different order. The startling vision comes abruptly, perhaps too abruptly to ensure that the comic ridicule which dominates the earlier parts of the poem can be shaped into unmistakable satire. With the addition of book 4 in 1742, there is no longer the possibility of the satire falling short. The defeated allegorical figures early in the book are effective preparation for the deaths to come in the conclusion. The more serious cultural criticism of the passages on education also creates the solemnity of implication and tone which effective satire needs to place in balance with comic techniques. Perhaps Pope realized that the earlier editions were too comic to convey the full impact of satire. And yet he realized that without the comic balance, the work would be an ineffectual tirade. The revisions the 1728 text underwent at all stages seem to make it more of a philosophical poem. The addition of book 4 completes the job.

What we see in *The Dunciad* from a thematic standpoint are the transformational powers of Dulness. Although she is an ancient goddess, Dulness has achieved particular effectiveness in conjunction with the modern dunces represented by Grub Street. The poem depicts the collapse of form and order from their earliest, seemingly insignificant, manifestations to the terrifying fall of the curtain of universal darkness. Each minor, particular event or personage adds to the cumulative effect at the conclusion of book 4.

In addition to important thematic metamorphoses, *The Dunciad* reveals the generic transformations typical of satire. Epic and a host of other generic structures and stylistic strategies are deformed in the transition to satire. In this process parody once again establishes itself as an essential reagent. Just as *The Dunciad* reveals on the thematic level how traditional genres have made way for deconstructed forms, the poem unites theme and form in the transformational process from epic, pastoral, and prophecy, among other structures, to satire. Thus theme and form establish the same insight, but on the formal level the transformation is traditional and normative. By means of this paradox, theme and form are held in balance. When we have recognized the abnormalities of prolegomenal excesses, extensive notes, and major generic disruptions as norms of the satiric tradition, *The Dunciad* reinforces our outrage at similar deviations in other genres. What is appropriate in satire is indecorous elsewhere. Thus satire is the form most commodious to the revelation of the decline of form.

7

SWIFT

A Tale of a Tub

Swift's extensive use of popular forms marks his satire out from that of Dryden and Pope. His work, however, gives us an especially valuable perspective on the relationship of satire to nonmimetic structures. It represents a varied range of parodies from relatively simple forms to the most complex and profound of satires, *Gulliver's Travels*.

Swift's "Project for the Advancement of Religion" (1709) should be regarded as a serious proposal because of the lack of elements sufficient to disrupt its rhetoric and turn it into fiction. Although *The Drapier's Letters* (1724–25) contains little in the way of such disruptive qualities, the employment of a persona moves it distinctly in the direction of fictive discourse.[1] Yet that may not be enough. To qualify as a satire rather than as satiric nonmimetic writing, *The Drapier's Letters* must reveal a more distinct pattern of textual disruption. Until this can be demonstrated, it must be thought of as belonging to a boundary genre, somewhere between natural discourse and the mimetic language proper to satire.[2] Whatever fictional elements it may have, *The Drapier's Letters* consists of real controversial letters, not feigned ones, and thus there is a strict balance preserved between the fictional elements and very real issues that are dealt with directly, not by the indirection of ironic design which characterizes all of the complex satires examined thus far. Further, if "The Project" is a generic satire, it reveals ineptness on Swift's part. To construct a satire without a clearly disruptive ironic design is wholly out of character for Swift, who was especially proud of his own refinement of irony.[3]

Although M. B. Drapier is a persona, we nonetheless hear another voice throughout the *Letters* as is so often the case in satire. In fact the establishment of a consistent voice can lead a prose satire directly into a more purely fictional form. Satire, with the need to maintain an outside object, cannot become too involved in the development of the internal fiction which leads away from the outside referent to an internally consistent aesthetic. Satire at its best is consistently inconsistent. It avoids plot development and invokes different generic tonalities as the demands of ridicule dictate. This shape-shifting imitates at times the confusion of the enemy under attack and also provides a difficult moving target for anyone planning a counterattack.

In approaching Swift, I have space to mention only a few of the many forms he has mastered both in and out of parody. In his poetry alone the following may be cited: "Phyllis; or the Progress of Love" is a "progress" poem; "Description of a City Shower" parodies the georgic in structure and the epic (Dryden's *Aeneis* [1697]) in diction and metrics. "The Humble Petition of Frances Harris" (1701) parodies a legal petition, and "An Elegy on the Death of Partrige" (1708) is a mock elegy. Among prose forms are the *Directions for Servants* (c. 1704–c. 1736), a parody of the rules of a great house, the Partridge-Bickerstaff papers (1708–9), a parody of almanac style, and "A Meditation Upon a Broom-Stick" (1703), Swift's spoof of a Boyle meditation. Indeed, the parody, although not the only form that Swift was proficient in, seems to be one that showed his genius to greatest advantage. The parody in which a single form, the treatise, is subjected to the most scathing satire is *A Tale of a Tub*.

Before turning to the formal patterns in *A Tale of a Tub*, a word or two needs to be said about the persona. The narrator of *A Tale* is admittedly something of a problem. I think it is a mistake to see him as a consistent fictional character. Such consistency is not appropriate to satire precisely because it distracts the reader from the satire and focuses him on the fiction. The fiction must always be subordinate to the rhetorical purpose of satire, since satire depends on maintaining a balance between concern with the real world and involvement with the imaginative one of its own making. An imbalance in either direction results in a generic change toward the purely rhetorical or the wholly mimetic fictional. Without any element of fiction, satire either does not exist or remains a rudimentary prototype.

The narrator of *A Tale of a Tub* identifies himself at one point as "a most devoted Servant of all Modern Forms," and so I shall refer to him, since that is particularly appropriate to his explicit and implicit regard for manifold structures. But since the more usual names of "Tale-teller" and Grub Street hack are applicable as well, I shall call him those too for variety's sake. I refer to Swift as the author behind the hack, and whatever artistic effects are achieved beyond the hack's stated intentions are attributed to him.

A *Tale of a Tub* is called a "treatise" several times in the course of its preface. Even to the somewhat muddled mind of the writer, the devoted servant of modern forms, generic distinctions are important. He begins with forms which are clearly subgeneric in modern practice. He will not, he tells us, declaim against the multitude of writers who use such forms, since he is one of them. Further, whatever cannot be understood must be presumed to have "something very useful and profound . . . coucht underneath . . ." (46).[4] Also, whatever "is Printed in a different Character," presumably in capitals or italics, "shall be judged to contain something extraordinary either of *Wit* or *Sublime*" (47). He also explains why he includes eulogy in his work, that is, self-praise: Moderns find it too much trouble to wait for the world to praise them.

Satire, however, is a genre to be avoided entirely. And even as the irony intensifies during a short disquisition on the popularity of satire, the servant of modern forms discloses his plans for A *Panegyrick upon the World* (53). Having declared himself the writer of a treatise and a connoisseur of panegyric, he nonetheless rejects much that is identified with the modern way. This can be illustrated at the conclusion of the preface when he explains why he has failed to append his panegyric and A *Modern Defence of the Proceeding of the Rabble in all Ages* to the treatise:

> finding my Common-Place-Book fill much slower than I had reason to expect, I have chosen to defer them to another Occasion. Besides, I have been unhappily prevented in that Design, by a certain Domestick Misfortune, in the Particulars whereof, tho' it would be very seasonable, and much in the *Modern* way, to inform the *gentle Reader,* and would also be of great Assistance towards extending this Preface into the Size now in Vogue, which by Rule ought to be *large* in proportion as the subsequent Volume is *small;* Yet I shall now dismiss our impatient Reader from any farther Attendance at the *Porch.* . . .   (54)

What should be noted here is that our servant does not follow the practice of the other moderns. He is devoted to the forms, but often, after calling our attention to them, he avoids their use. This is obviously a complicated rhetorical technique. But aside from that, it permits the servant of modern forms always to preserve his own extraordinary mercuriality. In order to become the great original he turns out to be, our servant must violate even his own cardinal precepts. This means also that the narrative voice is never that of a consistent fictional character. The flexibility the satirist needs is achieved here by a manipulation of forms, and as different forms come into play at various points, the voice we hear is appropriate to whatever form is preeminent. Thus our narrator is as protean as the work itself. The work is a treatise, but, even as parody, it does not always maintain its pose. Neither does the narrator remain a Grub Street hack, though at times he is that, to be sure. At other times, however, he becomes a satirist without irony. This sort of complexity is usual in satire. The form is flexible and adaptable. It fits every situation: it stretches like a rubber glove.

At the same time, there are discrepancies we ought to notice. The title of the work, *A Tale of a Tub,* does not entirely square with the format of the work. The preface and introduction prepare us for a treatise, but the title might suggest a narrative, were it not that "a tale of a tub" is a popular genre in its own right without having been legitimized by Aristotle or Scaliger. The fact is that by the time we reach section 2, we have both a treatise and a fairy tale, as far as overt genre is concerned. The combination is odd to say the least, especially since the tale of the three brothers is not prefaced by anything linking it to the treatise. Indeed, matters related to the treatise are confined for the most part to the digressions.

Many stylistic inconsistencies surface early in section 2. The tale of the brothers begins as a fairy tale: "Once upon a Time . . ." (73). After the fairy tale tone is established, however, a sudden introduction of irony changes the reader's attitude from one of sober hearing to a more guarded stance: "they travelled thro' several Countries, encountred a reasonable Quantity of Gyants, and slew certain Dragons" (74). Giants cannot, I suspect, be thought of in reasonable quantities, nor are dragons to be referred to as someone we might pass in the street. This irony serves as something of a transition to yet another change of tone and scene. What follows is suggestive of Restoration comedy. Coming up to town and falling in love with ladies marks a realm of activity at odds with giants and dragons. Indeed the apposition of generically incompatible motifs produces a tone appropriate to ridicule and burlesque.

In section 4 we turn to the account of Peter as projector and virtuoso. Many of Peter's projects are written works, and, as such, they represent modern productions of which Swift clearly disapproves. Other sorts of projects include inventions of the mechanical variety and merchandising. All may be regarded as forms under the modern dispensation. Since most were unknown to the ancient world, they have little or no relationship to nature. Rather, they are perverse structures, devised, not discovered, which lead the way to even greater corruption.

Peter's first project is one of buying and selling.[5] He purchases purgatory and then sells it over and over again to those he has duped. The image of Peter as modern entrepreneur emerges at nearly every point.

Peter's second project involves prescriptions and allows him to function as an apothecary. The "*Whispering-Office*" is another quasi-medical invention. The idea of insurance is ridiculed in Peter's project of an "*Office of Ensurance, for Tobacco-Pipe, Martyrs of the Modern Zeal . . .*" (107–8).

Next Peter is seen as "the Original Author of *Puppets* and *Raree-Shows*" (109), popular forms at best. A long passage on Peter's "Bulls" treats those compositions allegorically as though they were indeed animals of the male gender. The reference, however, is to Papal Bulls outlining the position of the papacy on matters of significance (110–13). Finally, another of Peter's compositions, the pardon, sold for a sum of money, comes under satiric attack. The pardon, like so much of what Peter invents, brings irreparable harm to its putative beneficiaries: "The Wretches trusting to this, lost their Lives and Money too" (114).

The digression, although recognized by the ancients as a component of the formal oration, becomes in A Tale of a Tub the epitome of modern form, or, more precisely, the modern departure from form. Irrelevant as it is to any unified design, the digression is analogous to modern literary contrivances, prefaces, abstracts, and collections of faults. All of these are fragmentary, all unrelated to any larger purpose or perspective. In "A Digression Concerning Criticks," criticism becomes "the very Quintessence of what is bad" since the true critic is "*a Discoverer and Collector of Writers Faults*" (95). In its form criticism is merely another debased modern invention: "the Whole appears to be nothing else but an *Abstract* of the *Criticisms* themselves have made" (96).

In "A Digression in the Modern Kind" there is even a greater concern with form. Here the servant of modern forms discloses his "very strange, new, and important Discovery; That the Publick Good of Mankind is performed by two Ways, *Instruction*, and *Diversion*" (124). Having arrived at this Horatian commonplace without benefit of reading Horace, the Tale-teller transcends that ancient poet by the discovery "that, as Mankind is now disposed, he receives much greater Advantage by being *Diverted* than *Instructed*" (124). Even while perverting the Horatian dictum, the Tale-teller accepts ancient authority nonetheless. Here he describes his art in terms of transcendentals and cake baking:

> However, in Compliance with a Lesson of Great Age and Authority, I have attempted carrying the Point in all its Heights; and accordingly throughout this Divine Treatise, have skilfully kneaded up both together with a *Layer* of *Utile* and a *Layer* of *Dulce*. (124)

Such forms as "Abstracts, Summaries, Compendiums, Extracts, Collections, Medulla's, Excerpta quaedam's, Florilegia's *and the like, all disposed into great Order, and reducible upon Paper*" (127) are central to our modern's attempt to comprehend "an universal System in a small portable Volume, of all Things that are to be Known, or Believed, or Imagined, or Practised in Life" (125). Seeing only Homer as a rival in this ambitious attempt, the servant of modern forms leaps to enumerate that poet's supposed deficiencies. True to his vocation in the service of modern forms, he denounces the author of the *Iliad* and the *Odyssey* for being unfamiliar with the pith of modern learning.

Next our author turns to yet another modern form: self-praise. This was formerly done in prefaces and brought to its height of perfection by Dryden:

> Our Great *Dryden* has long carried it as far as it would go, and with incredible Success. He has often said to me in Confidence, that the World would have never suspected him to be so great a Poet, if he had not assured them so frequently in his Prefaces, that it was impossible they could either doubt or forget it. (131)

Since the preface is a modern form, at least insofar as it is self-serving, the multiplication of prefaces to *A Tale* performs an essentially parodic function. But even here the servant of modern forms departs from the practice of such an illustrious modern as Dryden by filling the body of his work with the self-congratulation Dryden confined to his prefaces. Since our narrator professes to be one who skips over some forty or fifty pages of prefatory material, and yet "having the *Modern* Inclination to expatiate upon the Beauty of my own Productions, and display the bright Parts of my Discourse; I thought best to do it in the Body of the Work, where, as it now lies, it makes a very considerable Addition to the Bulk of the Volume, *a Circumstance by no means to be neglected by a skilful Writer*" (132).

As *A Tale* proper continues in section 6, the servant of modern forms raises a new generic issue when he refers to himself as an historian. The term, indeed, is not employed loosely in the sense of a narrator of a story. Rather it approximates a Lucianic view of history: "I shall by no means forget my Character of an Historian, to follow the Truth, step by step, whatever happens, or where-ever it may lead me" (133). This new approach to the work as a history seems hopelessly at odds with the other generic tendencies to this point. The work has been called a treatise; the tale of the three brothers has taken several generic directions. The hack's assumption of the role of historian adds yet another generic norm.

Section 7, "A Digression in Praise of Digressions," begins with a comparison of two kinds of work, the "*Iliad* in a *Nut-shell,*" which seems to belong to the ancients, and a "*Nutshell* in an *Iliad,*" which is owing "to the great *Modern* Improvement of *Digressions* . . ." (143). The digression as a modern form is one of those "late Refinements in Knowledge, running parallel to those of Dyet in our Nation, which among Men of judicious Taste, are drest up in various Compounds, consisting in *Soups* and *Ollio's, Fricassées* and *Ragousts*" (143).

Modern taste, then, is for compounds or olios, that is, generic mixtures epitomized by the digression. After recognizing that "there is a sort of morose, detracting, ill-bred People" (143), satirists like Swift perhaps, who disapprove of such compounds, our author affirms the need for making digressions allowable, since there would be few books if the restriction "of delivering nothing beyond what is to the Purpose" (144) were imposed. Such was possible among the Greeks, Romans, and English "when Learning was in its *Cradle,* to be reared and fed, and cloathed by *Invention* . . ." (144). But now, since the burden of the past has become intolerable, a new approach to writing books had to be found:

> THE whole Course of Things being thus entirely changed between *Us* and the *Ancients;* and the *Moderns* wisely sensible of it, we of this Age have discovered a shorter, and more prudent Method, to become *Scholars* and *Wits,* without the Fatigue of *Reading* or of *Thinking.* (144–45)

Such method is made possible by other forms of literature, including "*Systems* and *Abstracts,* in which the *Modern* Fathers of Learning, like prudent Usurers, spent their Sweat for the Ease of Us their Children" (145–46). Here again we see the identification of modern forms with corrupt business practices.

Both innovative forms and matter have had to be invented against the unhappy fact "that there is not at this present, a sufficient Quantity of new Matter left in Nature, to furnish and adorn any one particular Subject to the Extent of a Volume" (146). Since the infinity of matter cannot be expected to supply the modern author's needs, he must have recourse to "large *Indexes,* and little *Compendiums; Quotations* must be plentifully gathered, and bookt in Alphabet; To this End, tho' Authors need be little consulted, yet *Criticks,* and *Commentators,* and *Lexicons* carefully must" (147–48). Thus newfangled forms are substitutes for authors like Horace and Vergil who made use of the matter of nature, and are, in the opinion of some, identical with Nature herself.[6] Where a commonplace book can supply the lack of an intelligent mind, a body of literature will spring up to parody the great works of the past. When the servant of modern forms shows how moderns can compose "Collections listed under so many thousand Heads of a different Nature . . ." (148), he is not only specifying their hydra-headed multiplicity, but also that they do indeed belong to a different nature which parodies real Nature and conflicts with her. The "thousand Heads of a different nature" are not merely topics or subjects; they are the forms of bogus knowledge which delight and instruct the modern world.

Section 8 elaborates on the dissenter mode of oratory as observed in the practice of the Aeolists. The treatise format continues with the affectation of learning in the act of delineating a system.

The importance of forms, in the widest application of the word, and not excluding generic implications, is seen in section 9, "A Digression Concerning Madness." Indeed, sanity is defined as an acceptance of common forms:

the Brain, in its natural Position and State of Serenity, disposeth its Owner to pass his Life in the common Forms, without any Thought of subduing Multitudes to his own *Power,* his *Reasons* or his *Visions.* . . . (171)

"A Digression Concerning Madness," which carries us into the extravagance of modern form, even as we are reminded of the solidity of ancient precept, contains one of the significant cruxes in Swift's work. I am referring, of course, to the passage that concludes, "This is the sublime and refined Point of Felicity, called, *the Possession of being well deceived;* The Serene Peaceful State of being a Fool among Knaves" (174). F. R. Leavis, although recognizing no persona in *A Tale,* detected Swift's use of entrapment in this passage.[7]

Much more recently, the late Robert C. Elliott, in his eloquent defense of persona as a critical and aesthetic concept, has argued that our sense of entrapment in this digresson is sharpened by Swift's deliberate violation of the rules governing the employment of personae.[8] Elliott rightly points out that by the end of the passage, we are left as either fool or knave, depending on whether we have sided with the "Wisdom, which converses about the Surface" or Reason (173). The Tale-teller's position seems to be on the superficial side; thus we are unprepared for his assertion that we are fools to side with him and knaves to oppose. Elliott states the case succinctly:

> The shock to the reader is traumatic as he suddenly finds himself trapped in an intolerable dilemma: if he has chosen happiness and the surface of things he is a fool; if he has chosen reason he is a knave. There is no way out. No wonder he is shaken. But beyond that I think the reader has a strong sense that he has been not only trapped but booby-trapped. It is not part of the game that the Tale-teller should be able to speak in the savagely hostile accents which end the paragraph; they violate his mode of being, amorphous as it is. Instead, Swift has momentarily tossed the Tale-teller aside, speaking out in his own voice, breaking his own rules.[9]

Thus Elliott identifies what he sees as a conscious break in the persona. He insists on recognizing the existence of a persona in *A Tale of a Tub*, but that persona has certain inconsistencies about it. Such ambiguities, however, are acknowledged as intentional and functional.

The perception that the voice of the satirist sometimes can be heard over the fictive voice of the persona is an important one for the understanding of satire. What it proves, from another perspective, is the point I explained earlier: that satire always maintains the illusion of being nonmimetic. It is dealing with the real world in rhetorical patterns more readily associated with orations or discourses than with fiction. Such breaks in the consistency of the fictional speaker remind us of satire's relationship to the real world. Of course, this attempt to break the illusion which has been developed so carefully is just another aspect of mimesis. But it is a technique appropriate to satire's protean nature.

An excellent example of this same technique in Swift's late work can be found in *A Modest Proposal*.[10] Toward the end of this work, the proposer focuses on Ireland by making it clear that the proposal is intended for implementation in that country only. The wrath of the speaker descends upon all the abusers of that poverty-stricken nation:

Therefore, let no man talk to me of other Expedients: *Of taxing our Absentees at five Shillings a Pound: Of using neither Cloaths, nor Household Furniture except what is of our own Growth and Manufacture: Of utterly rejecting the Materials and Instruments that promote foreign Luxury: Of curing the Expensiveness of Pride, Vanity, Idleness, and Gaming in our Women: Of introducing a Vein of Parsimony, Prudence and Temperance: Of learning to love our Country, wherein we differ even from* LAPLANDERS, *and the Inhabitants of* TOPINAMBOO: *Of quitting our Animosities, and Factions; nor act any longer like the Jews, who were murdering one another at the very Moment their City was taken: Of being a little cautious not to sell our Country and Consciences for nothing: Of teaching Landlords to have, at least, one Degree of Mercy towards their Tenants. Lastly, Of putting a Spirit of Honesty, Industry, and Skill into our Shopkeepers; who, if a Resolution could now be taken to buy only our native Goods, would immediately unite to cheat and exact upon us in the Price, the Measure, and the Goodness; nor could ever yet be brought to make one fair Proposal of just Dealing, though often and earnestly invited to it.* (116–17)[11]

I have quoted at such length to stress what an extended departure this is from the rest of *A Modest Proposal*. The wrath apparent here marks a decided shift in tone from the dispassionate language of the proposer. These are clearly Swift's counterproposals, which, if adopted, would render the proposals of the persona impertinent. Indeed, the despair of these positive moral suggestions ever being implemented is made clear in the following lines, which mark a return from the author in propria persona to the personation which typifies the rest of the essay:

> Therefore I repeat, let no Man talk to me of these and the like Expedients; till he hath, at least, a Glimpse of Hope, that there will ever be some hearty and sincere Attempt to put *them in Practice*. (117)

Even the beginning of the next paragraph suggests an unwilling return to the mask by a writer exhausted by his many fruitless efforts to reform the Irish State:

> But, as to my self; having been wearied out for many Years with offering vain, idle, visionary Thoughts; and at length utterly despairing of Success, I fortunately fell upon this Proposal; which, as it is wholly new, so it hath something *solid* and *real*, of no Expence, and little Trouble, full in our own Power; and whereby we can incur no Danger in *disobliging* ENGLAND: For, this Kind of Commodity will not

bear Exportation; the Flesh being of too tender a Consistence, to admit a long Continuance in Salt. . . . (117)

At this point the return to the persona seems to have been completed, although the caveat about "*disobliging* England" seems more Swift than mask.
But if we think we have recurred to the consistency of the fiction, we are
wrong. For the next sentence draws the reader back to the righteous anger of
the satirist behind the mask, once again emphasized by italics: "*although, perhaps, I could name a Country, which would be glad to eat up our whole Nation
without it*" (117). Following hard upon this is the expected recurrence to
the mask.

A studied inconsistency of persona, then, is a trait of Swift's satires from *A
Tale of a Tub* to *A Modest Proposal*. Although the question is much too large
for consideration here, this intellectual inconsistency in the persona is a primary reason for the serious disagreements that exist in Swift scholarship over
Gulliver's Travels. Gulliver expresses in his own personated voice opinions
often at odds with Swift's views. But on many occasions the Swiftian wrath we
have just seen in *A Modest Proposal* breaks forth uncharacteristically from the
usually equanimous Gulliver. When Gulliver denounces prideful humanity at
the conclusion of the fourth voyage, the reader attuned to the complexities of
generic satire will hear the voice of Swift:

> the *Houyhnhnms*, who live under the Government of Reason, are no
> more proud of the good Qualities they possess, than I should be for not
> wanting a Leg or an Arm, which no Man in his Wits would boast of,
> although he must be miserable without them. I dwell the longer upon
> this Subject from the Desire I have to make the Society of an *English
> Yahoo* by any Means not insupportable; and therefore I here intreat
> those who have any Tincture of this absurd Vice, that they will not
> presume to appear in my Sight. (296)[12]

Those who prefer to read the persona as a consistent fiction may attribute
madness to Gulliver who seems to shriek such opinions. Those who deny the
concept of persona[13] will see this passage as a more direct and less ironic expression than, for example, Gulliver's waning trust of courtiers in the first
voyage.

Yet for those readers who accept the concept of persona and admit the
inconsistency of it in Swift's satires, the question as to the purpose of such
intrusions may still remain. The answer, I believe, has to do with the formal

complexities into which satire has the freedom to venture. The satirist cannot allow his fiction to move too far from the common sense of the real world. The intrusion of his own voice effectuates a kind of stability, even as it appears to lead to incongruity. It serves as an anchor to keep the fiction from moving too far away from the system of value which gives satire its impetus to begin with. That many subtle readers have allowed themselves to be seduced by the Tale-teller[14] may suggest that not enough has been done. But a better understanding of the generic norms of satire ought to be enough. If readers listen for the satirist's own voice, they are less likely to miss it. Reading a satire is the same delicate act of balancing generic clues that is required in the study of nearly all literature before the middle of the eighteenth century and much literature written thereafter. Readers bring the responsibility of learning to any literary work. They must know, to use Elliott's phrase, "the rules of the game."

When it can be seen that Swift's seeming inconsistency is indeed a studied attempt to follow a well-defined tradition of generic satire (while not denying that it may have other aesthetic values as well), this great controversy may be solved for most readers. Once it is understood that generic deviation, of which the shift from persona to authorial voice is only one aspect (fiction to rhetoric), the inconsistencies I have pointed to here will prove less troublesome. The entrapment defined by Elliott and many other students of Swift is less surprising when the readers understand it as a principle of satire as kind. But it is no less effective; indeed, perhaps it is more so, for readers will be less likely to miss what their understanding of the norms of satire prepares them for. Thus, when the trap is sprung in "A Digression Concerning Digressions," readers can avoid the dilemma of being either a fool or a knave. The pleasure of insight, not confusion, is more likely to result as the servant of modern forms fails even to notice that he has administered the coup de grace. Recurring immediately to his subject, madness, his mercurial mind seems particularly suited to modern irrelevancy. But this may be partly due to his not having administered a satiric blow. That has been done by Swift the satirist. When the Tale-teller utters the words, "BUT to return to *Madness*," (174) the readers will grasp what otherwise may have gone undetected: they have just completed a digression within a digression. This does the digression of ancient rhetoric and even the servant's own digression on digressions one better. It is, perhaps, the ultimate modern form.

Section 10 introduces yet another genre. This is "a pernicious Kind of Writings, called *Second Parts*" (183). The fear of the servant of modern forms that the ubiquitous author of "Second Parts" will produce an appropriate version of *A Tale of a Tub* leads him to "fly for Justice and Relief, into the Hands of that great *Rectifier of Saddles*, and *Lover of Mankind*, Dr. B——*tly*, begging he will take this enormous Grievance into his most *Modern* Consideration . . ." (183–84). This, like so many other generic themes throughout the book, permits a vigorous attack on the moderns and the bogus literary forms which embody forth their work.

It is also worthwhile to call attention to another literary kind in section 10, not dealt with thematically, but included as part of the episodic structure of *A Tale*. The symposium or banquet is almost inevitably found in complex satires. And, indeed, even in the parodied treatise form of *A Tale of a Tub*, which is not particularly suited to the banquet, we do find one, albeit in curtailed form. Though short, however, it is functional. Alluding to the mass of material available to the composer of a discourse, the hack considers it as food and nutriment:

> I do here give this publick Notice, that my Resolutions are, to circumscribe within this Discourse the whole Stock of Matter I have been so many Years providing. Since my *Vein* is once opened, I am content to exhaust it all at a Running, for the peculiar Advantage of my dear Country, and for the universal Benefit of Mankind. Therefore hospitably considering the Number of my Guests, they shall have my whole Entertainment at a Meal; And I scorn to set up the *Leavings* in the Cupboard. What the *Guests* cannot eat may be given to the *Poor*, and the *Dogs* under the table may gnaw the *Bones*; This I understand for a more generous Proceeding than to turn the Company's Stomachs by inviting them again to morrow to a scurvy Meal of *Scraps*. (184)

Here the banquet metaphor is used to attack the form of writing called "Second Parts." If the guests are fed properly at the first meal, there will be nothing left but scraps for a second. But what is even more interesting is the fact that Swift relates the reader and author to guest and host respectively. More and Rabelais had used it earlier, and Fielding was later to elaborate on it extensively in *Tom Jones*. In the conclusion of *A Tale* the servant of modern forms will pick out the strand of the banquet metaphor once again to close out his treatise: "The Conclusion of a Treatise, resembles the Conclusion of Human Life, which hath sometimes been compared to the End of a Feast; where few are satisfied to depart, *ut plenus vitae conviva:* For Men will sit down after the fullest Meal, tho' it be only to *doze*, or to *sleep* out the rest of the Day" (208).

In "A Digression in Praise of Digressions" a comparison between *A Tale* and Homer's *Iliad* is made explicit. *A Tale* represents modern culture. The "defective" poem of Homer's is the representative of the ancients. But Homer's virtues, his poetry, breadth of vision, or heroic excellence are not considered. The servant of modern forms rather judges Homer by corrupt modern standards. Homer's lack of acquaintance with modern works and concepts is a prime reason for his being held in disesteem. Logic and common sense, as well as aesthetics, are tossed aside. Although narrow and inapplicable, modern standards are the canon by which all the ancients must be judged. Thus the moderns assert their superiority.

In section 11 Jack takes "a fair Copy of his Father's *Will*, engrossed in Form upon a large Skin of Parchment" (190) and, ignoring the "plain, easy Directions" contained therein, "began to entertain a Fancy that the Matter was *deeper* and *darker*, and therefore must needs have a great deal more of Mystery at the Bottom" (190). Setting out to prove that the parchment is not merely what it seems to be but meat, drink, cloth, the philosopher's stone, and the universal medicine, Jack "had a Way of working it into any Shape he pleased; so that it served him for a Night-cap when he went to Bed, and for an Umbrello in rainy Weather. He would lap a Piece of it about a sore Toe, or when he had Fits, burn two Inches under his Nose . . ." (190). In satirizing the Calvinists' reshaping of scripture, Swift stresses the need for preserving both the meaning and form of a text. Even before the above antics began, Jack perverted the form of his father's will by having a fair copy made. The result of each excess is lost sight of in turn as he progresses to the next, and, at last, neither form nor meaning in its original state is recognizable. The same thing is true of the treatise that is called *A Tale of a Tub*. The servant of modern forms continually claims to be writing a treatise, but his multigeneric approach calls in doubt any strict definition. Nonetheless the claim persists to suggest that *A Tale* is a parody of a treatise, that is, very much a modern form, characterized by excessive prefatory material, constant digressions, and the failure ever to settle on a single logical point.

In its parodic relationship to the treatise or classical discourse, *A Tale of a Tub* functions more simply than has often been perceived. It diverges from the norms of the treatise only to be drawn back again to that essential structure. The movement back and forth between structures or the diction that identifies those structures creates a sense of chaos. But chaos is not the final impression that *A Tale of a Tub* should leave. Although we have a treatise that violates ancient prescriptions and serves modern forms, the classical discourse remains the model from which this modern parody diverges. Also there are the other forms, none of them modern, which are misused and misinterpreted by the narrator. They remain the touchstones against which the insanity of modern aberrations can be judged. Finally, there is the paradox of Augustan satire itself. Just as the narrator of A *Tale* parodies the classical treatise, Swift, the satirist, parodies that modern version. The result is not a chaotic modern treatise, but a coherent, devastating attack on the modern world. The very processes of modernity are subsumed in the attack and turned against their proponents. What is modern is condemned out of the mouth of its most devoted servant. Modern forms are so specious that their mere existence condemns them. But the glimpse we have of a more substantial world of forms suggests a coherence which the moderns can barely conceive. The existence of ancient form, even as glimpsed by a modern madman, condemns the modern alteration of form and therefore of thought. Because A *Tale of a Tub* is an incoherent treatise, it becomes a coherent satire. It does this by tracing the chaotic instincts of modernity to their source and reifying them in a substantial work of art which contains, nevertheless, a logic and rationality absent in the modern works it parodies and satirizes. The servant of modern forms unconsciously parodies the classical treatise, but Swift the satirist consciously parodies that modern aberration. The hostility of the narrator for Homer and other ancients is transcended by an even greater anger of the satirist against modern forms.

Those who admire the energy of the servant of modern forms fail to see that the real energy manifest in A *Tale of a Tub* has its origins in the hatred of the modern world, whether implicit or explicit, in the satiric attack. The servant of modern forms is merely a puppet who affects an undirected energy. Insofar as he is energized, it is by an involuntary self-condemnation. Finally we must remember that what energy we find in A *Tale of a Tub* comes not from a fictional narrator but from the satirist who gives him life and sets his convulsions into purposeful motion.

Gulliver's Travels

Hatred of the modern world is the unifying theme throughout nearly all of Swift's works from his early efforts to those of his maturity and decline. In *Gulliver's Travels* the mixture of popular and classical forms advances the satiric intention and creates an association of linked forms characteristic of generic satire.

Leo Strauss has suggested that Lilliput represents the modern world and Brobdingnag the ancient world.[15] Although some qualifications are in order, Strauss' insight is essentially correct. Indeed we may expand the notion by suggesting that part 3, the voyage to Laputa, is another example of the modern world, while part 4, the voyage to the land of the Houyhnhnms, represents a prelapsarian world prior even to the ancient world itself. These suppositions, I believe, are supported by specific details in each voyage.

Gulliver's Travels is, first and foremost, a parody of a travel book. Reference in the 1735 edition to William Dampier's *A Voyage Round the World* (1697) suggested that the parody was more specific than general, and, indeed, Swift adroitly imitates Dampier's concrete and matter-of-fact style. Also Nigel Dennis has drawn our attention to the possibility at least that Swift had *Robinson Crusoe* (1719) in mind as he wrote the *Travels*.[16] Yet if Swift intends the parody to point to the deficiencies of a particular work, that purpose is soon subsumed in a larger satiric design. Swift follows his normal practice of choosing a popular form as the vehicle for his satire. But he begins to include other forms, both classical and popular, very early in the first voyage.

Once we are properly rooted in the details of travel literature, the greatest of all classical travel books is evoked by a series of comic analogues. Gulliver, like Odysseus, is shipwrecked. But instead of remaining an epic hero, he becomes a victimized cyclops whose eyes are under threat, not from a fiery brand, but by the arrows of the Lilliputians.[17] The primary use of the parallel between two forms, the popular travel book and the ancient epic, is to underscore the discrepancy between Gulliver, the modern man, and the epic hero. Like Odysseus, Gulliver leaves behind him both wife and child. Like Odysseus he travels to fantastic lands, where he is almost constantly in danger. But unlike Odysseus, he plays the role of the cyclops and assumes the role of romance hero even from the very outset.[18] In the final voyage Gulliver's desire to remain among the Houyhnhnms contrasts with Odysseus' indomitable will to return home. Gulliver's self-exile from wife and family, after his enforced return, contrasts even more markedly with Odysseus' assumption of all his roles, father, son, husband, and king. Gulliver's decision to live with "fallen" Houyhnhnms (namely, horses) rather than with fallen humanity marks a major discrepancy between the success of an ancient hero and the degradation of modern man.

The *Odyssey* and *Gulliver's Travels*, however, do share a romance pattern. In the former, the romance pattern alters the epic structure. In Swift's work a mixture of genres, including romance, is exploited for the purposes of parody and satire. As romantic hero, Gulliver is a third son, a victim of shipwreck, neglect by his shipmates, and piratical depredation. He does not slay monsters, but manages to survive by killing rats and hornets in Brobdingnag. In Lilliput Gulliver makes much of his capacity for heroic action, whether in the act of urination or defecation, or merely in his heroic sexual proportions. Gulliver regards his acts of elimination as "adventures" and is clearly proud of his sexual dimensions in relation to those of the Lilliputians, even though he expresses some embarrassment and resorts to circumlocutions when sexual matters arise in the course of his narration. Finally, as romance hero, Gulliver comes as mock-Messiah from the land of the Houyhnhnms, bringing the message of the Houyhnhnm master that all human beings are really Yahoos, be they ever so gentle. Having returned from the underworld of Glubbdubdrib and the earthly paradise of part 4, Gulliver preaches the gospel of the fall of mankind.[19]

The way to read the *Travels* and other satires of this period is not by treating them as though they are realistic fiction. Rather they are mixtures of genres. Only by reading each work from several generic viewpoints can we grasp the discordant message: there is no orderly life to be lived among modern innovations. The modern world is merely a series of fragments. It is a perversion of ancient generic orders, no longer complete or able to sustain a full range of human behavior.

The reason critics have differed so widely on the essential pattern of *Gulliver's Travels*, some calling it a comedy and others a tragedy, is because it contains elements of so many generic patterns. But no matter what pattern we try to trace in the *Travels*, we shall always come up short. Each pattern is parodied and incomplete. Every generic pattern is truncated by another generic pattern, but not by chance. The design of satire brings together a generic mixture while ensuring that no genre represented will be a completed pattern. Just as one pattern reaches its apex, another begins. There is no completeness in generic representation because the world no longer furnishes appropriate models. If the actions of the world are incomplete, mimetic representations must be incomplete as well. But the imperfection is not total chaos; it represents coherence to a point. But only to a point. The total coherence of the ancient genres remains an ideal which cannot be achieved in a world far removed from the norms that governed them.

In the compendium of knowledge that Gulliver presents us with, we can expect a view of nearly every major social situation. We have seen in earlier discussions that the symposium is both an important theme and deliberative

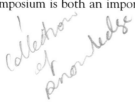

form in the satiric tradition. In the course of *Gulliver's Travels,* banquet situations will emerge as touchstones of behavior.

After Gulliver has arrived in Lilliput and been inhospitably tied down by his hosts, the "Demands of Nature" become so peremptory that he is forced to request food: "I could not forbear shewing my Impatience (perhaps against the strict Rules of Decency) by putting my Finger frequently on my Mouth, to signify that I wanted Food" (23).[20] The emphasis on nature's demands are reminiscent of Homeric procedure. After Odysseus' loss of six shipmates to Scylla, the survivors stop and cook a meal. This, as Aldous Huxley has pointed out, is exactly what would have happened.[21] Throughout the first voyage we have a comic mixture of probabilities and improbabilities. Gulliver's having kept his powder dry after a shipwreck and long swim is as improbable, perhaps, as his landing on an island inhabited by tiny people. But even while indulging in such incredible fictions, Swift gives us his version of "the whole truth," which includes a blend of the realistic and the probable. Looking past the fantastic aspects of Gulliver's situation, we must see him as a guest of the Lilliputians. Having reached the limits of his endurance, he can no longer patiently await his hosts' hospitality. He therefore consciously violates the rules of etiquette and decency. But where do these rules apply? Clearly not to Gulliver's situation. The fantastic situation in which he finds himself would seem to call for a suspension of the normal code of behavior. But Gulliver's mere partial awareness of an incongruity gives rise to the comedy of *Gulliver's Travels.* In this way generic dislocation creates tone and gives each episode its meaning. Once we realize that Gulliver's awkward devouring of meat and hogsheads of wine parodies a minor but important genre, the episode takes on new meaning.

What is even more extraordinary than Gulliver's breach of decorum is that a huge feast has been made ready by order of the king of Lilliput. Gulliver, however, devours this gigantic feast as quickly as it is supplied to him, to the "Wonder and Astonishment" of his "hosts." Here is no skimping of portions as we have seen in the banquet of Nasidienus or the feast of Virro in Juvenal. Gulliver consumes the king's largesse and even comments in the manner of a gourmet on the taste and method of preparation. After two hogsheads of wine, however, the supply is exhausted. Gulliver is overwhelmed by the admiration the people show for his gastronomical feats. Like a well-fed guest, he is grateful to his hosts for the delicacies they have lavished upon him: "I now considered my self as bound by the Laws of Hospitality to a People who had treated me with so much Expence and Magnificence" (24).

The fact that he is a prisoner under threat of imminent death does not seem to enter into Gulliver's assessment of his situation.

Even while supplying Gulliver with meat and drink, however, the Lilliputians have acted in character. For the hogsheads of wine contain a sleeping potion. Gulliver is, first and last, victimized by his diminutive hosts, just as guests at satiric banquets dine only at the pleasure of the symposiarch and lesser members of his household.

Although Gulliver's transportation to Mildendo intervenes between his eating and relieving himself, Gulliver's first opportunity to eliminate "that uneasy Load" must be linked to the feast itself. In the *Cena Trimalchionis*, for example, Trimalchio constantly leaves the hall to relieve himself and invites his guests to follow his example. Elimination is the obvious result of epulary activities. In the satiric world, the relationships between two necessary processes is not lost sight of. That no provision should be made for Gulliver's relief may seem as odd as Trimalchio's excessive providence and vulgar reminders. It is also strange that Gulliver should give us such a full account of his procedure, especially since he is so self-conscious about it. But in addition to his minute concern for truth, Gulliver may also be influenced by Lilliputian admiration for his digestive powers. Even elimination testifies to his heroic proportions. For example, after Gulliver's defecation and the hauling away of "the offensive Matter" in wheelbarrows, he refers to the episode as an "Adventure" (30). Here as in the banquet episode, epic and romance decorum is being applied to activities which never take place in those genres.

Later in part 1, when the king dines with Gulliver, we might expect a more proper banquet; but it is hardly less grotesque than the earlier dinner. The royal entourage sits on Gulliver's table with Flimnap, the treasurer, in attendance. While the base official looks at him with "a sour Countenance," Gulliver pretends not to see him and eats "more than usual, in Honour to my dear Country, as well as to fill the Court with Admiration" (64). There is no witty conversation here, just designing courtiers and heroic gastronomics. Indeed, the sour looks and deceit will win the day over omnivorous consumption, for this is indeed Lilliput.

Much of chapter six takes the form of an ancient politeia, that is, the elucidation of a system of government, laws, and education.[22] This format permits Swift to present some of his own ideas on these essential matters while comparing the present corruption of Lilliput with its own more ancient customs. The fact that modern practice is deficient and ancient practice ideal is no coincidence. Lilliput, except for a few archaisms, is essentially the modern world in which the good institutions of government and law have been beaten down and corrupted by the court. Monarchy has given place to what is essentially oligarchy. The weakness of the king allows court intrigues to replace the rule of a proper monarch and lawgiver.

In these respects Lilliput becomes a mirror of England. But in several other particulars the Lilliputians remain innocent of European innovation. Gunpowder, which will become such a large issue in book 2, is apparently unknown to them. Poisoned arrows are their most diabolical projectiles. Also the education of children, presumably an institution untouched by court intrigues, follows some ancient patterns favored by Swift. The essential modern evil seems to be the court, and what corruption of institutions there is stems from thence. Envy, jealousy, and malignity of every kind seem to breed naturally in the court atmosphere. This is the institution over which Sir Robert Walpole presides in England. In Lilliput it is the source of nearly everything that is bad.

In three of the four voyages, a judgment against Gulliver provides the climax, even in this relatively plotless potpourri of forms. It is appropriate that the court, the corruption of which occupies so much of the satire of the first part, should render the judgment. It is also appropriate that the judgment be clandestine and rendered without adequate evidence. The articles against Gulliver, which are cited verbatim, provide yet another subgenre in parody. Gulliver's inability to discern the injustice of the charges against him underscores his essential innocence and provides ironic commentary on the deception of the court party. The articles are indeed an exemplary deception among all deceptions emanating from the court. The court proceeds on the specious assumption that nothing is what it appears to be. Gulliver must be a "big-Endian" in his heart, whatever his deeds on behalf of the emperor may imply. From the perspective of the court greater innocence means greater guilt. The commonsense view of the world is totally rejected. Transforming all normal values, the court party conceives innovations that perfectly reflect the propensity of the modern world to see things·as it wishes, not as they are. Gulliver considers one result of this tendency:

> It was a Custom introduced by this Prince and his Ministry, (very different, as I have been assured, from the Practices of former Times) that after the Court had decreed any cruel Execution, either to gratify the Monarch's Resentment, or the Malice of a Favourite; the Emperor always made a Speech to his whole Council, expressing his *great Lenity and Tenderness, as Qualities known and confessed by all the World.* This Speech was immediately published through the Kingdom; nor

did any thing terrify the People so much as those Encomiums on his Majesty's Mercy; because it was observed, that the more these Praises were enlarged and insisted on, the more *inhuman* was the Punishment, and the *Sufferer more innocent.* (72)

Swift's implication is clear. The more intense and extensive the encomium, the more certain it is to be a lie. We may also glimpse here one of Swift's motives for turning away from panegyric and toward satire. The very panegyrics of the emperor and the ministry are satires against them. This is not exactly the same relationship Dryden saw between panegyric and satire in *Eleonora,* but, like his predecessor, Swift exploits the intimate connection between the two genres.

In the first book of *Gulliver's Travels,* then, we see the same relationship between form and theme which emerged in Dryden's *Mac Flecknoe.* Since the deceit of the king and the court party is the central theme of part 1, what more appropriate vehicle for the exposition of that theme than a travel book that is not a travel book, a narrative which is itself a deception?

Part 1 culminates in a deceit that far outweighs the playful deceptions of literature: the state trial. But Gulliver, who has had to become wiser about princes and courtiers than his birth and education might have warranted, resolves not to stay for his own trial, which he understands has already been held and himself already convicted:

But having in my Life perused many State-Tryals, which I ever observed to terminate as the Judges thought fit to direct; I durst not rely on so dangerous a Decision, in so critical a Juncture, and against such powerful Enemies. (73)

The party that employs this monumental deceit, however, is convicted by it. Even when their facts are correct, their political goals are so obnoxious to men of good will that they have no right to anyone's allegiance. Although Gulliver is guilty according to the letter of the law, the letter is the product of corrupt understanding. To be convicted by it is to be proclaimed innocent.

In part 2, the voyage to Brobdingnag, Gulliver finds himself from the beginning in the position of proving his humanity. His predicament is brought home to him when he compares it to his status in Lilliput:

In this terrible Agitation of Mind I could not forbear thinking of *Lilliput,* whose Inhabitants looked upon me as the greatest Prodigy that ever appeared in the World; where I was able to draw an Imperial

Fleet in my Hand, and perform those other Actions which will be re-
corded for ever in the Chronicles of that Empire, while Posterity shall
hardly believe them, although attested by Millions. I reflected what a
Mortification it must prove to me to appear as inconsiderable in this
Nation, as one single *Lilliputian* would be among us. (86–87)

It is Gulliver's fate to be unsuccessful in every attempt to rise above this peculiar station. Generic shifts chronicle Gulliver's efforts from different points
of view.

As in part 1 a "banquet" takes place early in the proceedings. This time it
is Gulliver who acts the Lilliputian role. His toast to his master's wife is
greeted with loud laughter. Next his very life and limb are threatened by the
curiosity of the youngest son, who picks our hero up by the legs and dangles
him on high. Even at dinner dangers threaten. Just as banquets serve as
touchstones of manners, taste, and morals in other satires, here the banquet
is a microcosm of Gulliver's plight in Brobdingnag. Whatever grace, wit, or
charm he may possess becomes subordinated and overshadowed by his concern for survival. His diminutive state diminishes everything else belonging
to him.

The next symposium is in the queen's chambers where Gulliver now
occupies the place formerly held by Lilliputians gawking at a colossal consumption of food and drink. While Gulliver eats "in Miniature," the queen
engorges incredible quantities of food:

> the Queen (who had indeed but a weak Stomach) took up at one
> Mouthful, as much as a dozen *English* Farmers could eat at a Meal,
> which to me was for some time a very nauseous Sight. She would
> craunch the Wing of a Lark, Bones and all, between her Teeth, al-
> though it were nine Times as large as that of a full grown Turkey; and
> put a Bit of Bread in her Mouth, as big as two twelve-penny Loaves.
> She drank out of a Golden Cup, above a Hogshead at a Draught. Her
> Knives were twice as long as a Scythe set strait upon the Handle. The
> Spoons, Forks, and other Instruments were all the same Proportion. I
> remember when *Glumdalclitch* carried me out of Curiosity to see some
> of the Tables at Court, where ten or a dozen of these enormous Knives
> and Forks were lifted up together; I thought I had never till then be-
> held so terrible a Sight. (106)

It is Swift's genius to make such an improbable situation believable. The details observed from the perspective of a Lilliputian make the queen seem less
than fastidious. Eating becomes a violent and savage act. The relatively re-

cent innovation of eating with knife and fork is reminiscent of Satan's infernal crew raising their arms on high. If not infernal, the raising of knives and forks here is a parody of the heroic. During the earlier dinner with the farm family, Gulliver takes out his own knife and fork, but we are not informed as to whether or not the members of the family are similarly equipped. If we can assume that a farm family is more likely to eat with their fingers, Gulliver's display of knife and fork may be an early attempt to establish his gentle status. Not everyone could afford the luxury of knife and fork, and so Gulliver may be anxious to show off his good breeding and social status.[23] At the court of Brobdingnag, knives, forks, and spoons, all the instruments of gracious dining are very much in evidence, as we might expect.

But the real significance of symposium emerges in Brobdingnag as it did in Lilliput. Every Wednesday when the king and queen dined together with their children in his majesty's apartments, the conversation with Gulliver turned on the "Manners, Religion, Laws, Government, and Learning of *Europe*" (106). Despite his contempt for the "diminutive Insects" of that continent, the king shows a philosophical interest in learning about the customs of other nations. This will lead to some of the most important episodes of part 2.

Although Swift employs the size discrepancy for the purposes of satirizing the diminutive Gulliver and the Europeans he represents, the admiration of size alone is also subjected to attack. After Gulliver is taken to view the chief temple "and particularly the Tower belonging to it, which is reckoned the highest in the Kingdom" (114), he comes away disappointed: "for, the Height is not above three thousand Foot, reckoning from the Ground to the highest Pinnacle top; which allowing for the Difference between the Size of those People, and us in *Europe*, is no great matter for Admiration, nor at all equal in Proportion, (if I rightly remember) to *Salisbury* Steeple" (114). Although Gulliver's chauvinism is probably at work here, jaded by having immensity always before him, our hero assumes the Horatian stance: *nil admirari.*

Yet some things seem much the worse when magnified by Brobdingnagian size. This is particularly true of evils. For example, the beggars with cancers of fantastic proportions and lice, all the more horrible because of their huge size, crawling on their clothes, are more shocking than they would be in normal measurements. Perhaps the most terrifying of all is the geyser of blood ejected by the execution of a malefactor.

Chapter 5 continues the trials of Gulliver, but here he is placed more fully and explicitly in the role of picaro. At the opening of the chapter his taunts directed at the envious dwarf result in a rain of apples tumbling about his ears. Indeed, one of the apples prostrates him.

Gulliver is next badly bruised by a hail shower, carried harmlessly in the mouth of a spaniel, threatened by a kite, soiled in a molehill, roundly boxed by a linnet, mortified by maids of honor, dropped by a governess, daubed with slime by a frog, and kidnapped by a monkey. The king ridicules him for his defenselessness, especially in the last escapade. Finally, his physical degradation is completed when he lands up to his knees in cow dung while striving to display his athletic prowess.

Gulliver's misfortunes recall those of picaresque heroes from Lazarillo to Don Quixote and Pablos of *El Buscón*. Although many events in chapters 1 and 2 contain picaresque elements, chapter 5 may be thought of as a miniature picaresque novel within the larger structure of the *Travels*.

With chapter 6 there is another generic shift. After some transitional material in which Gulliver displays his sycophancy towards the king and queen, Gulliver and the king enter into a formal deliberation regarding England, its constitution, government, and legal system. Gulliver begins the discourse and the king responds. We are not given the entire debate, which supposedly extended to five audiences. But rather we read a summation of major points in indirect discourse. The king's response is in the same format, but more of his very pointed language is reproduced verbatim.

Gulliver recognizes the relevance of an analogy to oratory when he "wished for the Tongue of *Demosthenes* or *Cicero*, that might have enabled me to celebrate the Praise of my own dear native Country in a Style equal to its Merits and Felicity" (127). Indeed, as the king of Brobdingnag recognizes, Gulliver does not deliver an objective account, but rather a panegyric: "My little Friend *Grildrig*; you have made a most admirable Panegyrick upon your Country" (132). But if that is so, the close relationship between panegyric and satire has once again been demonstrated. Although Gulliver delivers his speeches as panegyrics, the king's interpretation turns them to satire. For example, the king points to the real significance of Gulliver's praise: "You have clearly proved that Ignorance, Idleness, and Vice are the proper Ingredients for qualifying a Legislator" (132). In the king's brilliant mind, Gulliver's panegyric is turned to diatribe, and the truth becomes known.

Further, the king of Brobdingnag also recognizes that the dysfunction of the English system is not the result of weakness in the original conception. On the contrary, the king sees some merit in the ancient forms: "I observe among you some Lines of an Institution, which in its Original might have been tolerable; but these half erased, and the rest wholly blurred and blotted by Corruptions" (132). As in Lilliput, where modern innovation disrupted and effaced the customs and laws of antique times, modern England has rendered its "tolerable" institution vile and vicious. Again, Swift's hatred of the modern world echoes in the king's denunciation of England and her people. It is not so much human nature as human action that has resulted in the decline. The passion to tamper with a functioning system is what characterizes the modern mind and leads to collapse. Guilt, then, is widespread among modern men, but unlike original sin, it does not descend to all: "I cannot but conclude the Bulk of your Natives, to be the most pernicious Race of little odious Vermin that Nature ever suffered to crawl upon the Surface of the Earth" (132). The indictment is excoriating, but it is not all-encompassing. "The Bulk of your Natives" allows for some exclusions. The king, like Swift himself, leaves an opening for some of us who do not deserve to be objects of the diatribe, although we must not be too hasty in assuming that our own faces do not appear in the satiric mirror.

Gulliver's earlier attempts to display physical agility and courage were all to no effect. In the picaresque segment of part 2, he was degraded in a series of actions until he found himself knee deep in cow dung. Having failed so miserably to establish himself as a human being in a physical sense, Gulliver is given the opportunity to prove himself intellectually in his discussions with the king. This fails, too, as we have seen.

When Gulliver expresses resentment at the king's evaluation of England, his resentment is turned to ridicule (133). To avoid the king's expected bad opinion of England, Gulliver seeks to evade questions and extenuate the truth. But, he admits, all his efforts, by which he epitomizes the vices so deplorable to the king, are to no avail.

In one last, desperate effort to achieve respect, Gulliver seeks to provide the king of Brobdingnag with a knowledge of gunpowder and its military use. The king rejects the offer out of hand, but Gulliver persists in arguing his case to the reader, whom he implicates in his own disrespect for human life and liberty. Once again, Gulliver destroys his case, even as he pleads it.

From the discourse with the king, Gulliver moves to yet another genre. There follows a short disquisition or essay on the learning, laws, and government of Brobdingnag. Coming as it does after the denigration of the English politeia, this short "treatise" provides a positive ideal to compare with the crimes from which Gulliver has sought to exculpate his countrymen.

In the eighth and final chapter Swift returns to the voyage narrative and extricates Gulliver from the land of the giants by a deus ex machina worthy of a Sinbad adventure. Even in Gulliver's deliverance the limitless sense of space and perspective dominates our attention. A helpless Gulliver in his cage-box is carried away into the sky and unceremoniously dropped once again into the mediocre civilization from which he originated. The voyage ends as it began, in the realm of romance.

In part 2, as in the other voyages, Swift employs a combination of genres, popular and classical. Whether at sea, in picaresque adventures, or involved in a classical discourse or self-serving panegyric, Gulliver condemns himself and the nation he undertakes to represent. The shift from one genre to another allows for stylistic variations. But, even more important, it permits the inclusion of divergent material. The resulting incongruities permit ironies that would be impossible with a more unified style or subject matter. Yet if diversity alone were a virtue, we would admire satires merely for their chaotic effect. The voyage to Brobdingnag manages to subsume these varying styles or generic patterns under the larger rubric of the voyage. Generic shifting gives us a sense of verisimilitude appropriate to the realism expected in such a narrative. A voyage is necessarily episodic and ought to include exactly what happened. If the reality of those happenings can be identified under various genre headings, it really doesn't matter. The diversity we have seen makes the work seem realistic in certain respects despite the fact that *Gulliver's Travels'* major generic identification is with the imaginary or fabulous voyage; that is, a voyage that is not really a voyage. Coherence of genre in such a case would put the work into the category of fantasy; the mixing of fantastic forms with verisimilar ones, however, creates the paradox which dominates Swift's work. We are given the impression of fantasy and realism at the same time. The interplay of these two major imaginative structures helps to produce the ridicule we identify with satire.

The voyage to Laputa, part 3 of the *Travels*, owes more to Lucian than do the other three parts. Cosmic voyages did not appeal to Swift's imagination and so Laputa, or the flying island, is his only attempt to represent an extraterrestrial society. It is edifying to note that whatever high flying we may associate with the Laputians is under rigorous satiric scrutiny. Lucian's *True History* became the model for later imaginary voyages, even as it parodied and satirized the *Odyssey* itself. Some imaginary voyages standing between Lucian and Swift are Bishop Francis Godwin's *The Man in the Moon* (1638), Cyrano's *Les États et Empires de la Lune* (1656) and *Les États et Empires du Soleil* (1661) as well as Defoe's *The Consolidator* and a series of related works (1705).

Lucian's *True History* moves quickly from one episode to another, with little in the way of thematic unity or focus. Part 3 of *Gulliver's Travels* shares this episodic quality with its prototype. But at the same time part 3 is bound together by a thematic unity. Each episode is a critique of some form of a priori reasoning.

From the very outset of the *Travels* the expectation of the reader has been frustrated as he follows Gulliver through Lilliput and Brobdingnag. The doll-like Lilliputians are gentle in no sense of the word. Indeed they turn the tables on Gulliver who might ordinarily expect to rule over a people only six inches high. Instead, they dominate him, against all reason. On the other hand, the giants of Brobdingnag are far more gentle than their extraordinary size would seem to promise. When Gulliver first sets his eyes on the farm laborers, he is prepared to find no mercy: "For, as human Creatures are observed to be more Savage and cruel in Proportion to their Bulk; what could I expect but to be a Morsel in the Mouth of the first among these enormous Barbarians who should happen to seize me?" (87). But as it turns out, the Brobdingnagians, especially as represented by their king, are a good deal more civilized than Gulliver and the Europeans he represents. Whatever our expectations and Gulliver's may seem to be, they are invariably frustrated by reality.

As is true in the other voyages, the first chapter gives a realistic account and gets us to the destination that Swift, not Gulliver, has in mind. Very early in chapter 2 we see the problems of the flying island stemming directly from the abstract considerations of its ruling class. The Laputian king and his court are so absorbed by their speculations that ordinary everyday concerns are dangerously neglected.

The first subgenre to appear in part 3, a banquet, reflects the impracticality of mathematical and musical intelligence in the preparation of a meal:

> My Dinner was brought, and four Persons of Quality, whom I remembered to have seen very near the King's Person, did me the Honour to dine with me. We had two Courses, of three Dishes each. In the first Course, there was a Shoulder of Mutton, cut into an Æqui-lateral Triangle; a Piece of Beef into a Rhomboides; and a Pudding into a Cycloid. The second Course was two Ducks, trussed up into the Form of Fiddles; Sausages and Puddings resembling Flutes and Hautboys, and a Breast of Veal in the Shape of a Harp. The Servants cut our Bread into Cones, Cylinders, Parallelograms, and several other Mathematical Figures. (161)

Perhaps the various shapes satisfy a sublimated aesthetic sense of the inhabitants of Laputa. Gulliver fails to comment on the saporosity of his meal, so we do not know if the practical incompetence of the Laputians extends to their kitchens. It may be reasonable to assume, however, that so much con-cern for outward design must preclude proper attention to the intricacies of culinary science.

In chapter 3, the description of the flying island parodies scientific papers published in the *Philosophical Transactions of the Royal Society*. The style is matter-of-fact and sterile. What is interesting is not that Swift could imitate a scientific style so ably, but rather that the same prosaic and emotionless ap-proach is extended to a discussion of the military uses of the island. The abil-ity to state terrifying alternatives coolly looks ahead to the style of *A Modest Proposal*. Here Gulliver tells us of the king's act of last resort:

> But if they still continue obstinate, or offer to raise Insurrections; he proceeds to the last Remedy, by letting the Island drop directly upon their Heads, which makes a universal Destruction both of Houses and Men. (171)

Gulliver is also able to reveal, with the same mechanical lack of emotion, the king's practical concern disguised as mercy:

> And the King, when he is highest provoked, and most determined to press a City to Rubbish, orders the Island to descend with great Gentleness, out of a Pretence of Tenderness to his People, but indeed for fear of breaking the Adamantine Bottom. . . . (172)

Such hypocritical compassion is analogous to the Lilliputian king's expression of great lenity and tenderness even as he inflicts the most inhuman punish-ment upon innocent sufferers (72).

Swift's attack on the modern world gains momentum in chapters 4 and 5, where Lord Munodi's house, "built according to the best Rules of ancient Ar-chitecture" (176), and the surrounding estate are seen to flourish in compari-son with the poverty and barrenness of everything else planned and built according to modern principles. What is particularly distressing here is that commonsense judgments, including those of Munodi himself, seem to give way to the a priori assumptions behind the modern projects. Exponents of common sense, like Munodi, doubt the validity of their own insights when confronted with the authority of a priori dogma.

Chapter 7 begins with an attack on superstition, but it rapidly turns into a Lucianic revisionist critique of history. Great figures from the past, such as Alexander and Hannibal, come forward to correct the errors of historians.

Swift's presentation of the grand sextumvirate at the end of chapter 8 deserves brief comment. Five of the six figures presented, Brutus, Lucius Junius Brutus, Socrates, Epaminondas, and Cato the Younger, are ancients and distinguished for their struggles against tyranny. Sir Thomas More, the only modern in this group, is presumably chosen for his resistance to Henry VIII. The imbalance between ancients and moderns may be attributed to Swift's belief that few moderns had shown the courage to expose tyrants and defend liberty. Gulliver's commitment to brevity helps to achieve ironic point against the modern reader and the world he lives in:

> It would be tedious to trouble the Reader with relating what vast Numbers of illustrious Persons were called up, to gratify that insatiable Desire I had to see the World in every Period of Antiquity placed before me. I chiefly fed mine Eyes with beholding the Destroyers of Tyrants and Usurpers, and the Restorers of Liberty to oppressed and injured Nations. But it is impossible to express the Satisfaction I received in my own Mind, after such a Manner as to make it a suitable Entertainment to the Reader. (196)

Clearly this is dictated by Gulliver's pragmatic turn of mind. But just as surely we, as readers, are subjected to some brilliant Swiftian irony. We are not expected to take the same satisfaction in beholding these lovers of liberty. After all we are moderns who countenance, indeed thrive on, tyranny. Further, we are reading merely to be entertained, not to have our dull moral sense sharpened. Just how a prospect of the enemies of usurpation could be shaped to modern taste eludes our honest narrator. In his own way Swift had joined this honored group when he wrote his *Drapier's Letters*. He continues the battle here in *Gulliver's Travels*.

The Glubbdubdrib episodes follow a determinate pattern. Assumptions about historical figures are consistently discarded as the personages themselves tell the "true" story. The rejection of history is analogous to the dismissal of a priori method.

Chapters 7 and 8, though not in actual dialogue form, are influenced by the dialogues of Lucian and his later imitators. They reveal Swift's interest in history and in competing philosophical positions. The wide generic scope shown here reflects the broad interest in literary kinds manifested by both Lucian and Swift. Swift is largely an imitator here, but he is an original and interesting one.

Although Swift is sometimes critical of the ancients, he finds much more to disapprove of among the moderns. Gulliver presents himself as an admirer of old families during his visits with "the modern Dead," but he is unable to say very much good about them. The Swiftian objection to these families is on moral grounds. The scions of these families are too often given over to the worst excesses and most trivial pleasures. Gulliver discovers

> How Cruelty, Falshood, and Cowardice grew to be Characteristicks by which certain Families are distinguished as much as by their Coat of Arms. Who first brought the Pox into a noble House, which hath lineally descended in scrophulous Tumours to their Posterity. Neither could I wonder at all this, when I saw such an Interruption of Lineages by Pages, Lacqueys, Valets, Coachmen, Gamesters, Fidlers, Players, Captains, and Pickpockets. (198–99)

Again, ancient history contains errors, but Gulliver finds reason to be "chiefly disgusted with modern History" because it has perpetuated deception:

> I found how the World had been misled by prostitute Writers, to ascribe the greatest Exploits in War to Cowards, the wisest Counsel to Fools, Sincerity to Flatterers, *Roman* Virtue to Betrayers of their Country, Piety to Atheists, Chastity to Sodomites, Truth to Informers. (199)

Upon discovering the infirmities and deceits of the ruling class, Gulliver, the sycophant flatterer, concludes with irony more suited to Swift's own voice:

> I hope I may be pardoned if these Discoveries inclined me a little to abate of that profound Veneration which I am naturally apt to pay to Persons of high Rank, who ought to be treated with the utmost Respect due to their sublime Dignity, by us their Inferiors. (200)

There may be no more scathing indictment of favoritism in all of English literature than chapter 8 of the third part of the *Travels*. No society can survive and flourish with such a thoroughgoing disregard of merit. Once again the source of corruption is that modern innovation, the court. It sets up its mores in opposition to every ancient tradition and overcomes them both by deceit and by the force of luxury. The voice of the satirist may be heard above that of Gulliver in the concluding paragraph, where the "ancient" English Yeomen (Swift can stretch the concept when it serves his purpose) are compared with their modern descendants:

I DESCENDED so low as to desire that some *English* Yeomen of the old Stamp, might be summoned to appear; once so famous for the Simplicity of their Manners, Dyet and Dress; for Justice in their Dealings; for their true Spirit of Liberty; for their Valour and Love of their Country. Neither could I be wholly unmoved after comparing the Living with the Dead, when I considered how all these pure native Virtues were prostituted for a Piece of Money by their Grand-children; who in selling their Votes, and managing at Elections have acquired every Vice and Corruption that can possibly be learned in a Court. (201–2)

Having seen a court in Laputa oblivious to the practical needs of the people it rules and intent only upon refining the methods by which it enforces its oppression, we are treated to an anatomy of the corruption and vice which spring from privilege and are learned in a court. Now we proceed with Gulliver to the court of Luggnagg, where deceit leading to execution is nearly a daily occurrence. Gulliver thrives in this place, but rejects the offers of the king in order to return to his wife and children. Once again, the Odysseus theme emerges.

Chapter 10 is devoted to the extraordinary and immortal Struldbruggs. When Gulliver hears of these people, he launches into an epideictic oration in praise of immortality and outlines the life he would lead if such an advantage had been granted him. Gulliver's viewpoint has every weakness of a priori reasoning. As a result his panegyric is laughed at by persons who have a firsthand knowledge of the Struldbruggs. Gulliver has overlooked the obvious premise that perpetual life can only be worthwhile if it is coupled with eternal youth. But since it is unreasonable and unjust to suppose that such qualities could be joined, Gulliver's praise of perpetual life is the merest bubble. When the decrepitude of the Struldbruggs is fully revealed, sempiternity of mortal life is seen to be a terrible curse, not the valued gift which Gulliver initially took it to be.

Not without some justice, part 3 has long remained in the shadow of the other voyages. It is, in one sense, more derivative than the other three. As a fairly obvious imitation of Lucian's *True History*, the voyage to Laputa and the adventures that follow it rely on a series of satiric insights in different contexts. The unity of setting, which provides such a fecundifying backdrop to the satiric aim in the other three voyages, is lacking in part 3.

But having said this, it is important to note that part 3 gives us additional perspectives on the central issue and evil of part 1, the court. If Lilliput,

Laputa, and Luggnagg are unsatisfactory nations because of their courts, Brobdingnag and Houyhnhnmland are better because they have either no fully developed court, or no court whatsoever. Parts 1 and 3 are linked in that they both discover a single source of evil for corruption and vice in the governments of nations.

From beginning to end part 3 shows us a series of surmises or false assumptions (I have called them a priori) which are, in due time, shown for what they are. We expect the mathematical and musical geniuses of Laputa to be capable of rational thought, but we find them wholly defective when faced with practical problems. Their mode of a priori thinking bears no relationship to the everyday needs of the people. Rather the abstraction of the rulers results in a land poorly governed and ineptly tilled. The Academy of Lagado represents the a priori faith of the Laputian ruling class reduced to academic pursuits. The projectors attempt either what is impossible, or, if performed, useless.

Perhaps the most prominent false surmise, however, begins and ends the voyage. When the pirates capture his ship, Gulliver seeks mercy from a pirate who happens to be a Dutchman and a fellow Protestant. But when the Dutchman is pleased to be his worst enemy instead, Gulliver is surprised to find a degree of mercy at the hands of a Japanese captain. At the end of part 3, the Dutch are particularly resolute in insisting that every European trample on the crucifix. Again, it is the Japanese who permit Gulliver passage without performing that sacrilegious act. In each case we are to see that our prejudices are of little assistance to us. The truth is often what we least expect. In part 1 we may have anticipated the doll-like Lilliputians behaving perfectly. But they turned out to be aggressive and cruel beyond what their limited physical stature should allow. On the other hand, the gigantic Brobdingnagians, whom Gulliver expected to be brutal, prove to be eminently civilized for the most part. The dangerously mischievous ones are either young boys or dwarfs, the smallest members of the Brobdingnagian tribe. In Houyhnhnmland we may expect horses to be inferior to those who possess human shape. But once again we are wrong. The likely falsehood of a priori assumptions may be said to be a central theme in *Gulliver's Travels*. The fallacy of a priori thinking brings into relief the fallibility of the human intellect, its prejudices and misapprehensions.

Part 4 is essentially an animal fable in which expected roles are reversed. Gradually Gulliver becomes convinced of the rightness of this role reversal and thus denigrates himself as a Yahoo. The Yahoos, although they have a human shape, are extremely filthy and obnoxious. The Houyhnhnms, on the other hand, in the form of horses, are recognized early as completely rational and therefore superhuman creatures. As they proceed to affirm their superiority, Gulliver becomes a convert to their way of life.

What also becomes clear is that Houyhnhnm society is prelapsarian, that is, unfallen. Reason is in total control, there is no room for emotion, and lying, saying the thing that is not, is completely unknown. When Gulliver discourses with the Master Houyhnhnm, he is hard pressed to make him understand such concepts as power, government, war, law, and punishment, which have no words in his language.

By chapter 4 the animal fable is replaced by a "discourse" between Gulliver and his master in which the fallen state of European Yahoos is compared with the prelapsarian condition of the Houyhnhnms. The first subject for emphasis is lawyers and the legal system, both of which are offered as prime examples of the corruption of the rational faculty. In an unfallen state there is no need for a judicial system, since crime is unknown. In a fallen state, however, the judicial system becomes increasingly corrupt, marking the continued decline of humankind.

After the lawyers, physicians come in for satiric attack. Here Swift establishes a pattern of themes that will dominate satire for some time to come. Fielding particularly will use much the same approach to condemn virtually the identical societal groups. This is general satire. But Swift will come as close to particular satire as he ever does in *Gulliver's Travels* with the attack on the First Minister. Although Walpole is clearly meant, the satire remains explicitly general.

After Gulliver has presented his outline of English society, culminating in the attack on the Chief Minister of State, the Houyhnhnm master finds analogies for English customs, point by point, in the behavior of the Yahoos. The Yahoos' love of shiny stones is similar to the English love of gold. When a third Yahoo carries off a shining stone for which two others had been contending, the episode brings to mind the lawsuits Gulliver had previously described. The Yahoos' passion for a certain juicy root is analogous to the English love of wine or its potent substitute in the cups of the poor—gin. Gulliver's discourse on physicians is parallel to the observation that the Yahoos are the only animals subject to diseases, but that there is indeed a cure prescribed for their maladies: "a Mixture of *their own Dung* and *Urine,* forcibly put down the *Yahoo's* Throat" (262).

The Houyhnhnm master confesses an inability to find resemblances between English Yahoos and those of his own country when it comes to learning, arts, and manufactures; but the Leader Yahoo and his favorite, whose relationship the master describes in detail, parallels the earlier First or Chief Minister of State passage (262–63). The passage focuses on what Swift has, throughout the book, seen as the primary source of evil in the modern world: the court. When the master's description of the Yahoo leader and his favorite is concluded, Gulliver adds: "how far this might be applicable to our *Courts* and *Favourites*, and *Ministers of State*, my Master said I could best determine" (263).

The satire in chapters 6 and 7 has been couched in dialogue related by indirect discourse. The structure is nonetheless in the form of a deliberation wherein Gulliver presents the salient points of the English government and legal system, and the Houyhnhnm master attempts to understand things of which he has no conception. At this point the satire seems to be essentially demonstrative, although directed for the most part against general targets. But decisions are being reached which will surface significantly later on.

Chapters 8 and 9 are in the form of a politeia and give us a detailed account of the customs and governance of the Houyhnhnms. At the beginning of chapter 9 Swift integrates Gulliver's story with material of the politeia. The fate of the Yahoos and, therefore, Gulliver's fate as well, is debated in the General Assembly. The only debate ever to occur in a nation where pure reason dominates every aspect of life has to do directly with the Yahoos, who are the only irrational element in Houyhnhnmland. The subject of that debate is whether or not the Yahoos should be exterminated. Since the elimination of Yahoo unreason will return the country to its prelapsarian state, the result is a foregone conclusion. The only question to decide is the means by which such a desirable end might be realized. The Houyhnhnm master proposes an expedient, for which Gulliver had provided a hint, that Yahoos should be castrated in order to terminate their kind. After mentioning that what passed in the Grand Council was to have a profound effect upon him, Gulliver goes on to complete his essay on Houyhnhnm learning and customs.

The Houyhnhnms' use of stone tools (they "know not the Use of Iron," Gulliver tells us) places them in the primitive past as does their lack of letters, rudimentary astronomy, and excellent poetry. But even more specific evidence of their prelapsarian nature is the fact that they have no word for evil and consequently no clear concept of it. The behavior of Yahoos supplies them with the only notions of defect they have. The word "Yahoo" covereth a multitude of sins.

It is in the person of the Yahoos that evil enters into Houyhnhnmland. Although the Houyhnhnms themselves are unfallen and impervious to temptation, their well-being is threatened by the presence of the Yahoos. With the introduction of Gulliver, a Yahoo with some small measure of reason, the race of Yahoos becomes an even more serious threat than heretofore. The decision of the Council to send Gulliver back across the sea is the conclusion to the deliberation, but it has its judicial edge as well. Gulliver is evicted from Eden, as the other Yahoos assuredly will be, because he represents a fallen state. Although he is capable of some means of remedying the effects of the fall, he can never do so satisfactorily enough to merit a home in Eden. The Houyhnhnms recognize what he represents and act to expel him from their land. The remainder of part 4 is Gulliver's account of that expulsion and how he manages to live in a fallen world once he has glimpsed the joys of the earthly paradise.

Gulliver's mistake is not that he wants to preserve something of the unfallen world of the Houyhnhnms when he returns to the fallen world of England. Rather it is that he takes a too literal approach to achieving the ideal. The grandeur of the Houyhnhnms does not consist in their "horsiness," that is, their form, but rather in their unfallen nature. By the same token, the form of the Yahoos, both those in Houyhnhnmland and Europe, is not the reason for their degraded state. Their degradation results from their fallen nature.

At the same time, a fallen nature has a disastrous effect on the form of the creature involved. Although brute beasts, the Yahoos are unlike the other domesticated animals in Houyhnhnmland. They retain a wild, ungovernable quality which is foreign to rational creatures or creatures under the domination of reason. These inner qualities are reflected in their outer form, because form should be one with what it contains.

A distinction needs to be made here between ancient and modern form. For Swift, ancient form accurately reflects reality. Indeed, no Cartesian bifurcation of form and content is possible. In modern forms there is structure alone: shadow without substance. Beyond appearance there is nothing. Yet the form itself is chaotic and at best odd. Ancient forms, then, imitate nature; they are the coats the brothers are given in *A Tale of a Tub*. The brothers, however, seek to "modernize" their coats in order to follow fashion. These are corruptions of form, not of nature. But as the modern corruptions become more severe, there seems to be an effect on nature herself. Jack, we may recall, "rent the *main Body* of his *Coat* from Top to Bottom . . ." (138)

and later, "in a great Rage . . . tore off the whole Piece, Cloth and all, and flung it into the Kennel . . ." (138–39). This goes far beyond the earlier superficial decorating of the coats. At this point the very substance of the coat is altered.

An even greater perversion of nature is seen in the "unnatural" acts, which are peculiar to the modern world. Such appetites are unknown in Houyhnhnmland:

> I expected every Moment, that my Master would accuse the *Yahoos* of those unnatural Appetites in both Sexes, so common among us. But Nature it seems hath not been so expert a Schoolmistress; and these politer Pleasures are entirely the Productions of Art and Reason, on our Side of the Globe. (264)

Such unnamed evils are in themselves a form of madness. Having committed one excess after another, Jack of *A Tale of a Tub* runs mad. Madness for Swift is no mere formal aberration: it is a perversion of nature for which there is no cure.

It is important to notice that the essential form of *A Tale* is the classical treatise. It is an ancient form, not a modern one, as is usually assumed. What is modern in *A Tale* are the aberrations from classical design: the overuse of prefaces, the digressions, and, most of all, the inept logic or lack of logic throughout. The reader's recognition of the rhetorical soundness of the treatise being threatened, indeed, destroyed, by the introduction of modern forms and procedures is important to the effectiveness of the satire. Finally the modern forms hang on *A Tale* like so many fringes and silver points on the coats of the three brothers. And as the form continues to deteriorate, the narrator, insofar as he is a character at all, seems to fall off into the same madness as Jack the Aeolist. The servant of modern forms is effectively hoist with his own petard. Those forms threaten to pervert human nature and do in fact distort it almost beyond recognition. This is the core of the terrible message the Augustan satirists present to us.

Satire is by no means the chaotic, formless thing which so many critics have called it. It is indeed a mixture of forms, sometimes of prose and verse, but in complex satire there is a mixture of ancient forms with modern ones. The ancient forms reflect the natural order of things. The modern ones represent the corruption of that natural order. Within the satire the reader can see, at first hand, the terrible power of the modern forms to debase the ancient ones. Finally the modern forms accomplish a metamorphosis of the ancient forms with which they come into contact. Ancient and modern look the same—fragmentary, vague, unnatural.

In the simple structures of satire, however, the ancient form is not under the same kind of attack. Rather, the premises of logic are what is bad; the weak premises, the silly examples, conflict with the structure of the classical form, as in A *Modest Proposal.* Fanatical wrong-headedness belies the firm structure of the ancient pile. Like ancient architecture, antique formal structures of rhetoric and literature were molded by the logic and sanity of the ideas behind them. For Swift, modern forms rise out of madness. Madness is the ultimate distortion of nature and the moral ideas emanating from the Creator.

But the satiric voice can vary; it is not confined to a single pitch. It can assume the role of modern, at odds with classical form; or it can perform the role of the satirist who strikes out against modern forms and ideas, and takes his place beside the ancients in conformity with antique opinions and immemorial forms. Swift uses all four elements in A *Tale of a Tub* and *Gulliver's Travels:* ancient forms and antique voice; modern forms and modern voice. The interplay of these four elements helps to give Swift's satire its own unique texture, density, and complexity. Lesser satirists characteristically employ three elements: two of form and one of voice.

Just as *Gulliver's Travels* transforms from travel book to satire by the deformation of a series of generic strategies, it achieves a variety of metamorphoses within the narrative line. The most important of these is the transformation of Gulliver himself to would-be Houyhnhnm. What is changeable, whether institutions or persons, is, for Swift, essentially evil. Man's depravity is symbolized by his change. But in attempting to become a Houyhnhnm, Gulliver is looking to turn back the clock to a prelapsarian time. That, of course, is impossible. And it is precisely in that impossibility that mankind's tragedy resides. The tragedy of humankind is that our social salvation lies in earlier institutions which we cannot now recapture. Change has robbed us of the forms and structures which define our humanity. And yet people go on embracing change, encouraging it, to take us even farther from our heritage and source.

Swift's satiric bias against the modern world is illustrated most clearly in an idea cluster borrowed from Sir William Temple. Although Swift's regard for Temple has recently been questioned,[24] there seems no doubt that Temple's love of ancient learning and suspicion of things modern was shared by his young secretary.[25] In his essay "Some Thoughts Upon Reviewing the Essay of

Ancient and Modern Learning" (c. 1698), Temple observes that the moderns must be allowed the honor of two inventions unknown to the ancients: gunpowder (with a concession to the priority of the Chinese in this invention) and the lodestone, by which "navigation must be allowed to have been much improved and extended. . . ."[26] Temple goes on to aver that "both these have not served for any common or necessary use to mankind: one having been employed for their destruction, not their preservation; and the other, only to feed their avarice, or increase their luxury. . . ."[27]

In part 2 of the *Travels*, the ancient civilization of Brobdingnag has no knowledge of gunpowder. So it is with confidence inspired by evil that Gulliver seeks to ingratiate himself in the king's esteem. He offers him a secret by which that ruler can become the absolute master of his people: the secret of modern artillery. The king, of course, rebuffs Gulliver with numbing acerbity.

In part 3 the flying island of Laputa navigates by means of an immense lodestone. Although at first it seems a wonder, Gulliver soon realizes that the aeronautical dexterity of the island serves mainly to subjugate the denizens of the lands below.

Thus, while agreeing with Temple that modern inventions have dangerous consequences, Swift illustrates the perils much more concretely. Gulliver describes the use of gunpowder and cannon in terrifying detail and with obvious relish. But Swift takes the use of the lodestone one step farther than Temple did. Doubtless Swift had little fear that the moderns could contrive flying islands like the one he imagined. But he did greatly fear European imperialism directed against the rest of the world. For him the lodestone compass represented the ability of Europeans to get any place they wanted to go. But Laputa represented even more than that. It was a composite symbol of the navigational and military superiority which aggressive rulers could employ to subjugate their own people as well as the inhabitants of less advanced nations.

Just as the Augustan satirists reject modern accomplishments in science, trade, and the art of war, they scorn modern improvements in literature. They see literature as damaged irremediably by an unauthorized mixing of styles and forms. Ironically, satire is just such a mixed form, but it is not an innovation. It was so in ancient practice. To denounce the perversion of literature which mirrors the perversion of life, the Augustans employ that protean kind best adapted to grasping the horrific nuances of modernity. They do not simply choose satire, however. It is thrust upon them by the exigencies of their time. They are moved as Juvenal was: "si natura negat, facit indignatio versum."[28] If anger actuates the satirist, his subject matter is also provided to him:

> quidquid agunt homines, votum timor ira voluptas
> gaudia discursus, nostri farrago libelli est.[29]

The "farrago" of human concerns impinges on the senses in undifferentiated succession, just as Juvenal wrote the words on the page. That, at least, is the affectation of the satirists. But this, as I have argued, cannot be taken without the proverbial grain of salt. If satire is thought to have no determinate form, it begins somewhere in a basic rhetorical structure and develops its own norms.

Since satire emerges when literature and life are in disarray, it is not surprising that those norms are unlike those of other genres. Out of discord emerges a vision of discord which in turn becomes an affirmation of a possibility that was once, in some ancient imagination, a reality. However insubstantial that might appear, it is something of greater constancy than modern madness. This possibility is a past reality rooted in a tradition which extends back to such shadowy figures as Archilochus, Hipponax, Ananius, Hermippus, Kerkidas, and Aischrion. Satire, generic satire, came out of the shadows in republican Rome in the verses of Lucilius and rose to great heights in the imperial Romes of Horace, Persius, and Juvenal. Tradition makes satire more shapely than rhetorical form ever could.

In their quest for the essentials of the past, then, the great satirists are radicals in the original sense of the word. Since the future is merely a dangerous extension of an unacceptable present, satirists assume a somewhat reactionary stance. The greatest satire not only discredits perversity and evil wherever it is to be found, it also identifies that distortion of values as a particularly modern phenomenon. A certain nostalgia for a time less subject to change is an essential ingredient in Augustan satire. Particularly distressing to these satirists is the decline in literary form, for as the concept of genre slips away, so does a means of precise expression of the reality of things. Caught in a ferment of uncontrollable change, the satirists take solace and measure their own situation in the forms of satire. It is another paradox of satire that out of a vision of discord great literature can be made.

Good Satire depends on bad society.

8

CONCLUSION

There is little doubt that the culmination of generic satire can be found in the work of the authors who have been the focus of this study. The satires of Dryden and the great Scriblerians appeared just at a juncture when the high Renaissance regard for genre was giving way to formal promiscuity and the outright rejection of traditional forms. A protest against the decline of form could only come from men who possessed a command of genre and could see the implications of its demise for the culture as a whole. There is irony in the fact that great generic satire, written in opposition to the general decline of all that the kinds of literature represent, has often been read as further evidence of generic decline. Such a reading might seem to be justified by Menippean satire's sanction of a madcap disregard of form. But the neglect of form in satire is more shadow than substance, more appearance than reality.[1] The great satire, whether in the form of casual *sermo* or rigorous treatise, whether a single epistle or full-scale autobiography, faces in two directions like the Janus head. On the one hand, it may seem to turn generic differences inside out as it imitates the worst offenders in the rising popular literature. Once embarked on the chaos of reality, the great satirists must have seen that satire was precisely the right form to communicate lack of form in the objects of satire. But this is not the whole picture. Although the Janus head looks to chaos in one direction as its object of attack, the second face gazes intently toward the golden age of genre, when order prevailed and Astraea presided over human institutions.

Satire of the greatest substance, then, emerges along with a belief in the superiority of the past to the present and a fear of innovation as a threat to the institutions of the past. Thus the object of satire is a present danger or perversion of a hallowed norm. The past is essential because it is a known quantity: the object of profound interpretation, it has the sanctity of myth. The future, on the other hand, is much less substantial. A futurist must spend much of his time envisioning the utopia he proposes. That utopia necessarily lacks the solidity of the past. The satirist, therefore, rejects that vision and the present that may give it substance. As a result of this, the utopian vision that characterizes satire is almost invariably reactionary. That may be why the deliberative rhetorical form, which stresses the future, is so popular with satirists. Since satirists do not embrace change, they are particularly critical of those who sit in deliberation to plot future courses. Thus we see Flecknoe, Absalom, Achitophel, the servant of modern forms, the modest proposer, Dulness, and Cibber planning a future for humankind as well as for themselves. In one sense they are parodic utopians; they look, not to recover a valued past or to salvage what remains of it, but rather to march on thoughtlessly into the future. An expressed fear of change is so central to great satire that it may be regarded as a normative trait.

The major point of this study has been that satire occupies a unique position among the genres, but not one inconsistent with the fundamental mimetic theory of literature. Satire is essentially a borrower of forms, but as such it is not to be confused with those host structures. Indeed, it is the characteristic dynamic of satire to de-form those structures as part of their transformation to components of generic satire. The borrowed forms with which satire begins are never truly themselves, however. They are imitated structures, which, although often taken for themselves, are, from the very outset, in the process of being subsumed by the emerging form of satire.

There are a variety of methods by which generic satire comes into being, but the primary one is a pattern of ironies. Such a pattern or system is most clearly evident in complex satire where prolegomenal and suffixal material is added to a succession of internal constructions which give way to one another, sometimes with amazing rapidity. The apparent instability of satire, however, is a normative condition by which the host genres are deformed or restructured to compose the satire. But even in this restructuring those host genres do not lose their internal defining traits. What they do lose is their dominant and defining relationship to the overall literary structure. Instead of dominating, the host genre plays a subordinate role in relation to other generic strategies and to a deforming ironic pattern.

Although it does not provide an exact analogy, Lévi-Strauss's concept of *bricolage* may help us understand the structure of satire. In *La Pensée Sauvage,* Lévi-Strauss defines the art of the *bricoleur* as consisting of odds and ends or whatever is available.[2] What is produced, bricolage, is analogous to myth. Among the genres of traditional literary theory, satire is most like this form of art. Both employ fragments of an earlier civilizaton or culture to construct a contemporary pattern or system of signs. Satire adapts elements of other genres to create a form not far removed from pastiche in its outward appearance and method of composition. The essential meaning of this structure inheres in this method of composition or bricolage. By piecing together what is left over from a disintegrating past, the satirist forms a prism through which the present can be refracted. Just as the latest mythmaker uses outworn structures to construct his new perspectives, the satirist employs what is left over from a great literary tradition to reflect on contemporary shortcomings.

It is not so much the historical past, perhaps, as the ideal perception of pastness revealed in forms which attracts the great satirists. In other words, the conception of epic, tragedy, or the major nonmimetic structures—history, philosophy, and oratory—can be idealized even beyond any imagined past. Thus the historical past with which Homer deals is violent and cruel as well as heroic. But the generic ideal can be perfect in its kind. As formal construction and work of art, it has no moral limitations. Yet it has moral relevance both in the perfection or near perfection of its idealized form and the pattern of moral issues raised. The moral imperfections in Homer perceived by later thinkers[3] are resolved in the success of Homeric art. The perception of violence as a blemish in Homer is really only commentary on Homer's grasp of social realities both in his own time and in the time period of the setting of his poems. In the hands of a Homer and a Vergil, art reaches its highest realization. Literature, as Stephen Dedalus affirmed, is the record of man's triumphs while history records his defeats. For the great satirists, perfection of genre is an ideal representing nature. When the art of nature, that of Homer and Vergil, is beyond our grasp, satire can at least chronicle the reasons for it.

For these reasons, satire cannot be judged by its subject matter, which it presents as social reality. More pertinent is the art it employs to make that subject real and threatening. Once we have understood the intricate aesthetics of generic satire, we need not resort to contradictory qualifications of its generic status. Though it bears a unique relationship to nonmimetic verbal structures, satire is an imitation of such forms and therefore must be regarded as fictive discourse. It can then be understood that, like other genres, a satire is most importantly a work of art. Finally it must be judged as such according to its own unique but normative principles of composition.

NOTES

CHAPTER 1. INTRODUCTION

1. See my selected bibliography. The fact that Robert C. Elliott's excellent *Encyclopaedia Britannica* article appears in the "Macropaedia" instead of the "Micropaedia" may be indicative of wider general appeal. See Alvin Kernan, "Robert C. Elliott, 1914–1981," in *English Satire and the Satiric Tradition*, ed. Claude Rawson (Oxford: Basil Blackwell, 1984), 1–5.

2. Ibid., 4.

3. See John Traugott, "A Tale of a Tub" in *The Character of Swift's Satire: A Revised Focus*, ed. Claude Rawson (Newark: Univ. of Delaware Press, 1983), 83–126; and Irvin Ehrenpreis, "*Personae*," in *Restoration and Eighteenth-Century Literature: Essays in Honor of Alan Dugald McKillop*, ed. Carroll Camden (Chicago: Univ. of Chicago Press, 1963), 25–37. Reprinted in Ehrenpreis, *Literary Meaning and Augustan Values* (Charlottesville: Univ. Press of Virginia, 1974).

4. This is particularly true of studies of individual authors where the focus is on matters other than the aesthetics of satire.

5. Claude Lévi-Strauss, *The Savage Mind* (Chicago: Univ. of Chicago Press, 1966), 9.

6. Bernard Weinberg, *A History of Literary Criticism in the Italian Renaissance* (Chicago: Univ. of Chicago Press, 1961), 1:148.

7. Alastair Fowler, *Kinds of Literature: An Introduction to the Theory of Genres and Modes* (Cambridge, Mass.: Harvard Univ. Press, 1982), 45–48.

8. John Dryden, *Of Dramatic Poesy and Other Critical Essays*, ed. George Watson (New York: Everyman's Library, 1962), 2:143.

9. Ibid., 2:143. Howard D. Weinbrot, in *Alexander Pope and the Traditions of Formal Verse Satire* (Princeton: Princeton Univ. Press, 1982), passim, shows the impact of Dryden's views on later satirists. In *The Satires of Horace* (1966; rpt. Berkeley and Los

Angeles: Univ. of California Press, 1982), 258–73, Niall Rudd has shown how weak Dryden's case against Horace really is and that neither Horace's nor Juvenal's satire precisely fits Dryden's characterizations of them.

10. Ibid., 2:145.

11. Ibid., 1:59.

12. Ibid., 1:234.

13. Ibid., 1:159.

14. It is interesting to note that what has sometimes been taken for a misunderstanding by Dryden of Aristotle's distinction between action and plot is really an attempt to hew more closely to the principles of the ancients inherent in the plays themselves. Dryden is seldom influenced by critical authority. His authority is regularly the artistic success of literary works.

15. Ibid., 2:145.

16. Ibid., 2:145.

17. Ibid., 145.

18. Despite the vagueness of the term "Menippean Satire" a substantial amount of scholarly effort has been exerted to prove that various prose satires are "Menippean." J. P. Sullivan holds that Petronius' *Satyricon* belongs essentially to "the well-established genre of Menippean satire," although he recognizes that many other generic influences are present. See *The Satyricon of Petronius: A Literary Study* (Bloomington: Indiana Univ. Press, 1968), 82. For more recent scholarship on Menippean satire, see Eugene Korkowski, "Menippus and His Imitators: A Conspectus, Up to Sterne, for a Misunderstood Genre," Ph.D. diss., Univ. of California, San Diego, 1973. A number of relevant articles have proceeded from this dissertation, some of which are: "With an Eye to the Bunghole: Figures of Containment in *A Tale of a Tub*," *SEL* 15 (1975): 391–408; "Genre and Satiric Strategy in Burton's *Anatomy of Melancholy*," *Genre* 8 (1975): 74–87; and "Donne's *Ignatius* and Menippean Satire," *Studies in Philology* 72 (1975): 419–38. Northrop Frye has outlined the parameters of the Menippean form in *Anatomy of Criticism* (Princeton: Princeton Univ. Press, 1957), 309–12. Frye's influence can be seen in Robert A. Kantra, *All Things Vain: Religious Satirists and Their Art* (University Park: Pennsylvania State Univ. Press, 1984) who assumes that the qualities of Menippean satire are well-defined (121) as he finds examples of them in Chesterton, Belloc, and Arthur Hugh Benson.

19. Dryden, *Of Dramatic Poesy and Other Critical Essays*, 2:115.

20. Mikhail Bakhtin, *Problems of Dostoevsky's Poetics*, ed. and trans. Caryl Emerson (Minneapolis: Univ. of Minnesota Press, 1984), 118.

21. A. R. Heiserman, *Skelton and Satire* (Chicago: Univ. of Chicago Press, 1961), 305.

22. Ibid., 305. On the medieval inclination to mix serious and comic modes, see Ernst Robert Curtius, *European Literature and the Latin Middle Ages*, trans. Willard R. Trask (1953; rpt. New York: Harper Torch Books, 1963), 419–35.

23. Sullivan's description of the *Satyricon* as a "comic *Odyssey*" is an example of the recognition of multiple genres in the work (93).

24. Rosalie Colie, *The Resources of Kind: Genre-Theory in the Renaissance*, ed. Barbara K. Lewalski (Berkeley and Los Angeles: Univ. of California Press, 1973).

25. See these English Institute Essays in *New Approaches to Eighteenth-Century Literature*, ed. Phillip Harth (New York: Columbia Univ. Press, 1974). The most comprehensive awareness of genre mixing throughout "Augustan" poetry is in Margaret Anne Doody, *The Daring Muse: Augustan Poetry Reconsidered* (Cambridge: Cambridge Univ. Press, 1985).

26. For *Gargantua and Pantagruel* see Seidel, *Satiric Inheritance;* other works are Philip Holland, "Robert Burton's *Anatomy of Melancholy* and Menippean Satire, Humanist and English" (Ph.D. diss., Univ. of London, 1979), Robert H. Hopkins, *The True Genius of Oliver Goldsmith* (Baltimore: Johns Hopkins Univ. Press, 1969), and Melvyn New, *Laurence Sterne as Satirist: A Reading of Tristram Shandy* (Gainesville: Univ. of Florida Press, 1969).

27. My view of comedy owes much to Elder Olson, *The Theory of Comedy* (Bloomington: Indiana Univ. Press, 1968), 5–6.

28. Bywater's translation reads: "The ridiculous may be defined as a mistake or deformity not productive of pain or harm to others. . . ." *The Complete Works of Aristotle: The Revised Oxford Translation*, ed. Jonathan Barnes (Princeton: Princeton Univ. Press, 1984), 2:2319. The Greek words for "pain" and "harm" are ανώδυνου and φθαρτικόν.

29. *Philebus* (48c), trans. R. Hackforth, in *The Collected Dialogues of Plato*, ed. Edith Hamilton and Huntington Cairns (New York: Pantheon, 1961), 1129. "The ridiculous" is τὸ γελοῖον; "badness" is πονηρία.

30. Olson, *Theory of Comedy*, 16–17.

31. Ibid., 13.

32. W. Jackson Bate, "Johnson and Satire Manqué," in *Eighteenth-Century Studies in Honor of Donald F. Hyde* (New York: The Grolier Club, 1970), 147.

33. *The Twickenham Edition of the Poems of Alexander Pope*, ed. John Butt et al. (London and New Haven: Methuen and Yale Univ. Press, 1939–69), vol. 4. All subsequent citations to Pope's poetry are to this edition.

34. David B. Morris, *Alexander Pope: The Genius of Sense* (Cambridge, Mass.: Harvard Univ. Press, 1984), 216.

35. Barbara Herrnstein Smith, "Poetry as Fiction," *New Literary History* 2 (1971): 260. This article is reprinted in Smith's *On the Margins of Discourse* (Chicago: Univ. of Chicago Press, 1978). Smith's emphasis on language owes much to the Russian Formalists, I believe, as does my own explanation of satire's generic status. My debt is not in specifics, but rather in a more general theoretical approach. For recent accounts of the Russian Formalists see Victor Ehrlich, *Russian Formalism: History—Doctrine* (The Hague: Mouton, 1965) and Terry Eagleton, *Literary Theory: An Introduction* (Minneapolis: Univ. of Minnesota Press, 1983), 2–6. For a view compatible with Smith's see Tzvetan Todorov, *Theories of the Symbol*, trans. Catherine Porter (Ithaca, N.Y.: Cornell Univ. Press, 1982), chap. 5.

36. Smith, "Poetry as Fiction," 268–9.

37. This function is recognized by Frederick J. Stopp, *Evelyn Waugh: Portrait of an Artist* (London: Chapman and Hall, 1958), cited in Ronald Paulson, *The Fictions of Satire* (Baltimore: The Johns Hopkins Univ. Press, 1967), 4. Paulson agrees and elaborates on satire's borrowing procedure: "Satire enjoys the episodic forms, the collection

of stories or anecdotes, the list, the large dinner party or the group convention, the legal brief, the projector's pamphlet, the encyclopaedia, and the calendar," 5. See also Alastair Fowler, *Kinds of Literature*, 189, and David B. Morris, *Alexander Pope: The Genius of Sense*, 216.

38. Bate, "Johnson and Satire Manqué," 147.

39. D. H. Monro, *Argument of Laughter* (Notre Dame, Ind.: Univ. of Notre Dame Press, 1963), 235.

40. Colie, *Resources of Kind*, 114.

41. E. D. Hirsch, Jr., *Validity in Interpretation* (New Haven: Yale Univ. Press, 1967), 74. Hirsch later states that "All understanding of verbal meaning is necessarily genre-bound" (76).

42. Monro, *Argument of Laughter*, 235.

43. Alvin Kernan, *The Cankered Muse: Satire of the English Renaissance* (1959; rpt. Hamden, Conn.: Archon, 1976), 14.

CHAPTER 2. DEMONSTRATIVE SATIRE

1. *The Works of John Dryden*, ed. H. T. Swedenberg et al. (Berkeley and Los Angeles: Univ. of California Press, 1956–), vol. 3. All references to Dryden's poems are to this edition.

2. Aristotle, *Rhetoric*, trans. W. Rhys Roberts (New York: Modern Library, 1954), 32.

3. Ibid., 32.

4. *Hobbes's Thucydides*, ed. Richard Schlatter (New Brunswick, N.J.: Rutgers Univ. Press, 1975), 131.

5. See Fred Norris Robinson, "Satirists and Enchanters in Early Irish Literature," in *Studies in the History of Religions Presented to Crawford Howell Toy*, ed. D. G. Lyon and G. F. Moore (New York: Macmillan, 1912), 95–130; rpt. in *Satire: Modern Essays in Criticism*, ed. Ronald Paulson (Englewood Cliffs, N.J.: Prentice-Hall, 1971), 1–36. Another classic of its kind, influenced by the Robinson essay, is Robert C. Elliott, *The Power of Satire: Magic, Ritual, Art* (Princeton: Princeton Univ. Press, 1960).

6. Cited in Hermann Fränkel, *Early Greek Poetry and Philosophy*, trans. Moses Hadas and James Willis (New York and London: Harcourt Brace, 1973), 141.

7. Ibid., 142.

8. Elliott, *Power of Satire*, 105.

9. Northrop Frye, *Anatomy of Criticism* (Princeton: Princeton Univ. Press, 1957), 231.

10. *The Mabinogi and Other Welsh Tales*, trans. Patrick K. Ford (Berkeley and Los Angeles: Univ. of California Press, 1977), 177.

11. All citations to Cleveland's poems are to *The Poems of John Cleveland*, ed. Brian Morris and Eleanor Withington (Oxford: Clarendon Press, 1967).

12. See Hoyt Hopewell Hudson, trans., *The Praise of Folly* (1941; rpt. Princeton: Princeton Univ. Press, 1970), 131–42.

13. Walter Kaiser, *Praisers of Folly: Erasmus, Rabelais, Shakespeare* (London: Gollancz, 1964), 48–49.

14. Clarence H. Miller, "Introduction" to Erasmus, *The Praise of Folly* (New Haven: Yale Univ. Press, 1979), xiv–xv.

15. Gilbert Highet, *The Speeches in Vergil's Aeneid* (Princeton: Princeton Univ. Press, 1972).

16. Erasmus, *The Praise of Folly*, trans. Clarence H. Miller (New Haven: Yale Univ. Press, 1979), 9–10. All internal page references are to this edition.

17. See my "Socrates and Post-Socratic Satire," *Journal of the History of Ideas* 46 (1985): 3–12.

18. M. A. Screech, *Ecstasy and the Praise of Folly* (London: Duckworth, 1980), 10.

CHAPTER 3. DELIBERATIVE SATIRE

1. Ulrich Knoche, *Roman Satire*, trans. Edwin S. Ramage (Bloomington: Indiana Univ. Press, 1975), 22, 51.

2. *The Satires of Horace and Persius*, trans. Niall Rudd (New York: Penguin, 1973), II, i, 73.

3. Horace, *Satires, Epistles and Ars Poetica*, trans. H. Rushton Fairclough (London and Cambridge, Mass.: Loeb Classical Library, 1929), 229.

4. *Juvenal and Persius*, trans. G. G. Ramsay (London and Cambridge, Mass.: Loeb Classical Library, 1961), 337. The Latin texts for Persius and Juvenal are from this edition.

5. Rudd translation, 125. For *Alcibiades I*, see 131.

6. *The Satires of Juvenal*, trans. Rolfe Humphries (Bloomington: Indiana Univ. Press, 1958), 18.

7. Ibid., 25.

8. Ibid., 35.

9. Ibid., 64.

10. Ibid., 93.

11. Ibid., 118.

12. Knoche, *Roman Satire*, 149.

13. Humphries, *Satires of Juvenal*, 121.

14. Ibid., 134.

15. Ibid., 134.

16. Ibid., 134.

17. The translation is mine.

18. See Frederick M. Keener, *English Dialogues of the Dead: A Critical History, An Anthology, and A Check List* (New York: Columbia Univ. Press, 1973).

19. Northrop Frye, *Anatomy of Criticism* (Princeton: Princeton Univ. Press, 1957), 310.

20. Henry Fielding, *The History of Tom Jones a Foundling*, Introduction and Commentary by Martin C. Battestin, ed. Fredson Bowers (Middletown, Conn.: Wesleyan Univ. Press, 1975), 1:509.

21. Athenaeus, *The Deipnosophists or Banquet of the Learned*, trans. C. D. Yonge (London: Bohn, 1853), 1:29.

174 Notes to Pages 40–57

22. *Dio Chrysostom*, trans. J. W. Cohoon (London and Cambridge, Mass.: Loeb Classical Library, 1939), 2:427.

23. Petrarch, *Selected Sonnets, Odes and Letters*, ed. Thomas G. Bergin (Arlington Heights, Ill.: AHM Publishing, 1966), 2.

24. David Farley-Hills, *Rochester's Poetry* (London: Bell & Hyman, 1978), 157.

25. Dustin H. Griffin, *Satires Against Man: The Poems of Rochester* (Berkeley and Los Angeles: Univ. of California Press, 1973), 174.

26. Eduard Fraenkel, *Horace* (Oxford: Clarendon Press, 1957), 309.

27. See Howard D. Weinbrot, *The Formal Strain: Studies in Augustan Imitation and Satire* (Chicago: Univ. of Chicago Press, 1969), 129–64.

28. Andrew Marvell, *The Rehearsal Transpros'd and The Rehearsal Transpros'd, the Second Part*, ed. D. I. B. Smith (Oxford: Clarendon Press, 1971), 145.

29. James Sutherland, *English Literature of the Late Seventeenth Century* (Oxford: Clarendon Press, 1969), 341.

30. Ibid., 342–43.

31. See Mary Tom Osborne, *Advice-To-A-Painter Poems, 1633–1856: An Annotated Finding List* (Austin: Univ. of Texas Press, 1949).

32. J. H. Hexter, "Introduction" to *The Complete Works of St. Thomas More*, ed. Edward Surtz, S.J., and J. H. Hexter (New Haven: Yale Univ. Press, 1965), 4:xvi–xvii.

33. Ibid., 4:xvii–xviii.

34. A. R. Heiserman, "Satire in the *Utopia*," *PMLA* 78 (1963): 164.

35. All textual citations to the *Utopia* are from Surtz and Hexter, *The Complete Works of St. Thomas More*.

36. See John Higginbotham, "Satire," in *Greek and Latin Literature: A Comparative Study*, ed. John Higginbotham (London: Methuen, 1969), 225–26.

37. See Edward Surtz, S.J., *The Praise of Pleasure: Philosophy, Education, and Communism in More's "Utopia"* (Cambridge, Mass.: Harvard Univ. Press, 1957). Also see Richard Marius, *Thomas More: A Biography* (New York: Alfred A. Knopf, 1984), 160.

CHAPTER 4. JUDICIAL SATIRE

1. *The Complete Poetical Works of Byron*, ed. Paul E. More (Cambridge, Mass.: Riverside Press, 1933). All references to *The Vision of Judgment* are to this edition.

2. *The Complete Plays of Aristophanes*, ed. Moses Hadas (New York: Bantam Books, 1962), 147.

3. *Socrates' Defense (Apology)*, trans. Hugh Tredennick, in *The Collected Dialogues of Plato*, ed. Edith Hamilton and Huntington Cairns (New York: Pantheon, 1963), 5.

4. Ibid., 10.

5. Francis Macdonald Cornford, *The Origin of Attic Comedy*, ed. Theodore H. Gaster (Garden City, N.Y.: Anchor Books, 1961), 139.

6. *Socrates' Defense (Apology)*, 8.

7. Ibid., 8.

8. Ibid., 9.

9. Ibid., 9.

10. Ibid., 25.

11. Rabelais, *Oeuvres Complètes,* ed. Jacques Boulenger and Lucien Scheler (Paris: Gallimard, 1955), chap. 44, 484–86.

12. Miguel De Cervantes Saavedra, *Don Quijote De La Mancha,* ed. Martin De Riquer (Barcelona: Editorial Juventud, 1967), vol. 2, chap. 45, 858–65.

13. *Works of John Dryden,* vol. 2.

14. *The Works of Sir John Suckling: The Non-Dramatic Works,* ed. Thomas Clayton (Oxford: Clarendon Press, 1971).

15. Robert Southey, *The Poetical Works* (Boston: Houghton Mifflin, n.d.), 228–29.

16. See Vincent Carretta, *The Snarling Muse: Verbal and Visual Political Satire From Pope to Churchill* (Philadelphia: Univ. of Pennsylvania Press, 1983), 247.

17. *Poems on Affairs of State: Augustan Satirical Verse, 1660–1714,* ed. George deF. Lord et al. (New Haven: Yale Univ. Press, 1963–75), 2:328. Volume 2 is edited by Elias F. Mengel, Jr.

18. *Works of John Dryden,* 3:116.

19. Cited in René Huchon, *George Crabbe and His Times: 1754–1832* (1907; rpt. New York: Barnes and Noble, 1968), 273.

CHAPTER 5. DRYDEN

1. All citations to *Mac Flecknoe* are from *The Works of John Dryden,* ed. H. T. Swedenberg et al. (Berkeley and Los Angeles: Univ. of California Press, 1956–), vol. 2.

2. This is observed by Earl Miner, *The Restoration Mode From Milton to Dryden* (Princeton: Princeton Univ. Press, 1974), 344.

3. Paul J. Korshin, *Typologies in England: 1650–1820* (Princeton: Princeton Univ. Press, 1982), chap. 8, 269–327.

4. *Works of John Dryden,* 2:316–17.

5. Earl Miner, *Dryden's Poetry* (Bloomington: Indiana Univ. Press, 1967), 78–82.

6. By my count Shadwell employs it seven different times. See *The Complete Works of Thomas Shadwell,* ed. Montague Summers (1927; rpt. New York: Benjamin Blom, 1968), vol. 1. Stanford calls himself an owl on four separate occasions, three times in Act III, pp. 45, 48, and 51, and once in Act IV, p. 67. Sir Positive-at-all uses it twice: Act III, p. 40, and Act IV, p. 74. Emilia uses it once, in Act IV, p. 58.

7. There is a significant owl in Boileau's *Le Lutrin,* Chant III, which Dryden may have had in mind, particularly in the use of "reverend," since the owl was in the *lutrin* (lectern) and Boileau's mock-heroic poem is a satire on religious orders.

8. Thomas Shadwell, *The Virtuoso,* ed. Marjorie Hope Nicolson and David Stuart Rodes (Lincoln: Univ. of Nebraska Press, 1966), 2:i:27–30.

9. See *Virtuoso,* 2:i:146–47; 4:iv:12–13; 5:iv:19.

10. Shadwell, *Complete Works,* 1:254. The entire epilogue is in italics.

11. Harry Levin, "The Wages of Satire," in *Literature and Society: Selected Papers From the English Institute, 1978,* ed. Edward W. Said (Baltimore: Johns Hopkins Univ. Press, 1980), 3.

12. A. W. Verrall, *Lectures on Dryden* (1914; rpt. New York: Russell & Russell, 1963), 59. More recent attempts to assess the genre of *Absalom and Achitophel* are Chester Cable, "*Absalom and Achitophel* as Epic Satire," in *Studies in Honor of John Wilcox*, ed. A. D. Wallace and W. O. Ross (Detroit: Wayne State Univ. Press, 1958), 51–60; Morris Freedman, "Dryden's Miniature Epic," *Journal of English and Germanic Philology* 57 (1958): 211–19; R. G. Peterson, "Larger Manners and Events: Sallust and Virgil in *Absalom and Achitophel*, *PMLA* 82 (1967): 236–44.

13. Paul Ramsey, *The Art of John Dryden* (Lexington: Univ. of Kentucky Press, 1969), 96. See also Earl Miner, *Dryden's Poetry*, 141. More recently, Steven N. Zwicker, recognizing the multiplicity of genres in *Absalom and Achitophel*, concludes that "the poem, finally, [is] of no genre at all. . . ." (*Politics and Language in Dryden's Poetry: The Arts of Disguise* [Princeton: Princeton Univ. Press, 1984], 89). Although Zwicker's argument is complex and ingenious, a better explanation of the generic mixture in the poem is in Dryden's own identification of *Absalom and Achitophel* and *Mac Flecknoe* as Varronian satires (*Of Dramatic Poesy and Other Critical Essays*, 2:115). For an extended discussion of *Absalom and Achitophel* as a Varronian form, see W. K. Thomas, *The Crafting of "Absalom and Achitophel": Dryden's "Pen for a Party"* (Waterloo: Ont.: Wilfrid Laurier Univ. Press, 1978), chap. 9, 163–74.

14. For another discussion of the opening of the poem, with a different result, see Miner, *Dryden's Poetry*, 107–9. Norma Silbermintz, an M.A. candidate at City College, CUNY, in an unpublished essay, "Dryden's Distortion of the Old Testament in *Absalom and Achitophel*" (1984) has compared the relevant Hebrew Scriptures with Dryden's version and noted a number of discrepancies. See also my comments on the meaning of these distortions in "Dryden's Debasement of Scripture in *Absalom and Achitophel*," *SEL* 9 (1969): 395–413. Two valuable approaches to Dryden's "debasement" of Scripture and essentially secular meaning are George deF. Lord, "*Absalom and Achitophel* and Dryden's Political Cosmos," in *John Dryden*, ed. Earl Miner (Athens, Ohio: Ohio Univ. Press, 1972), 156–90, and Dustin Griffin, "Dryden's Charles: The Ending of *Absalom and Achitophel*," *Philological Quarterly* 57 (1978): 359–82.

15. Godfrey Davies, "The Conclusion of Dryden's *Absalom and Achitophel*," *Huntington Library Quarterly* 10 (1946–7): 69–82.

16. Samuel Johnson, "Life of Dryden," in *Lives of the English Poets*, ed. G. Birkbeck Hill (Oxford: Clarendon Press, 1905), vol. 1.

17. W. K. Thomas reads *Absalom and Achitophel* as having the form of a classical oration (*Crafting of "Absalom and Achitophel*," chap. 10, 175–213). The judicial quality of Dryden's satire has been widely recognized. *The Medal* borrows many elements of the classical oration: "there are grounds," Alan Roper writes, "for seeing the poem as a poetic version of forensic oratory in which Dryden, as royal advocate, reopens the case against Shaftesbury" (*Dryden's Poetic Kingdoms* [London: Routledge & Kegan Paul, 1965], 101). While recognizing (I think correctly) that "the *oratio*, or structure of classical debate is doubtless more closely patterned than satire's" (72), Edward A. and Lillian D. Bloom argue convincingly that in *Absalom and Achitophel* "rhetoric and satire reconcile their differences within a common design" (73) (*Satire's Persuasive Voice* [Ithaca: Cornell Univ. Press, 1979], 70–82).

CHAPTER 6. POPE

1. *The Twickenham Edition of the Poems of Alexander Pope*, ed. John Butt et al. (London and New Haven: Methuen and Yale Univ. Press, 1939–69), vol. 2. All subsequent references to *The Rape of the Lock* are to this text.

2. Earl Miner, *The Cavalier Mode From Jonson to Cotton* (Princeton: Princeton Univ. Press, 1971).

3. Philip Francis (*The Odes of Horace* [London and New York, n.d.], 23) translates this as:

Even while we talk in careless ease,
Our envious minutes wing their flight;
Then swift the fleeting pleasures seize,
Nor trust to-morrow's doubtful light.

4. Miner, *Cavalier Mode*, 104.

5. *The Poems of Thomas Carew*, ed. Rhodes Dunlap (Oxford: Clarendon Press, 1957), 5.

6. *The Greek Anthology*, trans. W. R. Paton (London and Cambridge, Mass.: Loeb Classical Library, 1916), 1:243–45.

7. *The Poetical Works of Robert Herrick*, ed. L. C. Martin (Oxford: Clarendon Press, 1956), 84.

8. Ibid., 84.

9. Andrew Marvell, *Complete Poetry*, ed. George deF. Lord (New York: Modern Library, 1968), 25.

10. *The Poems of Richard Lovelace*, ed. C. H. Wilkinson (Oxford: Clarendon Press, 1963), 48.

11. John E. Sitter, *The Poetry of Pope's Dunciad* (Minneapolis: Univ. of Minnesota Press, 1971), 94.

12. Aubrey L. Williams, *Pope's Dunciad: A Study of Its Meaning* (1955; rpt. Archon Books, 1968), 15.

13. *The Dunciad*, in *The Poems of Alexander Pope*, ed. James Sutherland, vol. 5. All citations from *The Dunciad* are to this edition.

14. Ibid., 283n.

15. Ibid., 284n.

16. Ibid., 286–87n.

17. Ibid., 287n.

18. See *Dunciad* 1.141, for an earlier mention of Ogilby.

19. Perhaps not so abruptly for Pope and his contemporaries as for us, since Ogilby had done a version of Aesop's fables.

20. See *Dunciad* 1.37–42, for earlier generic confusion.

21. Samuel Richardson, *Clarissa* (Oxford: Basil Blackwell, 1943), 3:153.

22. For the implicit sexuality of the pietà grouping see Leo Steinberg, "The Metaphors of Love and Birth in Michelangelo's Pietas," in *Studies in Erotic Art*, ed. Theodore Bowie and Cornelia V. Christenson (New York: Basic Books, 1970).

23. *Dunciad*, 182n.

24. Ian Jack, *Augustan Satire: Intention and Idiom in English Poetry, 1660–1750* (1952; rpt. London: Oxford Univ. Press, 1970), 133.

25. Williams, *Pope's Dunciad,* 89.

26. Ibid., 44.

27. *Dunciad,* 356, note to line 149.

28. See W. B. Carnochan, "Swift's *Tale:* On Satire, Negation, and the Uses of Irony," *Eighteenth Century Studies* 5 (1971): 122–44.

29. *Dunciad,* 391, note to lines 499, 500.

30. Miriam Leranbaum, *Alexander Pope's "Opus Magnum," 1729–1744* (Oxford: Clarendon Press, 1977).

31. *Dunciad,* 396, note to line 553.

CHAPTER 7. SWIFT

1. For a minority view of the "Project" see Leland D. Peterson, "Swift's *Project:* A Religious and Political Satire," *PMLA* 82 (1967): 54–63. For a range of viewpoints see Ronald Paulson, *The Fictions of Satire,* passim, and Irvin Ehrenpreis, *Acts of Implication: Suggestion and Covert Meaning in the Works of Dryden, Swift, Pope and Austen* (Berkeley and Los Angeles: Univ. of California Press, 1980), 51–82.

2. For an explanation of boundary genre, see Gary Saul Morson, *The Boundaries of Genre: Dostoevsky's "Diary of a Writer" and the Traditions of Literary Utopia* (Austin: Univ. of Texas Press, 1981).

3. "Verses on the Death of Dr. Swift, D.S.P.D" in *Poems,* ed. Harold Williams (Oxford: Clarendon Press, 1958), vol. 3:

Arbuthnot is no more my Friend,
Who dares to Irony pretend;
Which I was born to introduce,
Refin'd it first, and shew'd its Use. (55–8)

4. *A Tale of a Tub,* ed. A. C. Guthkelch and D. Nichol Smith, 2d ed. (Oxford: Clarendon Press, 1958). All citations are from this edition.

5. The essentially conservative satirists we have been studying object to the vulgarity of the marketplace and the new monied interests. F. P. Lock sees this bias as a characteristic of Swift's Tory sensibility (*Swift's Tory Politics* [Newark: Univ. of Delaware Press, 1983], 110–15, 168). This attitude underlies the obvious allegorical meaning of the passage, which has to do with the Catholic selling of indulgences prior to the Reformation.

6. Pope, "*Nature* and *Homer* were, he found, the same." *Essay on Criticism,* l. 135. See Emerson R. Marks, *The Poetics of Reason: English Neoclassical Criticism* (New York: Random House, 1968), 87–97.

7. F. R. Leavis, "The Irony of Swift," in *Swift: A Collection of Critical Essays,* ed. Ernest Tuveson (Englewood Cliffs, N.J.: Prentice-Hall, 1964), 15–29. Reprinted from *Determinations,* ed. F. R. Leavis (London: Chatto and Windus, 1934), 79–108.

8. Robert C. Elliott, *The Literary Persona* (Chicago: Univ. of Chicago Press, 1982), 128.

9. Ibid., 129.

10. On this Elliott (*Literary Persona*, 132) and Irvin Ehrenpreis, a principal opponent of the concept of persona, agree. See *Swift: The Man, His Works, and the Age* (Cambridge, Mass.: Harvard Univ. Press, 1962–83), 3:629.

11. *The Prose Works of Jonathan Swift*, ed. Herbert Davis (Oxford: Basil Blackwell, 1939–1968), vol. 12.

12. Swift, *Prose Works*, vol. 11.

13. For an analysis of this controversy see Elliott, *Literary Persona*, chap. 6, 107–23.

14. See John Traugott, "A Tale of a Tub," in *The Character of Swift's Satire: A Revised Focus*, ed. Claude Rawson (Newark: Univ. of Delaware Press, 1983), 83–126, for a spirited attack on the concept of the persona. For Traugott, the extravagances of the tale-teller are Swift's.

15. Leo Strauss, *The Political Philosophy of Hobbes* (Chicago: Univ. of Chicago Press, 1963), xv. Strauss's point is examined in Jack G. Gilbert, *Jonathan Swift: Romantic and Cynic Moralist* (Austin: Univ. of Texas Press, 1966), 120.

16. Nigel Dennis, *Jonathan Swift* (New York: Collier Books, 1967), 122–28.

17. For a discussion of possible meanings of the parallels between the *Odyssey* and *Gulliver's Travels*, see Thomas E. Maresca, *Epic to Novel* (Columbus: Ohio State Univ. Press, 1974), 171–73.

18. According to Northrop Frye, *Anatomy of Criticism*, 187, the romance hero is usually a third son. Odysseus is an only son; Gulliver, on the other hand, is indeed a third son.

19. Northrop Frye calls the descent narrative "the radical of satire" (*The Secular Scripture: A Study of the Structure of Romance* [Cambridge, Mass.: Harvard Univ. Press, 1976], 120).

20. All references to *Gulliver's Travels* are to *The Prose Works of Jonathan Swift*, ed. Herbert Davis (Oxford: Basil Blackwell, 1939–68), vol. 11.

21. Aldous Huxley, "Tragedy and the Whole Truth," in *Collected Essays* (New York: Harper & Brothers, 1959), 98.

22. See my "*Gulliver's Travels*, I, vi Reconsidered," *English Language Notes* 21 (1984): 44–53, for Swift's debt to Xenophon, especially to his *Politeia of the Spartans*.

23. See Fernand Braudel, *Civilization and Capitalism: 15th–18th Century*, trans. Siân Reynolds (New York: Harper & Row, 1979), 1:203–6.

24. A. C. Elias, Jr., *Swift At Moor Park: Problems in Biography and Criticism* (Philadelphia: Univ. of Pennsylvania Press, 1982).

25. The classic study of the ancients vs. moderns debate remains Richard Foster Jones, *Ancients and Moderns: A Study of the Rise of the Scientific Movement in Seventeenth-Century England* (1961; rpt. Berkeley and Los Angeles: Univ. of California Press, 1965).

26. Sir William Temple, *Five Miscellaneous Essays*, ed. Samuel Holt Monk (Ann Arbor: Univ. of Michigan Press, 1963), 95.

27. Ibid., 95.

28. Juvenal, Satire 1, 79. "Talent perhaps I lack, but anger's an inspiration . . ." (Humphries translation, 20).

29. Juvenal, Satire 1, 85–6. "I must cover it all in this olio, everything human, /

Passion and prayer and fear, pleasure, distraction, and rage." (Humphries translation, 20).

CHAPTER 8. CONCLUSION

1. For speculation on some reasons for satire's form, see my "Socrates and Post-Socratic Satire," *Journal of the History of Ideas* 46 (1985): 3–12.

2. Claude Lévi-Strauss, *The Savage Mind* (Chicago: Univ. of Chicago Press, 1966), 16–36.

3. Simone Weil, *The Iliad or The Poem of Force* (Wallingford, Pa.: Pendle Hill, n.d.).

SELECTED BIBLIOGRAPHY

Abrams, M. H. *The Mirror and the Lamp: Romantic Theory and the Critical Tradition.* New York: Oxford Univ. Press, 1953.

Adams, Robert P. *The Better Part of Valor: More, Erasmus, Colet, and Vives on Humanism, War, and Peace, 1496–1535.* Seattle: Univ. of Washington Press, 1962.

Aden, John M. *Pope's Once and Future Kings: Satire and Politics in the Early Career.* Knoxville: Univ. of Tennessee Press, 1978.

———. *Something Like Horace: Studies in the Art and Allusion of Pope's Horatian Satires.* Nashville, Tenn.: Vanderbilt Univ. Press, 1969.

Allinson, Francis G. *Lucian: Satirist and Artist.* New York: Longman, 1927.

Anderson, William S. *Essays on Roman Satire.* Princeton: Princeton Univ. Press, 1982.

———. "Juvenal and Quintilian." *Yale Classical Studies* 17 (1961): 3–93.

———. "The Mock-Heroic Mode in Roman Satire and Alexander Pope." In *Satire in the 18th Century.* Ed. J. D. Browning. New York: Garland, 1983, 198–213.

———. "Studies in Book I of Juvenal." *Yale Classical Studies* 15 (1957): 33–90.

Anselment, Raymond A. *"Betwixt Jest and Earnest": Marprelate, Milton, Marvell, Swift and the Decorum of Religious Ridicule.* Toronto: Univ. of Toronto Press, 1979.

Ariosto, Ludovico. *The Satires of Ludovico Ariosto: A Renaissance Autobiography.* Trans. Peter DeSa Wiggins. Athens, Ohio: Ohio Univ. Press, 1976.

Aristophanes. *The Complete Plays.* Ed. Moses Hadas. New York: Bantam Books, 1962.

Aristotle. *The Complete Works: The Revised Oxford Translation.* Ed. Jonathan Barnes. 2 vols. Princeton: Princeton Univ. Press, 1984.

Arrowsmith, William. "Luxury and Death in the *Satyricon.*" *Arion* 5 (1966): 304–31.

Athenaeus. *The Deipnosophists, or Banquet of the Learned.* Trans. C. D. Yonge. 3 vols. London: Bohn, 1853.

Auden, W. H. *The Dyer's Hand and Other Essays.* New York: Random House, 1962.

Auerbach, Erich. *Mimesis: The Representation of Reality in Western Literature.* Trans. Willard R. Trask. Princeton: Princeton Univ. Press, 1953.

Bakhtin, M. M. *The Dialogic Imagination: Four Essays.* Ed. Michael Holquist. Trans. Caryl Emerson and Michael Holquist. Austin: Univ. of Texas Press, 1981.

———. *Problems of Dostoevsky's Poetics.* Ed. and trans. Caryl Emerson. Minneapolis: Univ. of Minnesota Press, 1984.

———. *Rabelais and His World.* Trans. Helene Iswolsky. Cambridge, Mass.: MIT Press, 1968.

Baldwin, Barry. *Studies in Lucian.* Toronto: Hakkert, 1973.

Ball, Alan Perley. *The Satire of Seneca on the Apotheosis of Claudius.* New York: Columbia Univ. Press, 1902.

Bate, W. Jackson. "Johnson and Satire Manqué." In *Eighteenth-Century Studies in Honor of Donald F. Hyde.* Ed. W. H. Bond. New York: The Grolier Club, 1970, 145–60.

Bateson, F. W. *English Comic Drama, 1700–1750.* Oxford: Clarendon Press, 1929.

Batten, Charles L., Jr. *Pleasurable Instruction: Form and Convention in Eighteenth-Century Travel Literature.* Berkeley and Los Angeles: Univ. of California Press, 1978.

Beaty, Frederick L. *Byron the Satirist.* De Kalb: Northern Illinois Univ. Press, 1985.

Beaumont, Charles Allen. *Swift's Classical Rhetoric.* Athens, Ga.: Univ. of Georgia Press, 1961.

Birney, Alice Lotvin. *Satiric Catharsis in Shakespeare: A Theory of Dramatic Structure.* Berkeley and Los Angeles: Univ. of California Press, 1973.

Bjornson, Richard. *The Picaresque Hero in European Fiction.* Madison: Univ. of Wisconsin Press, 1977.

Bloom, Edward A. and Lillian D. Bloom. "Johnson's 'Mournful Narrative': The Rhetoric of 'London.'" In *Eighteenth-Century Studies in Honor of Donald F. Hyde,* ed. W. H. Bond. New York: The Grolier Club, 1970, 107–44.

———. *Satire's Persuasive Voice.* Ithaca, N.Y.: Cornell Univ. Press, 1979.

Bogel, Fredric V. "Dulness Unbound: Rhetoric and Pope's *Dunciad.*" *PMLA* 97 (1982): 844–55.

Booth, Wayne C. *A Rhetoric of Irony.* Chicago: Univ. of Chicago Press, 1974.

Boyd, John D. *The Function of Mimesis and Its Decline.* 2d ed. New York: Fordham Univ. Press, 1980.

Bramble, J. C. *Persius and the Programmatic Satire: A Study in Form and Imagery.* Cambridge: Cambridge Univ. Press, 1974.

Brant, Sebastian. *The Ship of Fools.* Trans. Edwin H. Zeydel. New York: Columbia Univ. Press, 1944.

Braudel, Fernand. *Civilization and Capitalism: 15th-18th Century.* Trans. Siân Reynolds. 3 vols. New York: Harper & Row, 1981–84.

Brooks-Davies, Douglas. *Pope's "Dunciad" and the Queen of Night: A Study in Emotional Jacobitism.* Manchester: Manchester Univ. Press, 1985.

Brower, Reuben Arthur. *Alexander Pope: The Poetry of Allusion.* Oxford: Clarendon Press, 1959.

Bryant, J. A., Jr. *The Compassionate Satirist: Ben Jonson and His Imperfect World.* Athens, Ga.: Univ. of Georgia Press, 1972.

Bullitt, John M. *Jonathan Swift and the Anatomy of Satire.* Cambridge, Mass.: Harvard Univ. Press, 1954.

Burke, Kenneth. *A Grammar of Motives.* New York: Prentice-Hall, 1954.

———. *Language as Symbolic Action: Essays on Life, Literature, and Method.* Berkeley and Los Angeles: Univ. of California Press, 1966.

———. *A Rhetoric of Motives.* Berkeley and Los Angeles: Univ. of California Press, 1969.

Butler, Marilyn. *Peacock Displayed: A Satirist in His Context.* London: Routledge & Kegan Paul, 1979.

Cable, Chester. "*Absalom and Achitophel* as Epic Satire." In *Studies in Honor of John Wilcox,* ed. A. D. Wallace and W. O. Ross. Detroit: Wayne State Univ. Press, 1958, 51–60.

Campbell, Oscar James. *Comicall Satyre and Shakespeare's "Troilus and Cressida."* San Marino, Calif.: Huntington Library, 1938.

———. *Shakespeare's Satire.* New York: Oxford Univ. Press, 1943.

Caputi, Anthony. *John Marston, Satirist.* Ithaca, N.Y.: Cornell Univ. Press, 1961.

Carnochan, W. B. *Confinement and Flight: An Essay on English Literature of the Eighteenth Century.* Berkeley and Los Angeles: Univ. of California Press, 1977.

———. *Lemuel Gulliver's Mirror for Man.* Berkeley and Los Angeles: Univ. of California Press, 1968.

———. "Satire, Sublimity, and Sentiment: Theory and Practice in Post-Augustan Satire." *PMLA* 85 (1970): 260–7.

———. "Swift's *Tale:* On Satire, Negation, and the Uses of Irony." *Eighteenth-Century Studies* 5 (1971): 122–44.

Carretta, Vincent. *The Snarling Muse: Verbal and Visual Political Satire From Pope to Churchill.* Philadelphia: Univ. of Pennsylvania Press, 1983.

Casaubon, Isaac. *De Satyrica Graecorum Poesi & Romanorum Satira.* Delmar, N.Y.: Scholars' Facsimiles and Reprints, 1973.

Cervantes, Miguel Saavedra de. *Don Quijote De La Mancha.* Ed. Martin De Riquer. 2 vols. Barcelona: Editorial Juventud, 1967.

Chernaik, Warren L. *The Poet's Time: Politics and Religion in the Work of Andrew Marvell.* Cambridge: Cambridge Univ. Press, 1983.

Clark, Arthur Melville. *Studies in Literary Modes.* Edinburgh and London: Oliver and Boyd, 1946.

Clark, John R. *Form and Frenzy in Swift's Tale of a Tub.* Ithaca, N.Y.: Cornell Univ. Press, 1970.

Cleveland, John. *The Poems.* Ed. Brian Morris and Eleanor Withington. Oxford: Clarendon Press, 1967.

Cohen, Ralph. "On the Interrelations of Eighteenth-Century Literary Forms." In *New Approaches to Eighteenth-Century Literature,* ed. Phillip Harth. New York: Columbia Univ. Press, 1974, 33–78.

Colie, Rosalie L. *The Resources of Kind: Genre-Theory in the Renaissance.* Ed. Barbara K. Lewalski. Berkeley and Los Angeles: Univ. of California Press, 1973.

Coffey, Michael. *Roman Satire.* London: Methuen, 1976.

Cook, Richard I. *Swift as a Tory Pamphleteer.* Seattle: Univ. of Washington Press, 1967.

Corbett, Philip B. *Petronius.* New York: Twayne, 1970.

Cornford, Francis Macdonald. *The Origin of Attic Comedy.* Ed. Theodore H. Gaster. Garden City, N.Y.: Anchor Books, 1961.

Courtney, E. "Parody and Literary Allusion in Menippean Satire." *Philologus* 106 (1962): 86–100.

Culler, Jonathan. *Structuralist Poetics: Structuralism, Linguistics, and the Study of Literature.* Ithaca, N.Y.: Cornell Univ. Press, 1975.

Curtius, Ernst Robert. *European Literature and the Latin Middle Ages.* Trans. Willard R. Trask. 1953; rpt. New York: Harper Torchbooks, 1963.

Dane, Joseph A. "Parody and Satire: A Theoretical Model." *Genre* 13 (1980): 145–59.

Davies, Godfrey. "The Conclusion of Dryden's *Absalom and Achitophel.*" *Huntington Library Quarterly* 10 (1946–47): 69–82.

Davis, Herbert. *Jonathan Swift: Essays on His Satire and Other Studies.* New York: Oxford Univ. Press, 1964.

Dennis, Nigel. *Jonathan Swift: A Short Character.* New York: Collier Books, 1964.

De Porte, Michael. *Nightmares and Hobbyhorses: Swift, Sterne, and Augustan Ideas of Madness.* San Marino: Huntington Library, 1974.

———. "Swift and the License of Satire." In *Satire in the 18th Century*, ed. J. D. Browning. New York: Garland, 1983, 53–69.

Dessen, Cynthia S. *Junctura Callidas Acri: A Study of Persius' Satires.* Illinois Studies in Language and Literature 59. Urbana: Univ. of Illinois Press, 1968.

Dio Chrysostom. [*Works*]. Trans. J. H. Cohoon and H. Lamar Crosby. 5 vols. London and Cambridge, Mass.: Loeb Classical Library, 1939–51.

Dixon, Peter. *The World of Pope's Satires: An Introduction to the Epistles and Imitations of Horace.* London: Methuen, 1968.

Donne, John. *Ignatius His Conclave.* Ed. T. S. Healy. Oxford: Clarendon Press, 1969.

Donoghue, Denis. *Jonathan Swift: A Critical Introduction.* Cambridge: Cambridge Univ. Press, 1969.

Doody, Margaret Anne. *The Daring Muse: Augustan Poetry Reconsidered.* Cambridge: Cambridge Univ. Press, 1985.

Dover, K. J. *Aristophanic Comedy.* Berkeley and Los Angeles: Univ. of California Press, 1972.

Dryden, John. *Of Dramatic Poesy and Other Critical Essays.* Ed. George Watson. 2 vols. New York: Everyman's Library, 1962.

———. *The Works.* Ed. E. N. Hooker et al. 20 vols. Berkeley and Los Angeles: Univ. of California Press, 1956–.

Duff, J. Wight. *Roman Satire: Its Outlook on Social Life.* Berkeley: Univ. of California Press, 1936.

Duisit, Lionel. *Satire, parodie, calembour: esquisse d'une théorie des modes dévalués.* Stanford French and Italian Studies 11. Saratoga, Calif.: Anima Libri, 1978.

Dyson, A. E. *The Crazy Fabric: Essays in Irony.* London: Macmillan, 1966.

Eagleton, Terry. *Literary Theory: An Introduction.* Minneapolis: Univ. of Minnesota Press, 1983.

Edwards, Thomas R. *Imagination and Power: A Study of Poetry on Public Themes.* New York: Oxford Univ. Press, 1971.

———. *This Dark Estate: A Reading of Pope.* Berkeley and Los Angeles: Univ. of California Press, 1963.

Ehrenpreis, Irvin. *Acts of Implication: Suggestion and Covert Meaning in the Works of Dryden, Swift, Pope, and Austen.* Berkeley and Los Angeles: Univ. of California Press, 1980.
———. *Literary Meaning and Augustan Values.* Charlottesville: Univ. Press of Virginia, 1974.
———. *"Personae."* In *Restoration and Eighteenth-Century Literature Essays in Honor of Alan Dugald McKillop,* ed. Carroll Camden. Chicago: Univ. of Chicago Press, 1963, 25–37.
———. *Swift: The Man, His Works, and the Age.* 3 vols. Cambridge, Mass.: Harvard Univ. Press, 1962–83.
———. *"Swiftian Dilemmas."* In *Satire in the 18th Century,* ed. J. D. Browning. New York: Garland, 1983, 214–31.
Ehrlich, Victor. *Russian Formalism: History, Doctrine.* 2d ed. The Hague: Mouton, 1965.
Elias, A. C., Jr. *Swift at Moor Park: Problems in Biography and Criticism.* Philadelphia: Univ. of Pennsylvania Press, 1982.
Elkin, P. K. *The Augustan Defence of Satire.* Oxford: Clarendon Press, 1973.
Elliott, Robert C. *The Literary Persona.* Chicago: Univ. of Chicago Press, 1982.
———. *The Power of Satire: Magic, Ritual, Art.* Princeton: Princeton Univ. Press, 1960.
———. *The Shape of Utopia: Studies in a Literary Genre.* Chicago: Univ. of Chicago Press, 1970.
Engell, James. *The Creative Imagination: Enlightenment to Romanticism.* Cambridge, Mass.: Harvard Univ. Press, 1981.
England, A. B. *Energy and Order in the Poetry of Swift.* Lewisburg, Pa.: Bucknell Univ. Press, 1980.
Erasmus, Desiderius. *The Julius Exclusus.* Trans. Paul Pascal. Bloomington: Indiana Univ. Press, 1968.
———. *The Praise of Folly.* Trans. Clarence H. Miller. New Haven: Yale Univ. Press, 1979.
———. *The Praise of Folly.* Trans. Hoyt Hopewell Hudson. Princeton: Princeton Univ. Press, 1941.
Erskine-Hill, Howard. *The Augustan Idea in English Literature.* London: Edward Arnold, 1983.
Fairer, David. *Pope's Imagination.* Manchester: Manchester Univ. Press, 1984.
Farley-Hills, David. *Rochester's Poetry.* London: Bell & Hyman, 1978.
Feinberg, Leonard. *Introduction to Satire.* Ames: Iowa State Univ. Press, 1967.
———. *The Satirist: His Temperament, Motivation, and Influence.* Ames: Iowa State Univ. Press, 1963.
Ferguson, Oliver W. *Jonathan Swift and Ireland.* Urbana: Univ. of Illinois Press, 1962.
Fergusson, Francis. *The Human Image in Dramatic Literature.* Garden City, N.Y.: Anchor Books, 1957.
———. *The Idea of a Theater.* Princeton: Princeton Univ. Press, 1949.
———. *Literary Landmarks: Essays on the Theory and Practice of Literature.* New Brunswick, N.J.: Rutgers Univ. Press, 1975.
Fielding, Henry. *The Wesleyan Edition.* Ed. Martin C. Battestin et al. 6 vols. Middletown, Conn.: Wesleyan Univ. Press, 1967–.

Fischer, John Irwin. *On Swift's Poetry.* Gainesville: Univ. Presses of Florida, 1978.
Fiske, George Converse. *Lucilius and Horace: A Study in the Classical Theory of Imitation.* Wisconsin Studies in Language and Literature, No. 7. Madison: Univ. of Wisconsin Press, 1920.
Ford, Patrick K., trans. *The Mabinogi and Other Welsh Tales.* Berkeley and Los Angeles: Univ. of California Press, 1977.
Fowler, Alastair. *Kinds of Literature: An Introduction to the Theory of Genres and Modes.* Cambridge, Mass.: Harvard Univ. Press, 1982.
Fraenkel, Eduard. *Horace.* Oxford: Clarendon Press, 1957.
Fränkel, Hermann. *Early Greek Poetry and Philosophy.* Trans. Moses Hadas and James Willis. New York: Harcourt Brace, 1973.
Francis, Philip. *The Odes of Horace.* London and New York, n.d.
Freedman, Morris. "Dryden's Miniature Epic." *Journal of English and Germanic Philology* 57 (1958): 211–19.
Frye, Northrop. *Anatomy of Criticism.* Princeton: Princeton Univ. Press, 1957.
———. "The Nature of Satire." *University of Toronto Quarterly* 14 (1944–45): 75–89.
———. *The Secular Scripture: A Study of the Structure of Romance.* Cambridge, Mass.: Harvard Univ. Press, 1976.
Fuess, Claude Moore. *Lord Byron as a Satirist in Verse.* New York: Columbia Univ. Press, 1912.
Fussell, Paul. *The Rhetorical World of Augustan Humanism: Ethics and Imagery From Swift to Burke.* Oxford: Clarendon Press, 1965.
Garrison, James D. *Dryden and the Tradition of Panegyric.* Berkeley and Los Angeles: Univ. of California Press, 1975.
Gilbert, Jack G. *Jonathan Swift: Romantic and Cynic Moralist.* Austin: Univ. of Texas Press, 1966.
Goldgar, Bertrand A. *Walpole and the Wits: The Relation of Politics to Literature, 1722–1742.* Lincoln: Univ. of Nebraska Press, 1976.
Goodman, Paul. *The Structure of Literature.* Chicago: Univ. of Chicago Press, 1954.
Greek Anthology, The. Trans. W. R. Paton. 5 vols. London and Cambridge, Mass.: Loeb Classical Library, 1916.
Griffin, Dustin H. *Alexander Pope: The Poet in the Poems.* Princeton: Princeton Univ. Press, 1978.
———. "Dryden's Charles: The Ending of *Absalom and Achitophel.*" *Philological Quarterly* 57 (1978): 359–82.
———. "Satiric Closure." *Genre* 18 (1985): 173–89.
———. *Satires Against Man: The Poems of Rochester.* Berkeley and Los Angeles: Univ. of California Press, 1973.
Grube, G. M. A. *The Greek and Roman Critics.* London: Methuen, 1965.
Guilhamet, Leon. "Dryden's Debasement of Scripture in *Absalom and Achitophel.*" *SEL* 9 (1969): 395–413.
———. "*Gulliver's Travels,* I, vi Reconsidered." *English Language Notes* 21 (1984): 44–53.
———. "Socrates and Post-Socratic Satire." *Journal of the History of Ideas,* 46 (1985): 3–12.

Guillén, Claudio. *Literature as System: Essays Toward the Theory of Literary History.* Princeton: Princeton Univ. Press, 1971.

Guite, Harold. "An 18th-Century View of Roman Satire." In *The Varied Pattern: Studies in the 18th Century,* ed. Peter Hughes and David Williams. Publications of the McMaster University Association for 18th-Century Studies, vol. 1. Toronto: Hakkert, 1971, 113–20.

Haight, Elizabeth Hazelton. *Essays on Ancient Fiction.* New York: Longman, 1936.

Halsband, Robert. *Lord Hervey: Eighteenth-Century Courtier.* New York: Oxford Univ. Press, 1974.

Hamburger, Käte. *The Logic of Literature.* 2d ed. Trans. Marilynn J. Rose. Bloomington: Indiana Univ. Press, 1973.

Hammond, Paul. *John Oldham and the Renewal of Classical Culture.* Cambridge: Cambridge Univ. Press, 1983.

Harth, Phillip. *Contexts of Dryden's Thought.* Chicago: Univ. of Chicago Press, 1968.

———. *Swift and Anglican Rationalism: The Religious Background of "A Tale of a Tub."* Chicago: Univ. of Chicago Press, 1961.

Heiserman, Arthur. *The Novel Before the Novel: Essays and Discussions About the Beginnings of Prose Fiction in the West.* Chicago: Univ. of Chicago Press, 1977.

———. "Satire in the *Utopia.*" PMLA 78 (1963): 163–74.

———. *Skelton and Satire.* Chicago: Univ. of Chicago Press, 1961.

Hernadi, Paul. *Beyond Genre: New Directions in Literary Classification.* Ithaca, N.Y.: Cornell Univ. Press, 1972.

Herrick, Robert. *Poetical Works.* Ed. L. C. Martin. Oxford: Clarendon Press, 1956.

Hester, Thomas M. *Kinde Pitty and Brave Scorn: John Donne's Satyres.* Durham, N.C.: Duke Univ. Press, 1982.

Higginbotham, John, ed. *Greek and Latin Literature: A Comparative Study.* London: Methuen, 1969.

Highet, Gilbert. *The Anatomy of Satire.* Princeton: Princeton Univ. Press, 1962.

———. *Juvenal The Satirist: A Study.* Oxford: Clarendon Press, 1954.

———. "Petronius the Moralist." *Transactions of the American Philological Association* 72 (1941): 176–94.

———. *The Speeches in Vergil's Aeneid.* Princeton: Princeton Univ. Press, 1972.

Hirsch, E. D., Jr. *The Aims of Interpretation.* Chicago: Univ. of Chicago Press, 1976.

———. *Validity in Interpretation.* New Haven: Yale Univ. Press, 1967.

Hodgart, Matthew. *Satire.* New York: McGraw-Hill, 1969.

Hoffman, Arthur W. *John Dryden's Imagery.* Gainesville: Univ. of Florida Press, 1962.

Holden, William P. *Anti-Puritan Satire, 1572–1642.* New Haven: Yale Univ. Press, 1954.

Holland, Philip. "Robert Burton's *Anatomy of Melancholy* and Menippean Satire, Humanist and English." Ph.D. diss., Univ. of London, 1979.

Holloway, John. "The Well-Filled Dish: An Analysis of Swift's Satire." *Hudson Review* 9 (1956): 20–37.

Hope, A. D. "The Satiric Muse." In *The Cave and the Spring.* Chicago: Univ. of Chicago Press, 1970, 61–67.

Hopkins, Kenneth. *Portraits in Satire.* London: Barrie Books, 1958.

Hopkins, Robert H. *The True Genius of Oliver Goldsmith*. Baltimore: Johns Hopkins Univ. Press, 1969.

Horace, *Satires, Epistles and Ars Poetica*. Ed. and trans. H. Rushton Fairclough. London and Cambridge, Mass.: Loeb Classical Library, 1929.

Horace and Persius. *Satires*. Trans. Niall Rudd. New York: Penguin, 1973.

Huchon, René. *George Crabbe and His Times: 1754–1832*. London, 1907; rpt. New York: Barnes & Noble, 1968.

Hume, Robert D. *The Rakish Stage: Studies in English Drama, 1660–1800*. Carbondale and Edwardsville: Southern Illinois Univ. Press, 1983.

Hunter, J. Paul. *Occasional Form: Henry Fielding and the Chains of Circumstance*. Baltimore: Johns Hopkins Univ. Press, 1975.

Jack, Ian. *Augustan Satire: Intention and Idiom in English Poetry, 1660–1750*. Oxford: Clarendon Press, 1952.

Jaffe, Nora Crow. *The Poet Swift*. Hanover, N.H.: Univ. Press of New England, 1977.

Jebb, Sir Richard. *Essays and Addresses*. Cambridge: Cambridge Univ. Press, 1907.

Jemielity, Thomas. "*The Vanity of Human Wishes*: Satire Foiled or Achieved." *Essays in Literature* 11 (1984): 35–45.

Jensen, H. James, and Malvin R. Zirker, Jr. *The Satirist's Art*. Bloomington: Indiana Univ. Press, 1972.

Jones, Richard Foster. *Ancients and Moderns: A Study of the Rise of the Scientific Movement in Seventeenth-Century England*. St. Louis, 1961; rpt. Berkeley and Los Angeles: Univ. of California Press, 1965.

Juvenal. *The Satires*. Trans. Rolfe Humphries. Bloomington: Indiana Univ. Press, 1958.

Kaiser, Walter. *Praisers of Folly: Erasmus, Rabelais, Shakespeare*. London: Gollancz, 1964.

Kallen, Horace M. *Liberty, Laughter, and Tears: Reflections on the Relations of Comedy and Tragedy to Human Freedom*. De Kalb: Northern Illinois Univ. Press, 1968.

Kantra, Robert A. *All Things Vain: Religious Satirists and Their Art*. University Park, Pa.: Pennsylvania State Univ. Press, 1984.

Keener, Frederick M. *The Chain of Becoming: The Philosophical Tale, the Novel, and A Neglected Realism of the Enlightenment: Swift, Montesquieu, Voltaire, Johnson, and Austen*. New York: Columbia Univ. Press, 1983.

———. *English Dialogues of the Dead: A Critical History, An Anthology, and a Check List*. New York: Columbia Univ. Press, 1973.

Kern, Jean B. *Dramatic Satire in the Age of Walpole, 1720–1750*. Ames: Iowa State Univ. Press, 1976.

Kernan, Alvin. *The Cankered Muse: Satire of the English Renaissance*. New Haven, 1959; rpt. Hamden, Conn.: Archon, 1976.

———. *The Plot of Satire*. New Haven: Yale Univ. Press, 1965.

Kierkegaard, Søren. *The Concept of Irony: With Constant Reference to Socrates*. Trans. Lee M. Capel. Bloomington: Indiana Univ. Press, 1968.

Kirk, Eugene P. *Menippean Satire: An Annotated Catalogue of Texts and Criticism*. New York: Garland, 1980.

Knoche, Ulrich. *Roman Satire*. Trans. Edwin S. Ramage. Bloomington: Indiana Univ. Press, 1975.

Knox, Ronald. *Essays in Satire*. 1928; rpt. Port Washington, N.Y.: Kennikat, 1968.

Korkowski, Eugene. "Donne's *Ignatius* and Menippean Satire." *Studies in Philology* 72 (1975): 419–38.

———. "Genre and Satiric Strategy in Burton's *Anatomy of Melancholy.*" *Genre* 8 (1975): 74–87.

———. "Menippus and His Imitators: A Conspectus, Up to Sterne, for a Misunderstood Genre." Ph.D. diss., Univ. of California, San Diego, 1973.

———. "With an Eye to the Bunghole: Figures of Containment in *A Tale of a Tub.*" *SEL* 15 (1975): 391–408.

Korshin, Paul J. *Typologies in England: 1650–1820.* Princeton: Princeton Univ. Press, 1982.

Kupersmith, William. *Roman Satirists in Seventeenth-Century England.* Lincoln: Univ. of Nebraska Press, 1985.

Lall, Rama Rani. *Satiric Fable in English: A Critical Study of the Animal Tales of Chaucer, Spenser, Dryden, and Orwell.* New Delhi: New Statesman Publishing, 1979.

Lawlor, John. "Radical Satire and the Realistic Novel." *Essays and Studies* 9 (1955): 58–75.

Leavis, F. R. "The Irony of Swift." In *Determinations,* ed. F. R. Leavis. London: Chatto and Windus, 1934, 79–108.

Lee, Jae Num. *Swift and Scatological Satire.* Albuquerque: Univ. of New Mexico Press, 1971.

Leranbaum, Miriam. *Alexander Pope's "Opus Magnum," 1729–1744.* Oxford: Clarendon Press, 1977.

Lesky, Albin. *A History of Greek Literature.* Trans. James Willis and Cornelis de Heer. New York: Crowell, 1966.

Levin, Harry. "The Wages of Satire." In *Literature and Society: Selected Papers From the English Institute, 1978,* ed. Edward W. Said. Baltimore: Johns Hopkins Univ. Press, 1980, 1–14.

Lévi-Strauss, Claude. *The Savage Mind.* Chicago: Univ. of Chicago Press, 1966.

Leyburn, Ellen Douglas. *Satiric Allegory: Mirror of Man.* New Haven: Yale Univ. Press, 1956.

Lock, F. P. *The Politics of "Gulliver's Travels."* Oxford: Clarendon Press, 1980.

———. *Swift's Tory Politics.* Newark: Univ. of Delaware Press, 1983.

Lockwood, Thomas. *Post-Augustan Satire: Charles Churchill and Satirical Poetry, 1750–1800.* Seattle: Univ. of Washington Press, 1979.

Loftis, John. *Comedy and Society From Congreve to Fielding.* Stanford: Stanford University Press, 1959.

———. *The Politics of Drama in Augustan England.* Oxford: Clarendon Press, 1963.

Logan, George M. *The Meaning of More's "Utopia."* Princeton: Princeton Univ. Press, 1983.

Lord, George deF. "*Absalom and Achitophel* and Dryden's Political Cosmos." In *John Dryden,* ed. Earl Miner. Athens, Ohio: Ohio Univ. Press, 1972.

———. *Heroic Mockery: Variations on Epic Themes from Homer to Joyce.* Newark: Univ. of Delaware Press, 1977.

——— et al., eds. *Poems on Affairs of State: Augustan Satirical Verse, 1660–1714.* 7 vols. New Haven: Yale Univ. Press, 1963–75.

Lovelace, Richard. *The Poems*. Ed. C. H. Wilkinson. Oxford: Clarendon Press, 1963.

Lyles, Albert M. *Methodism Mocked: The Satiric Reaction to Methodism in the Eighteenth Century*. London: Epworth, 1960.

Mack, Maynard. *Alexander Pope: A Life*. New York and London: W. W. Norton, in association with New Haven and London: Yale Univ. Press, 1985.

——. *"Collected In Himself"*: *Essays Critical, Biographical, and Bibliographical on Pope and Some of His Contemporaries*. Newark: Univ. of Delaware Press, 1983.

——, ed. *Essential Articles for the Study of Alexander Pope*. Rev. ed. Hamden, Conn.: Archon, 1968.

——. *The Garden and the City: Retirement and Politics in the Later Poetry of Pope, 1731–1743*. Toronto: Univ. of Toronto Press, 1969.

——. "The Muse of Satire." *Yale Review* 41 (1951): 80–92.

—— and James A. Winn, eds. *Pope: Recent Essays by Several Hands*. Hamden, Conn.: Archon, 1980.

——. " 'Wit and Poetry and Pope': Some Observations on His Imagery." In *Pope and His Contemporaries: Essays Presented to George Sherburn*, ed. James L. Clifford and Louis A. Landa. New York: Oxford Univ. Press, 1949, 20–40.

Mahoney, John L. *The Whole Internal Universe: Imitation and the New Defense of Poetry in British Criticism, 1660–1830*. New York: Fordham Univ. Press, 1985.

Maresca, Thomas E. *Epic to Novel*. Columbus: Ohio State Univ. Press, 1974.

——. *Pope's Horatian Poems*. Columbus: Ohio State Univ. Press, 1966.

Marius, Richard. *Thomas More: A Biography*. New York: Knopf, 1984.

Marks, Emerson R. *The Poetics of Reason: English Neoclassical Criticism*. New York: Random House, 1968.

Martin, Josef. *Symposion: Die Geschichte einer literarischen Form*. Studien zur Geschichte und Kultur des Altertums, vol. 17. Paderborn: Verlag Ferdinand Schöningh, 1931.

Marvell, Andrew. *Complete Poetry*. Ed. George deF. Lord. New York: Modern Library, 1968.

——. *The Rehearsal Transpros'd and The Rehearsal Transpros'd the Second Part*. Ed. D. I. B. Smith. Oxford: Clarendon Press, 1971.

McCabe, Richard A. *Joseph Hall: A Study in Satire and Meditation*. Oxford: Clarendon Press, 1982.

Miller, Stuart. *The Picaresque Novel*. Cleveland: Press of Case Western Reserve Univ., 1967.

Miner, Earl. *The Cavalier Mode From Jonson to Cotton*. Princeton: Princeton Univ. Press, 1971.

——. *Dryden's Poetry*. Bloomington: Indiana Univ. Press, 1967.

——. "In Satire's Falling City." In *The Satirist's Art*, ed. H. James Jensen and Malvin Zirker, Jr. Bloomington: Indiana Univ. Press, 1972, 3–27.

——. *The Restoration Mode From Milton to Dryden*. Princeton: Princeton Univ. Press, 1974.

Monro, D. H. *Argument of Laughter*. Melbourne, 1951; rpt. Notre Dame, Ind.: Univ. of Notre Dame Press, 1963.

More, St. Thomas. *The Complete Works.* Vol. 4. Ed. Edward Surtz and J. H. Hexter. New Haven: Yale Univ. Press, 1965.

Morris, David B. *Alexander Pope: The Genius of Sense.* Cambridge, Mass.: Harvard Univ. Press, 1984.

Morson, Gary Saul. *The Boundaries of Genre: Dostoevsky's "Diary of a Writer" and the Traditions of Literary Utopia.* Austin: Univ. of Texas Press, 1981.

Muecke, D. C. *The Compass of Irony.* London: Methuen, 1969.

Murray, Gilbert. *Aristophanes: A Study.* Oxford: Clarendon Press, 1933.

———. *A History of Ancient Greek Literature.* 1897; rpt. New York: Ungar, 1966.

Murry, John Middleton. *Jonathan Swift: A Critical Biography.* 1955; rpt. New York: Farrar, Straus and Giroux, 1967.

New, Melvyn. *Laurence Sterne as Satirist: A Reading of Tristram Shandy.* Gainesville: Univ. of Florida Press, 1969.

Nichols, James W. *Insinuation: The Tactics of English Satire.* The Hague: Mouton, 1971.

Nussbaum, Felicity A. *The Brink of All We Hate: English Satires on Women, 1660–1750.* Lexington: Univ. Press of Kentucky, 1984.

Nuttall, A. D. *A New Mimesis: Shakespeare and the Representation of Reality.* London: Methuen, 1983.

O'Gorman, Donal. *Diderot the Satirist.* Toronto: Univ. of Toronto Press, 1971.

Olson, Elder. *The Theory of Comedy.* Bloomington: Indiana Univ. Press, 1968.

Osborne, Mary Tom. *Advice-To-A-Painter Poems, 1633–1856: An Annotated Finding List.* Austin: Univ. of Texas Press, 1949.

Palmeri, Frank A. "'To Write Upon Nothing': Narrative Satire and Swift's A *Tale of a Tub.*" *Genre* 18 (1985): 151–72.

Paratore, Ettore. *Biografia e poetica di Persio.* Florence, 1968.

Paulson, Ronald. *The Fictions of Satire.* Baltimore: Johns Hopkins Univ. Press, 1967.

———. *Hogarth: His Life, Art and Times.* 2 vols. New Haven: Yale Univ. Press, 1971.

———, ed. *Satire: Modern Essays in Criticism.* Englewood Cliffs, N.J.: Prentice-Hall, 1971.

———. *Rowlandson: A New Interpretation.* New York: Oxford Univ. Press, 1972.

———. *Satire and the Novel in Eighteenth-Century England.* New Haven: Yale Univ. Press, 1967.

———. *Theme and Structure in Swift's Tale of a Tub.* New Haven: Yale Univ. Press, 1960.

Payne, F. Anne. *Chaucer and Menippean Satire.* Madison: Univ. of Wisconsin Press, 1981.

Peter, John Desmond. *Complaint and Satire in Early English Literature.* Oxford: Clarendon Press, 1956.

Peterson, Leland D. "Swift's *Project:* A Religious and Political Satire." *PMLA* 82 (1967): 54–63.

Peterson, R. G. "Larger Manners and Events: Sallust and Virgil in *Absalom and Achitophel.*" *PMLA* 82 (1967): 236–44.

Petrarch, *Selected Sonnets, Odes and Letters.* Ed. Thomas G. Bergin. Arlington Heights, Ill.: AHM Publishing, 1966.

Petro, Peter. *Modern Satire: Four Studies.* Berlin: Mouton, 1982.

Pinkus, Philip. "Satire and St. George." *Queen's Quarterly* 70 (1963): 30–49.

———. *Swift's Vision of Evil.* 2 vols. English Literary Studies, No. 3. Victoria, B.C.: Univ. of Victoria, 1975.

Plato. *Collected Dialogues.* Ed. Edith Hamilton and Huntington Cairns. New York: Pantheon, 1963.

Pollard, Arthur. *Satire.* London: Methuen, 1970.

Pope, Alexander. *The Twickenham Edition of the Poems.* Ed. John Butt et al. 11 vols. London and New Haven: Methuen and Yale Univ. Press, 1939–69.

Powers, Doris C. *English Formal Satire: Elizabethan to Augustan.* The Hague: Mouton, 1971.

Preston, Thomas R. *Not in Timon's Manner: Feeling, Misanthropy, and Satire in Eighteenth-Century England.* University, Ala.: Univ. of Alabama Press, 1975.

Price, Martin. *Swift's Rhetorical Art: A Study in Structure and Meaning.* New Haven: Yale Univ. Press, 1953.

———. *To the Palace of Wisdom: Studies in Order and Energy from Dryden to Blake.* Garden City, N.Y.: Doubleday, 1964.

Quintana, Ricardo. *The Mind and Art of Jonathan Swift.* New York: Oxford Univ. Press, 1936.

Rabelais, François. *Oeuvres Complètes.* Ed. Jacques Boulenger and Lucien Scheler. Paris: Gallimard, 1955.

Rader, Ralph W. "The Concept of Genre and Eighteenth-Century Studies." In *New Approaches to Eighteenth-Century Literature,* ed. Phillip Harth. New York: Columbia Univ. Press, 1974, 79–115.

Ramage, Edwin S., et al. *Roman Satirists and Their Satire: The Fine Art of Criticism in Ancient Rome.* Park Ridge, N.J.: Noyes Press, 1974.

Ramsey, Paul. *The Art of John Dryden.* Lexington: Univ. of Kentucky Press, 1969.

Randolph, Mary Claire. "'Candour' in XVIIIth-Century Satire." *Review of English Studies* 20 (1944): 45–62.

———. "The Medical Concept in English Renaissance Satiric Theory." *Studies in Philology* 38 (1941): 125–57.

———. "The Structural Design of the Formal Verse Satire." *Philological Quarterly* 21 (1942): 368–84.

Rankin, H. D. *Petronius the Artist: Essays on the Satyricon and Its Author.* The Hague: Martinus Nijhoff, 1971.

Rawson, Claude, ed. *The Character of Swift's Satire: A Revised Focus.* Newark: Univ. of Delaware Press, 1983.

———, ed. *English Satire and the Satiric Tradition.* Oxford: Basil Blackwell, 1984.

———. *Gulliver and the Gentle Reader: Studies in Swift and Our Time.* London: Routledge & Kegan Paul, 1973.

———. "Pope's Waste Land: Reflections on Mock-Heroic." *Essays and Studies* (1982), 45–65.

Robinson, Fred Norris. "Satirists and Enchanters in Early Irish Literature." In *Studies in the History of Religions Presented to Crawford Howell Toy.* Ed. D. G. Lyon and G. F. Moore. New York: Macmillan, 1912, 95–130.

Roper, Alan. *Dryden's Poetic Kingdoms.* London: Routledge & Kegan Paul, 1965.

Rosenheim, Edward W., Jr. *Swift and the Satirist's Art.* Chicago: Univ. of Chicago Press, 1963.

Rosmarin, Adena. *The Power of Genre.* Minneapolis: Univ. of Minnesota Press, 1985.

Rothstein, Eric. "Jonathan Swift as Jupiter: 'Baucis and Philemon.'" In *The Augustan Milieu: Essays Presented to Louis A. Landa,* ed. Henry Knight Miller et al. Oxford: Clarendon Press, 1970, 205–24.

Rudd, Niall. *The Satires of Horace.* Cambridge, 1966; rpt. Berkeley and Los Angeles: Univ. of California Press, 1982.

Russell, D. A. *Criticism in Antiquity.* Berkeley and Los Angeles: Univ. of California Press, 1981.

Sacks, Sheldon. *Fiction and the Shape of Belief: A Study of Henry Fielding, With Glances at Swift, Johnson, and Richardson.* Berkeley and Los Angeles: Univ. of California Press, 1964.

Schakel, Peter J. "Dryden's *Discourse* and 'Bi-Partite Structure' in the Design of Formal Verse Satire." *English Language Notes* 21 (1984): 33–41.

———. *The Poetry of Jonathan Swift: Allusion and the Development of a Poetic Style.* Madison: Univ. of Wisconsin Press, 1978.

Scholes, Robert. "An Approach Through Genre." In *Towards a Poetics of Fiction,* ed. Mark Spilka. Bloomington: Indiana Univ. Press, 1977, 41–51.

———. *Structuralism in Literature: An Introduction.* New Haven: Yale Univ. Press, 1974.

Scholes, Robert, and Robert Kellogg. *The Nature of Narrative.* New York: Oxford Univ. Press, 1966.

Screech, M. A. *Ecstasy and The Praise of Folly.* London: Duckworth, 1980.

Seidel, Michael. *Satiric Inheritance: Rabelais to Sterne.* Princeton: Princeton Univ. Press, 1979.

Selden, Raman. *English Verse Satire, 1590–1765.* London: Allen & Unwin, 1978.

Shadwell, Thomas. *The Complete Works.* Ed. Montague Summers. 4 vols. London, 1927; rpt. New York: Benjamin Blom, 1968.

———. *The Virtuoso.* Ed. M. H. Nicolson and D. S. Rodes. Lincoln: Univ. of Nebraska Press, 1966.

Sitter, John E. *The Poetry of Pope's "Dunciad."* Minneapolis: Univ. of Minnesota Press, 1971.

Skulsky, Harold. *Metamorphosis: The Mind in Exile.* Cambridge, Mass.: Harvard Univ. Press, 1981.

Smith, Barbara Herrnstein. *On the Margins of Discourse.* Chicago: Univ. of Chicago Press, 1978.

———. "Poetry as Fiction." *New Literary History* 2 (1971): 259–81.

Smith, Frederik N. *Language and Reality in Swift's "A Tale of a Tub."* Columbus: Ohio State Univ. Press, 1979.

Smith, Hallett. *Elizabethan Poetry: A Study in Conventions, Meaning, and Expression.* Cambridge, Mass.: Harvard Univ. Press, 1966.

Smith, R. Jack. "Shadwell's Impact Upon John Dryden." *Review of English Studies* 20 (1944): 29–44.

Southey, Robert. *The Poetical Works*. Boston: Houghton Mifflin, n.d.
Spacks, Patricia Meyer. *An Argument of Images: The Poetry of Alexander Pope*. Cambridge, Mass.: Harvard Univ. Press, 1971.
————. "Some Reflections on Satire." *Genre* 1 (1968): 13–20.
Starkman, Miriam K. "Swift's Rhetoric: The 'Overfraught Pinnace'?" *The South Atlantic Quarterly* 68 (1969): 188–97.
————. *Swift's Satire on Learning in "A Tale of a Tub."* Princeton: Princeton Univ. Press, 1950.
Startzman, Louis Eugene. "Images of Evil in the Formal Verse Satire of Joseph Hall, John Marston, John Donne, and Alexander Pope." Ph.D. diss., Ohio University, Athens, 1970.
Steele, Peter. *Jonathan Swift: Preacher and Jester*. Oxford: Clarendon Press, 1978.
Stein, Arnold. "Donne and the Satiric Spirit." *ELH* 11 (1944): 266–82.
————. "The Second English Satirist." *Modern Language Review* 38 (1943): 273–78.
Steinberg, Leo. "The Metaphors of Love and Birth in Michelangelo's Pietas." In *Studies in Erotic Art*, ed. Theodore Bowie and Cornelia V. Christenson. New York: Basic Books, 1970, 231–85.
Stopp, Frederick J. *Evelyn Waugh: Portrait of an Artist*. London: Chapman and Hall, 1958.
Strauss, Leo. *The Political Philosophy of Hobbes*. Chicago: Univ. of Chicago Press, 1963.
Strelka, Joseph P., ed. *Theories of Literary Genre*. Yearbook of Comparative Criticism, vol. 8. University Park, Pa.: Pennsylvania State Univ. Press, 1978.
Suckling, Sir John. *The Non-Dramatic Works*. Ed. Thomas Clayton. Oxford: Clarendon Press, 1971.
Sullivan, J. P., ed. *Satire: Critical Essays on Roman Literature*. Bloomington: Indiana Univ. Press, 1963.
————. *The Satyricon of Petronius: A Literary Study*. Bloomington: Indiana Univ. Press, 1968.
Surtz, Edward, S.J. *The Praise of Pleasure: Philosophy, Education, and Communism in More's Utopia*. Cambridge, Mass.: Harvard Univ. Press, 1957.
Sutherland, James. *English Literature of the Late Seventeenth Century*. Oxford: Clarendon Press, 1969.
————. *English Satire*. Cambridge: Cambridge Univ. Press, 1962.
Sutherland, W. O. S. *The Art of the Satirist: Essays on the Satire of Augustan England*. Austin: Univ. of Texas Press, 1965.
Swift, Jonathan. *Poems*. Ed. Harold Williams. 3 vols. Oxford: Clarendon Press, 1958.
————. *The Prose Works*. Ed. Herbert Davis. 14 vols. Oxford: Basil Blackwell, 1939–68.
————. *A Tale of a Tub*. Ed. A. C. Guthkelch and D. Nichol Smith. 2d ed. Oxford: Clarendon Press, 1958.
Taylor, Donald S. *Thomas Chatterton's Art: Experiments in Imagined History*. Princeton: Princeton Univ. Press, 1978.
Temple, Sir William. *Five Miscellaneous Essays*. Ed. Samuel Holt Monk. Ann Arbor: Univ. of Michigan Press, 1963.

Thomas, W. K. *The Crafting of "Absalom and Achitophel": Dryden's "Pen for a Party."* Waterloo, Ont.: Wilfrid Laurier Univ. Press, 1978.

Thompson, C. R. *The Translations of Lucian by Erasmus and St. Thomas More.* Ph.D. diss., Princeton Univ., 1937. Ithaca, N.Y.: privately printed, 1940.

Thompson, Sister Geraldine. *Under Pretext of Praise: Satiric Mode in Erasmus' Fiction.* Toronto: Univ. of Toronto Press, 1973.

Thucydides. *Hobbes's Thucydides.* Ed. Richard Schlatter. New Brunswick, N.J.: Rutgers Univ. Press, 1975.

Tillotson, Geoffrey. *Augustan Studies.* London: Athlone Press, 1961.

———. *On the Poetry of Pope.* 2d ed. Oxford: Clarendon Press, 1950.

———. *Pope and Human Nature.* Oxford: Clarendon Press, 1958.

Todorov, Tzvetan. *The Fantastic: A Structural Approach to a Literary Genre.* Trans. Richard Howard. Ithaca, N.Y.: Cornell Univ. Press, 1975.

———. *Theories of the Symbol.* Trans. Catherine Porter. Ithaca, N.Y.: Cornell Univ. Press, 1982.

Tomlinson, Charles. *Poetry and Metamorphosis.* Cambridge: Cambridge Univ. Press, 1983.

Traugott, John. "*A Tale of a Tub.*" In *The Character of Swift's Satire: A Revised Focus,* ed. Claude Rawson. Newark: Univ. of Delaware Press, 1983, 83–126.

Trickett, Rachel. *The Honest Muse: A Study in Augustan Verse.* Oxford: Clarendon Press, 1967.

Trimpi, Wesley. *Muses of One Mind: The Literary Analysis of Experience and Its Continuity.* Princeton: Princeton Univ. Press, 1983.

Uphaus, Robert W. *The Impossible Observer: Reason and the Reader in Eighteenth-Century Prose.* Lexington: Univ. of Kentucky Press, 1979.

Valle-Killeen, Suzanne Dolores. *The Satiric Perspective: A Structural Analysis of Late Medieval, Early Renaissance Satiric Treatises.* New York: Senda Nueva de Ediciones, 1980.

Van Rooy, C. A. *Studies in Classical Satire and Related Literary Theory.* Leiden: E. J. Brill, 1965.

Verrall, A. W. *Lectures on Dryden.* London, 1914; rpt. New York: Russell & Russell, 1963.

Vieth, David. "Divided Consciousness: the Trauma and Triumph of Restoration Culture." *Tennessee Studies in Literature* 22 (1977): 46–62.

———. "Shadwell in Acrostic Land: The Reversible Meaning in Dryden's *Mac Flecknoe.*" In *Studies in Eighteenth-Century Culture,* vol. 9, ed. Roseann Runte. Madison: Univ. of Wisconsin Press, 1979, 503–16.

Viëtor, Karl. *Geist und Form: Aufsätze zur deutschen Literaturgeschicte.* Bern: A. Francke AG Verlag, 1952.

Walsh, P. G. *The Roman Novel: The 'Satyricon' of Petronius and the 'Metamorphoses' of Apuleius.* Cambridge: Cambridge Univ. Press, 1970.

Wardroper, John. *Kings, Lords and Wicked Libellers: Satire and Protest, 1760–1837.* London: John Murray, 1973.

Weil, Simone. *The Iliad or The Poem of Force.* 1945; rpt. Wallingford, Pa.: Pendle Hill, n.d.

Weinberg, Bernard. *A History of Literary Criticism in the Italian Renaissance.* 2 vols. Chicago: Univ. of Chicago Press, 1961.

Weinbrot, Howard D. *Alexander Pope and the Traditions of Formal Verse Satire.* Princeton: Princeton Univ. Press, 1982.

———. *Augustus Caesar in "Augustan" England: The Decline of a Classical Norm.* Princeton: Princeton Univ. Press, 1978.

———. *The Formal Strain: Studies in Augustan Imitation and Satire.* Chicago: Univ. of Chicago Press, 1969.

Weinsheimer, Joel. *Imitation.* London: Routledge & Kegan Paul, 1984.

Welsford, Enid. *The Fool: His Social and Literary History.* 1935; rpt. Garden City, N.Y.: Anchor Books, 1961.

Weston, Arthur H. *Latin Satirical Writing Subsequent to Juvenal.* Lancaster, Pa.: privately printed, 1915.

Whitman, Cedric H. *Aristophanes and the Comic Hero.* Cambridge, Mass.: Harvard Univ. Press, 1964.

Wiesen, David S. *St. Jerome as a Satirist: A Study in Christian Latin Thought and Letters.* Ithaca, N.Y.: Cornell Univ. Press, 1964.

Willeford, William. *The Fool and His Scepter: A Study in Clowns and Jesters and Their Audience.* Evanston: Northwestern Univ. Press, 1969.

Williams, Aubrey L. *Pope's Dunciad: A Study of Its Meaning.* London, 1955; rpt. Hamden, Conn.: Archon, 1968.

Williams, Kathleen. *Jonathan Swift and the Age of Compromise.* Lawrence: Univ. Press of Kansas, 1958.

Witke, Charles. *Latin Satire: The Structure of Persuasion.* Leiden: E. J. Brill, 1970.

Worcester, David. *The Art of Satire.* Cambridge, Mass., 1940; rpt. New York: Russell & Russell, 1960.

Zetzel, J. E. G. "Horace's *Liber Sermonum:* the Structure of Ambiguity." *Arethusa* 13 (1980): 59–77.

Zimbardo, Rose A. *Wycherley's Drama: A Link in the Development of English Satire.* New Haven: Yale Univ. Press, 1965.

Zimmerman, Everett. *Swift's Narrative Satires.* Ithaca, N.Y.: Cornell Univ. Press, 1983.

Zwicker, Steven N. *Politics and Language in Dryden's Poetry: The Arts of Disguise.* Princeton: Princeton Univ. Press, 1984.

INDEX